SINNERS AND SAINTS

AMS PRESS
NEW YORK

SINNERS AND SAINTS

*A TOUR ACROSS THE STATES, AND
ROUND THEM;*

WITH

THREE MONTHS AMONG THE MORMONS.

BY

PHIL ROBINSON,
AUTHOR OF "UNDER THE SUN."

BOSTON:
ROBERTS BROTHERS.
1883.

Reprinted from the edition of 1883, Boston
First AMS EDITION published 1971
Manufactured in the United States of America

International Standard Book Number: 0-404-08444-3

Library of Congress Catalog Number: 75-134400

AMS PRESS INC.
NEW YORK, N.Y. 10003

CONTENTS.

CHAPTER I.

FROM NEW YORK TO CHICAGO.

CHAPTER II.

FROM CHICAGO TO DENVER.

CHAPTER III.

IN LEADVILLE.

CHAPTER IV.

FROM LEADVILLE TO SALT LAKE CITY.

CHAPTER V.

THE CITY OF THE HONEY-BEE.

CHAPTER VI.

LEGISLATION AGAINST PLURALITY.

CHAPTER VII.

SUA SI BONA NÔRINT.

CHAPTER VIII.

COULD THE MORMONS FIGHT?

CHAPTER IX.

THE SAINTS AND THE RED MEN.

CHAPTER X.

REPRESENTATIVE AND UNREPRESENTATIVE MORMONISM.

CHAPTER XI.

THROUGH THE MORMON SETTLEMENTS

CHAPTER XII.

FROM NEPHI TO MANTI.

CHAPTER XIII.

FROM MANTI TO GLENWOOD.

CHAPTER XIV.

FROM GLENWOOD TO MONROE.

CHAPTER XIX.

MORMON VIRTUES.

CHAPTER XX.

CHAPTER XXI.

FROM UTAH INTO NEVADA.

CHAPTER XXII.

FROM NEVADA INTO CALIFORNIA.

CHAPTER XXIII.

SINNERS AND SAINTS.

CHAPTER I.

FROM NEW YORK TO CHICAGO.

By the Pennsylvania Limited—Her Majesty's swine—Glimpses of
Africa and India—"Eligible sites for Kingdoms"—The Phœnix
city—Street scenes—From pig to pork—The Sparrow line—
Chicago Mountain—Melancholy merry-makers.

"DOES the fast train to Chicago *ever stop ?*" was the question of a bewildered English fellow-passenger, Westward-
bound like myself, as I took my seat in the car of the
Pennsylvania Limited mail that was to carry me nearly
half the distance from the Atlantic to the Pacific. "Oh,
yes," I replied, "it stops— *at Chicago.*"

By this he recognized in me a fellow-innocent, and so we
foregathered at once, breakfasted together, and then went
out to smoke the calumet together.

To an insular traveller, it is a prodigiously long journey
this, across the continent of America, but I found the
journey a perpetual enjoyment. Even the dull country
of the first hour's travelling had many points of interest for
the stranger—scattered hamlets of wooden houses that were
only joined together by straggling strings of cocks and hens ;
the others that seemed to have been trying to scramble over
the hill and down the other side but were caught just as

B

they got to the top and pinned down to the ground with lightning conductors ; the others that had palings round them to keep them from running away, but had got on to piles as if they were stilts and intended (when no one was looking) to skip over the palings and go away ; the others that had rows of dwarf fir-trees in front of them, through which they stared out of both their windows like a forward child affecting to be shy behind its fingers. These fir-trees are themselves very curious, for they give the country a half-cultivated appearance, and in some places make the hillsides and valleys look like immense cemeteries, and only waiting for the tombstones. Even the levels of flooded land and the scorched forests were of interest, as significant of a country still busy over its rudiments

"All charcoal and puddles," said a fellow-traveller disparagingly ; "I'm very glad we're going so fast through it."

Now for my own part I think it looks very uncivil of a train to go with a screech through a station without stopping, and I always wish I could say something in the way of an apology to the station-master for the train's bad manners. No doubt people who live in very small places get accustomed to trains rushing past their platforms without stopping even to say "By your leave." But at first it must be rather painful. At least I should think it was. On the other hand, the people " in the mofussil " (which is the Anglo-Indian for " all the country outside one's own town ") did not pay much attention to our train. Everybody went about their several works for all the world as if we were not flashing by. Even the dogs trotted about indifferently, without even so much as noticing us, except occasionally some distant mongrel, who barked at the train as if it was a stray bullock, and smiled complacently upon the adjoining landscape when he found how thoroughly he had frightened it away.

There seemed to me a curious dearth of small wild life. The English " country " is so full of birds that all others seem, by comparison, birdless.   Once, I saw a russet-winged hawk hovering over a copse of water-oak as if it saw something worth eating there ; once, too, I saw a blue-bird brighten a clump of cedars. Now and again a vagabond crow drifted across the sky.   But, as compared with Europe or parts of the East which I know best, bird-life was very scanty.

And presently Philadelphia came sliding along to meet us with a stately decorum of metalled roads and well-kept public grounds, and we stopped for the first of the twelve halts, worth calling such, which I had to make in the 3000 miles between the Atlantic and the Pacific.

How treacherously the trains in America start ! There is no warning given, so far as an ordinary passenger can see, that the start is under contemplation, and it takes him by surprise.   The American understands that " All aboard " means " If you don't jump up at once you'll be left behind." But to those accustomed to a " first " and a " second " and a " third " bell—and accustomed, too, not to get up even then until the guard has begged them as a personal favour to take their seats—the sudden departure of the American locomotive presents itself as a rather shabby sort of practical joke.

The quiet, unobtrusive scenery beyond Philadelphia is English in character, and would be still more so if there were hedges instead of railings.   By the way, whenever reading biographical notices of distinguished Americans I have been surprised to find that so many of them at one time or other had " split rails " for a subsistence.   But now that I have followed " the course of empire " West, I am not the least surprised.   I only wonder that *every* American has not split rails, at one time or another, or, indeed, gone on doing it all his life. For how such a prodigious quantity of rails ever got split (even supposing distinguished men to have assisted in the industry in early life) passes my feeble comprehension. All the way from New York to Chicago there are on an average twenty lines of split rails running parallel with the railway track, in sight all at once! And after all, this is only one narrow strip across a gigantic continent. In fact, the two most prominent " natural features " of the landscape along this route are dwarf firs and split rails. But no writer on America has ever told me so. Nor have I ever been told of the curious misapprehension prevalent in the States as to the liberty of the subject in the British Isles.

In America, judging at any rate from the speech of " the average American," I find that there is a belief prevalent that the English nation " lies prostrate under the heel of a tyrant." What a shock to those who think thus, must have been that recent episode of the queen's pigs at Slough!

Six swine and a calf belonging to her Majesty found themselves, the other day, impounded by the Slough magistrates for coming to market without a licence. Slough, from geographical circumstances over which it has no control, happens to be in Buckinghamshire, and this country has been declared " an infected district," so that the bailiff who brought his sovereign's pigs to market, without due authority to do so, transgressed the law. Two majesties thus came into collision over the calf, and that of the law prevailed. Such a constitutional triumph as this goes far to clear away the clouds that appeared to be gathered upon the political horizon, and the shadows of a despotic dictatorship which seemed to be falling across England begin to vanish. The written law, contained probably in a very dilapidated old copy in the possession of these rural magistrates, a dogs'-eared and, it may be, even a ragged volume, asserted itself supreme over a monarch's farmyard stock, and dared to break down that divinity which doth hedge a Sovereign's swine. There are some who say that in the British Isles men are losing their reverence for the law, and that justice wears two faces, one for the rich and another for the poor. They would have us believe that only the parasites of princes sit in high place, and that the scales of justice rise or fall according to the inclinations of the sceptre, with the obsequious regularity of the tides that wait upon the humours of the moon. But such an incident as this, when the Justices of Slough, those intrepid Hampdens, sate sternly in their places, and, fearless of Royal frowns and all the displeasure of Windsor, dispensed to the pigs, born in the purple, and to the calf that had lived so near a throne, the impartial retribution of a fine—with costs—gives a splendid refutation to these calumnies. Where shall we look in Republican history for such another incident? or where search for dauntless magistrates like those of Slough, who shut their eyes against the reflected glitter of a Court, who fined the Royal calf for risking the health of Hodge's miserable herd, and gave the costs against the Imperial pigs for travelling into Buckinghamshire without a licence? Fiat justitia, ruat cœlum. There was no truckling here to borrowed majesty, no sycophant adulation of Royal ownership; but that fine old English spirit of courageous independence which has made tyrants impossible in our island and our law supreme. It was of no use before such men as these, the stout-hearted champions of equal justice, for the bailiff to plead manorial privilege, or to threaten the thunders of the House of Brunswick. They were as implacable as a bench of Rhadamanthuses, and gave these distinguished

hogs the grim choice between paying a pound or going to
one.   Nor, to their credit be it said, did either bailiff, calf,
or pigs exhibit resentment.   On the contrary, they accepted
judgment with that respectful acquiescence which characterizes our law-abiding race, and the swine turned without
a murmur from the scene of their repulse, and trotted cheerfully before the bailiff out of Buckinghamshire back to
Windsor.

The bailiff, no doubt, bethought him of the past, and
wished the good old days of feudalism were back, when a
King's pig was a better man than a Buckinghamshire
magistrate.   But if he did, he abstained from saying so.   On
the contrary, he paid his fine like a loyal subject, and gathering his innocent charges round him went forth, more in
sorrow than in anger, from the presence of the magisterial
champions of the public interests.   The punished pigs, too,
may have felt, perhaps, just a twinge of regret for the days
when they roamed at will over the oak-grown shires, infecting
each other as they chose, without any thought of Contagious
Diseases Acts or vigilant justices.   But they said nothing ;
and the spectacle of an upright stipendiary dispensing impartial   justice   to   a   law-abiding   aristocracy   was   thus
complete.

To return to my car.   Beyond Philadelphia the country
was waking up for Spring.   The fields were all flushed with
the first bright promise of harvest ; blackbirds—reminding
me of the Indian king-crows in their sliding manner of
flight and the conspicuous way in which they use their tails
as   rudders—were   flying   about   in   sociable   parties ;   and
flocks of finches went jerking up the hill-sides by fits and
starts after the fashion of these frivolous little folk.

A mica-schist (it may be gneiss) abounds along the railway track, and it occurred to me that I had never, except

in India, seen this material used for the ornamentation of houses. Yet it is very beautiful. In the East they beat it up into a powder—some is white, some yellow—and after mixing it with weak lime and water, wash the walls with it, the result being a very effective although subdued sparkle, in some places silvery, in others golden.

Nearing Harrisburg the country begins to resemble upper Natal very strongly, and when we reached the Susquehanna, I could easily have believed that we were on the Mooi, on the borders of Zululand. But the superior majesty of the American river soon asserted itself, and I forgot the comparison altogether as I looked out on this truly noble stream, with the finely wooded hills leaning back from it on either side, as if to give its waters more spacious way.

And then Harrisburg, and the same stealthy departure of the train. But outside the station our having started was evident enough, for a horse that had been left to look after a buggy for a few minutes, took fright, and with three frantic kangaroo-leaps tried to take the conveyance whole over a wall. But failing in this, it careered away down the road with the balance of the buggy dangling in a draggle-tail sort of way behind it.

Nature works with so few ingredients that landscape repeats itself in every continent. For there is a limit, after all, to the combinations possible of water, mountain, plain, valley, and vegetation. This is strictly true, of course, only when we deal with things generically. Specific combinations go beyond arithmetic. But even with her species, Nature delights in singing over old songs and telling the tales she has already told. For instance here, after passing Harrisburg, is a wonderful glimpse of Naini Tal in the Indian hills—memorable for a terribly fatal landslip three years ago—with its oaks and rhododendrons and scattered pines.

In the valleys the streams go tumbling along with willows on either bank, and here and there on the hillsides, shine white housés with orchards about them.

The houses men build for themselves when they are thinking only of shelter are ugly enough. Elegance, like the nightingale, is a creature of summer-time, when the hard-working months of the year are over and Nature sits in her drawing-room, so to speak, playing the fine lady, painting the roses and sweetening the peaches. But, ugly though they are, these scattered homesteads are by far the finest lines in all the great poem of this half-wild continent, and lend a grand significance to every passage in which they occur. And the pathos of it! Look at those two horses and a man driving a plough through that scrap of ground yonder. There is not another living object in view, though the eye covers enough ground for a European principality. Yet that man dares to challenge all this tremendous Nature! It is David before Goliath, before a whole wilderness of Goliaths, with a plough for a sling and a ploughshare for a pebble.

Here all of a sudden is another man, all alone with some millions of trees and the Alleghanies. And he stands there with an axe in his hands, revolving in that untidy head of his what he shall do next to the old hills and their reverend forest growth. The audacity of it, and the solemnity!

It would be as well perhaps for sentiment if every man was quite alone. For I find that if there are two men together one immediately tries to sell the other something; and to inform him of its nature, he goes and paints the name of his disgusting commodities on the smooth faces of rocks and on tree-trunks. Now, any landscape, however grand, loses in dignity if you see " Bunkum's Patent " inscribed in the foreground in whitewash letters six feet high.

What a mercy it is these quacks cannot advertise on the sky—or on running water !

For the river is now at its grandest and it keeps with us all the afternoon, showing on either side splendid waterways between sloping spurs of the hills densely wooded and strewn with great boulders. But on a sudden the mountains are gone and the river with them, and we speed along through a region of green grass-land and abundant cultivation. Land agents might truthfully advertise it in lots as " eligible sites for kingdoms."

And so on, past townships, whose names running (at forty miles an hour) no man can read, and round the famous " horseshoe curve "—where it looks as if the train were trying to get its head round in order to swallow its tail— down into valleys already taking their evening tints of misty purple, and pink, and pale blue. And then Derry.

Just before we arrived there, two freight trains had selected Derry as an opportune spot for a collision, and had collided accordingly. There could have been very little reservation about their collision, for the wreck was complete, and when we got under way again we could just make out by the moonlight the scattered limbs of carriages lying heaped about on the bank. In some places it looked as if a clumsy apprentice had been trying to make packing-cases out of freight wagons, but had given up on finding that he had broken the pieces too small. And they were too big for matches. So it was rather a useless sort of collision, after all—and no one was hurt.

But " the Pennsylvania Limited " has very little leisure to think about other people's collisions, and so we were soon on our way again through the moonlit country, with the hills in the distance lying still and black, like round-backed monsters sleeping, and the stations going by in sudden snatches of lamplight, and every now and then a train, its bell giving a wail exactly like the sound of a shell as it passes over the trenches. And so to Pittsburg, and, our "five minutes" over, the train stole away like a hyena, snarling and hiccoughing, and we were again out in the country, with everything about us beautified by the gracious alchemy of the moonlight and the stars.

And the Ohio River rolled alongside, with its steamers ploughing up furrows of ghostly white froth, and unwinding as they went long streamers of ghostly black smoke—and then I fell asleep.

When I awoke next morning I was in Indiana, and very sunny it looked without a hill in sight to make a shadow. The water stood in lakes on the dead level of the country, and horses, cattle, sheep, and here and there a pig—a pre-gustation of Chicago—grazed and rooted, very well satisfied apparently with pastures that had no ups and downs to trouble them as they loitered about. And as the morning wore on, the people woke up, and were soon as busy as their windmills. In the fields the teams were ploughing; in the towns, the children were trooping off to school. But the eternal level began at last, apparently, to weary the Penn-sylvania Limited, for it commenced slackening speed and finding frivolous pretexts for coming nearly to a standstill— the climax being reached when we halted in front of a small, piebald pig. We looked at the pig and the pig looked at us, and the pig got the best of it, for we sneaked off, leaving the porker master of the situation and still looking.

But these great flats—what a paradise of snipe they are, and how golf-players might revel on them! Birds were abundant. Crows went about in bands recruiting "black marauders" in every copse; blackbirds flew over in flocks, and small things of the linnet kind rose in wisps from the sedges and osiers. And there was another bird of which I did not then know the name, that was a surprise every time it left the ground, for it sate all black and flew half scarlet. Could not these marsh levels be utilized for the Indian water-nut, the singhara? In Asia where it is cultivated it ranks almost as a local staple of food, and is delicious.

A noteworthy feature of the country, by the way, is the sudden appearance of *hedge-rows*. No detail of landscape that I know of makes scenery at once so English. And then we find ourselves steaming along past beds of osiers, with long waterways stretching up northwards, with here and there a painted duck, like the European sheldrake, floating under the shadows of the fir-trees, and then I became aware of a great green expanse of water showing through the trees, and I asked " What is that? The water must be very deep to be such a colour." "That is Lake Michigan," was the answer, "and this is Chicago we are coming to now."

And very soon we found ourselves in the station of the great city by the lake, with the masts of shipping alongside the funnels of engines. But not a pig in sight!

I had thought that Chicago was *all pigs*.

And what a city it is, this central wonder of the States! As a whole, Chicago is nearly *terrific*. The real significance of this phœnix city is almost appalling. Its astonishing resurrection from its ashes and its tremendous energy terrify jelly-fishes like myself. Before they have got roads that are fit to be called roads, these Chicago men have piled up the new County Hall, to my mind one of the most imposing structures I have ever seen in all my wide travels.

Chicago does not altogether seem to like it, for every one spoke of it as " too solid-looking," but for my part I think it *almost* superb. The architect's name, I believe, is Egan ;

but whence he got his architectural inspiration I cannot say. It reminds me in part of a wing of the Tuileries, but why it does I could not make up my mind.

Then again, look at this Chicago which allows its business thoroughfares to be so sumptuously neglected—some of them are almost as disreputable-looking as Broadway—and goes and lays out imperial "boulevards" to connect its "system of parks." These boulevards, simply if left alone for the trees to grow up and the turf to grow thick, will before long be the finest in all the world. The streets in the city, however, if left alone much longer, would be a disgrace to —well, say Port Said. The local administration, they say, is "corrupt." But that is the standing American explanation for everything with which a stranger finds fault. I was always told the same in New York—and would you *seriously* tell me that the municipal administration of New York is corrupt?—to account for congestion of traffic, fat policemen, bad lamps, sidewalks blocked with packing-cases, &c , &c. And in Chicago it accounts for the streets being more like rolling prairie than streets, for cigar stores being houses of assignation, for there being so much orange peel and banana skin on the sidewalks, &c., &c. But I am not at all sure that "municipal corruption" is not a scapegoat for want of public spirit.

But let the public spirit be as it may, there can be no doubt as to the private enterprise in Chicago. Take the iron industry alone — what prodigious proportions it is assuming, and how vastly it will be increased when that circum-urban "belt line" of railways is completed! Take, again, the Pullman factories. They by themselves form an industry which might satisfy any town of moderate appetite. But Chicago is a veritable glutton for speculative trade.

The streets at all times abound with incident. Here at one corner was a Hansom cab, surely the very latest development of European science, with two small black children, looking like imps in a Drury Lane pantomime, trying to pin "April Fool" on to the cabman's dependent tails. Could anything be more incongruous? In the first place, what have negro children to do with April fooling? and in the next, imagine these small scraps in ebony taking liberties with a Hansom! A group of cowboy-and-miner looking men were grouped in ludicrous attitudes of sentimentality before a concertina-player, who was wheezing out his own version of "old country" airs. On the arm of one of the group languished a lady with a very dark skin, dressed in a rich black silk dress, with a black satin mantle trimmed with sumptuous fur, and half an ostrich on her head by way of bonnet and feathers. The men there, as in most of America, strike me as being very judicious in the arrangement of their personal appearance, especially in the trimming of their hair and moustachios; but many of the women—I speak now of Chicago—sacrificed everything to that awful Amercan institution, the "bang."

I know of no female head-dress in Asia, Africa, or Europe so absurd in itself or so lunatic in the wearer as some of the Chicago bangs. Ugliness of face is intensified a thousand-fold by "the ring-worm style" of head-dress with which they cover their foreheads and half their cheeks. Prettiness of face can, of course, never be hidden; but I honestly think that neither a black skin, nor lip-rings and nose-rings, nor red teeth, nor any other fantastic female fashion that I have ever seen in other parts of the world, goes so far towards concealing beauty of features as that curly plastering which, from ignorance of its real name, I have called "the ring worm style of bang."

Here, too, in Chicago I found a man selling "gophers."
Now, I do not know the American name for this vanish-
into-nothing sort of pastry, but I do know that there is one
man in London who declares that he, and he alone in all the
world, is aware of the secret of the gopher. And all London
believes him. His is supposed to be a lost art—but for him
—and I should not be surprised if some lover of the antique
were to bribe him to bequeath the precious secret to an
heir before he dies. But in Chicago peripatetic vendors of
this cate are an every-day occurrence, and even the juvenile
Ethiop sometimes compasses the gopher. What its American name is I cannot say ; but it is a very delicate kind of
pastry punched into small square depressions, and every
mouthful you eat is so inappreciable in point of matter that
you look down on your waistcoat to see if you have not
dropped it, and when the whole is done you feel that you
have consumed about as much solid nutriment as a fish
does after a nibble at an artificial bait. Have you ever
given a dog a piece of warm fat off your plate and seen him
after he had swallowed it *look on the carpet for it?* So rapid
is the transit of the delicious thing that the deluded animal
fancies that he has as yet enjoyed only the foretaste of a
pleasure still to be, the shadow only of the coming event,
the promise of something good. It is just the same with
yourself after eating a gopher.

Of course I went to see the stock-yards, and my visit, as
it happened, had something of a special character, for I saw
a pig put through its performances in *thirty-five seconds*. A
lively piebald porker was one of a number grunting and
quarrelling in a pen, and I was asked to keep my eye on
him. And what happened to that porker was this. He

[1] Need I say that I do *not* refer to the small field-rat of that
name?

was suddenly seized by a hind leg, and jerked up on to a
small crane. This swung him swiftly to the fatal door
through which no pig ever returns. On the other side stood
a man —

> That two-handed engine at the door
> Stands ready to smite once, and smite no more,

and the dead pig shot across a trough and through another
doorway, and then there was a *splash !* He had fallen head
first into a vat of boiling water. Some unseen machinery
passed him along swiftly to the other end of the terrible
bath, and there a water-wheel picked him up and flung him
out on to a sloping counter. Here another machine seized
him, and with one revolution scraped him as bald as a nut.
And down the counter he went, losing his head as he slid
past a man with a hatchet, and then, presto ! he was up
again by the heels. In one dreadful handful a man emptied
him, and while another squirted him with fresh water, the
pig—registering his own weight as he passed the teller's
box—shot down the steel bar from which he hung, and
whisked round the corner into the ice-house. One long cut
of a knife made two "sides of pork" out of that piebald
pig. Two hacks of a hatchet brought away his backbone.
And there, in thirty-five seconds from his last grunt—dirty,
hot-headed, noisy—the pig was hanging up in two pieces,
clean, tranquil, *iced !*

The very rapidity of the whole process robbed it of all its
horrors. It even added the ludicrous to it. Here one
minute was an opinionated piebald pig making a prodigious
fuss about having his hind leg taken hold of, and lo ! before
he had even made up his mind whether to squeal or only
to squeak, he was hanging up in an ice-house, split in two !
He had resented the first trifling liberty that was taken with
him, and *in thirty-five seconds* he was ready for the cook !

That the whole process is virtually painless is beyond all
doubt, for it is only for the first fraction of the thirty-odd
seconds that the pig is sentient, and I doubt if even
electricity could as suddenly and painlessly extinguish life
as the lightning of that unerring poniard, "the dagger of
mercy" and the instantaneous plunge into the scalding
bath.

Of the Chicago stock-yards, a veritable village, laid out
with its miniature avenues intersecting its mimic streets and
numbered blocks, it is late in the day to speak. But it was
very interesting in its way to see the poor doomed swine
thoughtlessly grunting along the road, and inquisitively
asking their way, as it seemed, of the sheep in Block 9 or of
the sulky Texan steer looking out between the palings of
Block 7 ; to watch the cattle, wild-eyed from distress and
long journeying, snorting their distrust of their surroundings,
and trying at every opportunity to turn away from the
terribly straight road that leads to death, into any crossway
that seemed likely to result in freedom ; to see for the first
time the groups of Western herdsmen lounging at the
corners, while their unkempt ponies, guarded in most cases
by drowsy shepherd-dogs, stood tethered in bunches against
the palings. All day long the air is filled with porcine
clamour, and some of the pens are scenes of perpetual riot.
For the pig does not chant his "nunc dimittis" with any
seemliness. His last canticles are frivolous. It is impossible to translate them into any "morituri te salutant," for
they are wanting in dignity, and even self-respect. With
the cattle it is very different. But few of them were in such
good case as to make high spirits possible, and many were
wretched objects to look at. Dead calves lay about in the
pens, and there was a general air of distress that made the
scene abundantly pathetic. But, after all, it does not *pay*

to starve or overdrive cattle, and we may confidently expect therefore, that in Chicago, of all places in the world, they are neither starved nor overdriven systematically.

The English sparrow has multiplied with characteristic industry in Chicago, but further west I lost it. I saw none between Omaha and Salt Lake City. So the sparrow line, I take it, must be drawn for the present somewhere west of Clinton. I do not *think* it has crossed the Mississippi yet from the east. But it is steadily advancing its frontiers—this aggressive fowl—from both sea-boards, and just as it has pushed itself forward from the Atlantic into Illinois, so from the Pacific it has got already as far as Nevada. The tyranny of the sparrow is the price men pay for civilization. Only savages are exempt. Here in America, they have developed into a multitudinous evil, dispossessing with a high hand the children of the soil, thrusting their Saxon assumption of superiority upon the native feathered flock of grove and garden, and driving them from their birthright. They have no respect for authorities, and entertain no awe even for the Irish aldermen of New York. In Australia it is the same. Imported as a treasure, they have presumed upon the sentiment of exiled Englishmen until they have become a veritable calamity. So they have been publicly proclaimed as " vermin," and a price set upon their heads " per hundred." Indeed, legislatures threaten to stand or fall upon the sparrow question. Here in America, men and women began by putting nesting-boxes for the birds in the trees and at corners of houses ; I am much mistaken if before long they do not end by putting up ladders against the trees to help the cats to get up to catch the sparrows.

I looked everywhere for " Chicago Mountain "—a New England joke against the Phœnix City—and at last found it

c

behind a house at the corner of Pine and Colorado streets. They say (in Boston) that Chicago, being chaffed about having no high land near it, set to work to build itself a mountain, but that when it had reached its present moderate elevation of a few feet, the city abandoned the project. But I am inclined to think that this fiction is due to the spite of the New Englanders, who, it is notorious, have to sharpen the noses of their sheep to enable them to reach the grass that grows between the stones; for on looking at the mountain in question I perceived it to be merely a natural sand-dune which it has not been thought worth while to clear away. Further to acquaint myself with the city, I went into sundry "penny gaffs," or cafés chantants, and found them to my surprise patronized by groups of men sad almost to melancholy. It was the music, I think, that made them feel so. Its effect on me I know was very chastening. I felt inclined to lift up my voice and howl. But the intense gravity of the company restrained me, and I left. Yet I am told that inside these very places men stab each other with Bowie knives and shoot each other with revolvers, and are even sometimes quite disagreeable in their manners. But so far as my own experience goes I seldom saw a gathering so unanimously solemn. I might even say so tearful. It is possible, of course, that the music eventually maddens them, that it works them up about midnight into a homicidal melancholy. But there was no profligacy of blood-shedding while I was there.

They did not even offer to murder a musician.

CHAPTER II.

FROM CHICAGO TO DENVER.

Fathers of Waters—"Rich Lands lie Flat"—The Misery River—
Council Bluffs—A "Live" town, sir—Two murders : a contrast—
Omaha—The immorality of "writing up"—On the prairies—The
modesty of "Wish-ton-Wish"—The antelope's tower of refuge
—Out of Nebraska into Colorado—Man-eating Tiger..

FROM Chicago to Omaha by the "Chicago and North-
western" route is not an exhilarating journey. When
Nature begins to make anything out here in America she
never seems to know when to stop. She can never make
a few of anything. For instance, it might have been
thought that one or two hundred miles of perfectly flat land
was enough at a time. But Nature, having once commenced flattening out the land, cannot leave off. So all
the way from Chicago to Omaha there is the one same
pattern of country, a wilderness of maize-stubble and virgin
land, broken only for the first half of the way by occasional
patches of water-oak, and for the second half of willows.

Just on the frontier-line of these two vegetable divisions of
the country lies a tract of bright turf-land. What a magician
this same turf is! It is Wendell Holmes, I think, who
says that Anglo-Saxons emigrate only *" in the line of turf."*

The better half of the journey passed on Sunday, and the
people were all out in loitering, well-dressed groups " to see
the train pass," and at the stations where we stopped, to see

the passengers, too. Where they came from it was not easy
to tell, for the homesteads in sight were very few and far
between. Yet there they were, happy, healthy, well-to-do
contented-looking families, enjoying the Day of Rest—the
one dissipation of the hard-worked week. What a comfortable connecting link with the outer world the railway
must be to these scattered dwellers on this prairie-land !

So through Illinois to the Mississippi. How wonderfully
it resembles the Indus where it flows past Lower Sind. A
minaret or two, a blue-tiled cupola and a clump of palms
would make the resemblance of the Mississippi at
Clinton to the Indus below Rohri complete. And both
rivers claim to be "the Father of Waters." I would not
undertake to decide between them. In modern annals, of
course, the American must take pre-eminence ; but what
can surpass the historic grandeur that dignifies the Indian
stream ?

And so into Iowa, just as flat, and as rich, and as monotonous as Illinois, and with just the same leagues of maize-
stubble, unbroken soil, water-oaks and willows. And then,
in the deepening twilight, to Cedar Rapids, with the
pleasant sound of rushing water and all the townsfolk waiting " to see the train " on their way from church, standing in
groups, with their prayer-books and Bibles in their hands.

By the way, what an admirable significance there is in
the care with which these young townships discharge their
duties to their religion and the dead. The church or
prayer-house seems to be always one of the first and finest
buildings. With only half-a-dozen homesteads in sight in
some places, there is " the church," and while all the rest
are of the humblest class of frame houses, the church is
of brick. The cemeteries again. Before even the plots
round the living are set in order, " God's acre " (often

the best site in the neighbourhood) is neatly fenced and laid out.

And I thought it somehow a beautiful touch of national character, this reverent providence for the dead that are to come. And just before I went to sleep, I saw out in the moonlit country a cemetery, and on the crest of the rising ground stood one solitary tombstone, the pioneer of the many—the first dead settler's grave. In this new country the living are as yet in the majority !

Awakening, find myself still in Iowa, and Iowa still as flat as ever. Not spirit enough in all these hundred miles of land to firk up even a hillock, a mound, a pimple. But to make a new proverb, "Rich lands lie flat;" and Iowa, in time, will be able to feed the world—aye, and to clothe it too

In the mean time we are approaching the Missouri, through levels in which the jack-rabbit abounds, and every farmer, therefore, seems to keep a greyhound for coursing the long-eared aborigines. The willows, conscious of secret resources of water, are already in leaf, and overhead the wild ducks and geese are passing to their feeding-grounds. Here I saw " blue " grass for the first time, and I must say I am glad that grass is usually green. Elsewhere in the States, *English* grass is called " blue grass ;" but in some parts, as here in this part of Iowa, there is a native grass which is literally blue. And it is not an improvement, so far as the effect on the landscape goes, upon the old fashioned colour for grass. And then the Missouri, a muddy, shapeless, dissipated stream. The people on its banks call it "treacherous," and pronounce its name " Misery." It is certainly a most unprepossessing river, with its ill-gotten banks of ugly sand, and its lazy brown waters gurgling along in an overgrown, self-satisfied way. It is a bullying stream ; gives nobody peace that lives near it ; and is perpetually trying in an underhanded sort of way to "scour" out the foundations of the hollow columns on which the bridges across it are built. But the abundance of water-fowl upon its banks and side-waters is a redeeming feature for all who care to carry a gun, and I confess I should like to have had a day's leisure at Council Bluffs to go out and have a shot. The inhabitants of the place, however, do not seem to be goose-eaters, for, close season or not, I cannot imagine their permitting flocks of these eminently edible birds to fly circling about over their houses, within forty yards of the ground. The wild-goose is proverbially a wary fowl, but here at Council Bluffs they have apparently become from long immunity as impertinent and careless as sparrows.

Council Bluffs, as the pow-wow place of the Red Men in the days when Iowa was rolling prairie and bison used to browse where horses plough, has many a quaint legend of the past; and in spite of the frame houses that are clustered below them and the superb cobweb bridge—it has few rivals in the world—that here spans the Missouri, the Bluffs, as the rendezvous of Sagamore and Sachem, stand out from the interminable plains eloquent of a very picturesque antiquity. And so to Omaha.

"But I guess, sir, Om'a's a *live* town. Yes, sir, *a live town*."

My experiences of Omaha were too brief for me to be just, too disagreeable for me to be impartial. Before breakfast I saw a murder and suicide, and between breakfast and luncheon a fire and several dog-fights. Perhaps I might have seen something more. But a terrible dust-storm raged in the streets all day. Besides, I went away.

I am beginning already to hate "live" towns.

I.

It was during the Afghan War. I had just ridden back from General Roberts' camp in the Thull Valley, on the frontiers of Afghanistan, and found myself stopped on my return at the Kohat Pass. " It is the orders of Government," said the sentry: " the Pass is unsafe for travellers."

But I *had* to get through the Pass whether it was " safe " or not, for through it lay the only road to General Browne's camp, to which I was attached. So I dismounted, and after a great deal of palaver, partly of bribes, partly of un-truths, I not only got past the native sentries, but got a guide to escort me, through the thirty miles of wild Afridi defiles that lay before me. The scenery is, I think, among the finest in the world, while, added to all is the strange fascination of the knowledge that the people who live in the Pass have cherished from generation to generation the most vindictive blood feuds. The villages are surrounded by high walls, loopholed along the top, and the huts in the inside are built against the wall, so that the roofs of them can be used by the men of the village as lounges during the day, and as ramparts for sentries during the night. Within these sullen squares each clan lives in perpetual siege. The women and children are at all times permitted to go to and fro ; but for the men, woe to him who happens to stray within reach of the jezails that lie all ready loaded in the loopholes of the next village. The crops are sown and reaped by men with guns slung on their backs, and in the middle of every field stands a martello-tower, in which the peasants can take shelter if neighbours sally out to attack them while at work. Rope-ladders hang from a doorway half-way up the tower, and up this, like lizards, the men scramble, one after the other, as soon as danger threatens, draw in the ladder, and through the loop-holes overlook their menaced crops.

A wonderful country truly, and something in the air to day that makes my guide ride as hard as the road will permit, with his sword drawn across the saddle before him. My revolver is in my hand. And so we clatter along, mile after mile, through the beautiful series of little valleys, grim villages, and towers. Now and again a party of women will step aside to let us pass, or a dog start up to bark at us, but not a single man do we see. Yet I know very well that hundreds of men see us ride by, and that a jezail is lying at every loophole, and covering the very path we ride on.

We reach a sudden turn of the path; my guide gallops round it. He is hardly out of my sight when *Bang! bang!* It is no use pulling up, and the next instant I am round the corner too. A man, with his jezail still smoking from the last shot, starts up from the undergrowth almost under my horse's feet, and narrowly escapes being ridden down. Another man comes running down the hillside towards him. In front of me, some fifty yards off, is my guide, with his horse's head towards me and his sword in his hand, and on the path, midway between us, lies a heap of brightly-coloured clothing—a dead Afridi! For a second both guide and I thought that it was we who had drawn the fire from the ambushed men. But no, it was the poor Afridi lad lying there in the path before us, and the victim of a blood feud. He had tried, no doubt, to steal across from his own village to some friendly hamlet close by, but his lynx-eyed enemies had seen him, and, lying there on either side of his path, had shot him as he passed.

But what a group we were! Myself, with my revolver

in my hand, looking, horror-stricken, now at the dead, and now at his murderers ; my guide, in the splendid uniform of the Indian irregular cavalry, emotionless as only Orientals can be ; the two murderers talking together excitedly ; in the middle of us the dead lad ! But there was still another figure to be added, for suddenly, along the very path by which the victim had come, there came running an old woman—perhaps she had followed the lad with a mother's tender anxiety for his safety—and in an instant she saw the worst. Without a glance at any of us, she flung herself down with the cry of a breaking heart, by the dead boy's side, and as my guide turned to ride on and I followed him, as the murderers slipped away into the undergrowth, we all heard her crooning, between her sobs, over the body of her murdered son.

II.

I was in Omaha. I had just crossed Thirteenth Street, and, turning to look as I passed, at the Catholic church, had caught an idle glimpse of the folk in the street. Among them was a woman at the wooden gateway of a small house, hesitating, so it seemed to me afterwards, about pushing it open, for though she had her hand upon the latch, yet she did not lift it, but appeared to me, at the distance I passed and the cursory glance I gave, to be listening to what some-body was saying to her through the window. Had I been only a few yards nearer ! At the moment that I saw her, the wretched woman was gazing with fixed and horrified eyes upon a face—a grim and cruel face—that glared at her from a window, and at a gun that she saw was pointed full at her breast. And the next instant, just as I had turned the corner, there was the report of fire-arms. It did not occur to me to stop. But suddenly I heard a cry, and then a second shot, and somehow there flashed upon my mind the picture of that hesitating woman by the wicket, with her knitted shawl over her head, and the wind blowing her light dress to one side.

I did not turn back, however. For the woman and the shots had only the merest flash of a connexion in my mind. But after a few steps a man came running past me, going perhaps for the doctor, or the police, or the coroner, and the scared look on his face suddenly once more wrenched back to my imagination the woman at the wicket.

So I turned back into Thirteenth Street, and there, in the middle of the road, with a man stooping over her and two women, transfixed by sudden terror into attitudes that were most tragic, I saw the woman lying. Her face was turned up to the bright sunlit sky, her shawl had fallen back about her neck, and her hair lay in the dust. She was already dead. And her murderer? He too had gone to his last account; and as I stood there in that dreary Omaha road, with the wind raising wisps of dust about the horror-stricken group, and thought of the two dead bodies lying there, one in the roadway, the other in the house close by, my mind reverted involuntarily to the fancy that at that very moment the two souls, man and wife, were standing before their Maker, and that perhaps she, the poor mangled woman, was pleading for mercy for the man, her husband, the lover of her youth—her murderer.

———

In the evening, when a cool breeze was blowing, and imagination pictured the trees holding up screens of green foliage before the hotel windows to shut out the ugly views of half-built streets, I entertained feelings that were almost kindly towards Omaha; but the memory of the day that was

happily past, as often as it recurred to me, changed them to
gall again. All day long there had been a flaring, glaring
sun overhead and the wind that was blowing would have done
credit to the deserts through which I have since marched with
the army in Egypt. It went howling down the street with the
voices of wild beasts, and carried with it such simooms of
sand as would probably in a week overwhelm and bury in
Ninevite oblivion the buildings of this aspiring town. And
not only sand, but whirlwinds of vulgar dust also, with occasional discharges of cinders, that came rushing along the
road, picking up all the rubbish it could find, dodging up
alleys and coming out again with accumulations of straw,
rampaging into courtyards in search of paper and rags,
standing still in the middle of the roadway to whirl, and
altogether behaving itself just as a disreputable and aggressive vagabond may be always expected to behave. Of
course I was told it was a " very exceptional " day.
It always *is* a " very exceptional day " wherever a
stranger goes. But I must confess that I never saw any
place—except Aden, and perhaps East London, in South
Africa—that struck me on short acquaintance as so
thoroughly undesirable for a lengthened abode. The big
black swine rooting about in the back yards, the little black
boys playing drearily at " marbles " with bits of stone, the
multitude of dogs loafing on the sidewalks, the depressing
irregularity of the streets, the paucity of shade-trees, the
sandy bluffs that dominate the town and hold over the heads
of the inhabitants the perpetual threat of siroccos, and the
general appearance (however false it may have been) of
disorder—all combined with various degrees of force to give
the impression that Omaha is a place that had from some cause
or another been suddenly checked in its natural expansion.

Its geographical position is indisputably a commanding

one, and already the great smelting works, with one exception the busiest in the States, the splendid workshops of
the Union Pacific Railway, and the thriving distillery close
by, give promise of the great industries which in the future
this town, with its wonderful advantages of communication,
as the meeting-point of great railway high-roads, will attract
to itself. Omaha has an admirable opera-house, and when
its hotel is rebuilt it will be able to offer visitors good
accommodation. It has also an imposing school-house im-
posingly advertised by being on top of a hill, and the
refining grace of gardens is not completely absent, while the
" stove-pipe " hat gives fragmentary evidence of advanced
civilization. But all this affords encouragement for the
future only; at present Omaha is a depressing spot. And
so I left the town without regret ; but I did not make
any effort to shake off the dust of Omaha. That was impossible; it had penetrated the texture of my clothing so
completely that nothing but shredding my garments into
their original threads would have sufficed.

Now I had read something of Omaha before I went
there, had seen it called "a splendid Western city," and
been invited to linger there to examine its " dozens of noble
monuments to invincible enterprise," which, with "the dozen
or more church spires," are supposed to break the sky-line
of the view of this " metropolis of the North-western States
and Territories." It is possible, therefore, that my profound
disappointment with the reality, after reading such exagge-
rated description, may have tinged my opinion of Omaha,
and, combined with the unfortunately " exceptional " day
I spent there, have made me think very poorly of the former
capital of Nebraska. That it has a great future before it, its
position alone guarantees, and the enterprise of Nebraska
puts beyond all doubt ; but the sight-seer going to Omaha,

and expecting to find it anything but a very new town on a very unprepossessing site, will be as greatly disappointed as I was.

Equally unfortunate is the " writing up " which the Valley of the .Platte has received. Who, for instance, that has travelled on the railway along that great void can read without annoyance of " beautiful valley landscapes, in which thousands of productive farms, fine farm-houses, blossoming orchards, and *thriving cities* " are features of the country traversed? No one can charge me with a want of sympathy with the true significance of this wonderful Western country. And I can say, therefore, without hesitation that the dreariness of the country between Omaha and Denver Junction is almost inconceivable. There is hardly even a *town* worth calling such in sight, much less " thriving cities." The original prairie lies there spread out, on either hand, in nearly all its original barrenness. Interminable plains, that occasionally roll into waves, stretch away to the horizon to right and left, dotted with skeletons of dead cattle and widely scattered herds of living ones. Here and there a cow-boy's shed, and here and there a ranch of the ordinary primitive type, and here and there a dug-out, are all the " features " of the long ride. An occasional emigrant waggon perhaps breaks the dull, dead monotony of the landscape, and in one place there is a solitary bush upon a mound. A hawk floats in the air above a prairie-dog village. A plover sweeps past with its melancholy cry.

No, the journey to North Platte—where a very bad breakfast was put before us at a dollar a head—is *not* attractive. But here again it is the Possible in the future that makes the now desolate scene so full of interest and so splendidly significant. As a grazing country it can never, perhaps, be very populous ; but in time, of course, those ranches, now

struggling so bravely against terrible odds, will become
" fine farm-houses," and have " blossoming orchards " about
them.   But as yet these things are not, and for good, all-
round dreariness I would not know where to send a friend
with such confidence as to the pastures between Omaha and
North Platte.

Oh ! *when* are we to have Pullman palace balloons ?
Condemned to travel, my soul and my bones cry out for
air-voyaging.

That some day man should fly like a bird has been, in
spite of superstition, an article of honest belief from the
beginning of time, and in the dove of Archytas alone we
have proof enough that, even in those days, the successful
accomplishment of flight was accepted as a fact of science.
During the Middle Ages so common was this belief that
every man who dabbled in physics was pronounced a magician, and as such was credited with the power of transport-
ing himself through the air at will.   Some, indeed, actually
claimed the enviable privilege, Friar Bacon among others.
But history records no practical illustration of their control
of the air, while more than one death is chronicled of daring
men who, with insufficient apparatus, launched themselves
in imitation of birds upon space, and fell, more or less
precipitately, to earth.   The Italian who flapped himself off
Stirling Castle trusted only to a pair of huge feather wings,
which he had tied on to his arms, and got no farther on his
way to France than the heads of the spectators at the bottom
of the wall; while the Monk of Tübingen started on his
journey from the top of his tower with apparatus that immediately turned inside out, and increased by its weight the
momentum with which he came down plumb into the street.

Beyond North Platte the same melancholy expanses again
commence, the same rolling prairies, with the same dead

cattle and the same herds of live ones, an occasional waggon or a stock-yard or snow-fence being all that interrupts the flat monotony. But approaching Sterling a suspicion of verdure begins in places to steal over the grey prairie, and flights of "larks," with a bright, pleasant note, give something of an air of animation to isolated spots. Here is a plough at work, the first we have passed, I think, since we left Omaha, and the plover piping overhead seem to resent the novelty. Cattle continue to dot the landscape, and all the afternoon the Platte rolls along a sluggish stream parallel to the track.

The train happened to slacken pace at one point, and a man came up to the cars. He was a beggar, and asked our help to get along the road "eastward." One of his arms was in a sling from an accident, and his whole appearance eloquent of utter destitution. And the very landscape pleaded for him. Beggary at any time must be wretchedness, but here in this bleak waste of pasturage it must almost be *despair*. And as the train sped on, the one dismal figure creeping along by the side of the track, with the dark clouds of a snowstorm coming up to meet him, was strangely pathetic.

And then Sterling. May Sterling be forgiven for the dinner it set before us!

And then on again, across long leagues of level plain, thickly studded with prickly pear patches and seamed with the old bison and antelope tracks leading down from the hills to the river. There are no bison now. They cannot stand before the stove-pipe hat. The sombreroed hunter, with his lasso, the necklace of death, was an annoyance to them; they spent their lives dodging him. The befeathered Indian, "the chivalry of the prairie," who pincushioned their hides full of arrows, was a terror to them, and they fell by thousands. But before the stove-pipe hat the bison fled incontinently by the herd, and have never returned.

The prairie-dogs peep out of their holes at us as we passed. The bashfulness of "Wish-ton-Wish," as the Red Man calls the prairie-dog, is as nearly impudence as one thing can be another. It sits up perkily on one end at the edge of its hole till you are close upon it, and then, with a sudden affectation of being shocked at its own immodesty, dives headlong into its hole ; but its hind-legs are not out of sight before the head is up again, and the next instant there is the prairie-dog sitting exactly where you first saw it ! Such a burlesque of shyness I never saw in a quadruped before.

A solitary coyote was loitering in a hungry way along a gulch, and I could not help thinking how the most important epochs of one's life may often turn upon the merest trifles. Now, here was a coyote ambling lazily up a certain gulch because it had happened to see some white bones bleaching a little way up it. But in the very next gulch, which the coyote had *not* happened to go up, were three half-bred greyhounds idling about, just in the humour for something to run after. But they could not see the coyote, though it was really only a few yards off, nor could the coyote see them. So the dogs lounged about in a listless, do-nothing, tired-of-life sort of way, thinking existence as dull as ditch water, while the coyote, unconscious of the narrow escape of its life that it ran, trotted slowly along—scrutinized the old bones—scratched its head—yawned out of sheer ennui, and then trotted along again. Now, what a difference it would have made to those three dogs if they had only happened to loaf into the next gulch ! And what a prodigious difference it would have made to the coyote if it had happened to loaf into the next gulch !

The prickly pear, that ugly, fleshy little cactus, with its sudden summer glories of crimson and golden blossoms, fulfils a strange purpose in the animal economy of the prairies. In itself it appears to be one of the veriest outcasts among vegetables, execrated by man and refused as food by beast. Yet if it were not for this plant the herds of prairie antelope would have fared badly enough, for the antelope, whenever they found themselves in straits from wolves or from dogs, made straight for the prickly pear patches and belts, and there, standing right out on the barren, open plain, defied their swift but tender-footed pursuers to come near them. For the small, thick pads of the cactus, though they lie so flat and insignificantly upon the ground, are studded with tufts of strong, fierce spines, and woe to the wolf or the dog that treads upon them. The antelope's hoofs, however, are proof against the spines, and one leap across such a belt suffices to place the horned folk in safety. These patches and belts, then, so trivial to the eye, and in some places almost invisible to the cursory glance, are in reality Towers of Refuge to the great edible division of the wild prairie nations, and as impassable to the eaters as was that girdle of fire and steel which Von Moltke buckled so closely round the city of the Napoleons.

But here we are approaching Denver. The cottonwood has mustered into clusters, a prototype of the future of these now scattered ranches. Dotted about here and there in suitable corners, on river bank or under sheltering bluff, single trees are growing side by side with single stockyards or single cow-boys' huts, but every now and again, where nature offers them a good site for a colony, the trees congregate, select lots, and permanently locate. It is not very different after all, with human beings.

Nature here is undoubtedly tempting, and **Denver**

D

itself must surely be one of the most beautiful towns in the States. Through great reaches of splendid farm-land, with water in abundance and the cottonwood and willow growing thickly, we pass to our destination as the twilight settles on the country.

A whole day has again been spent in the train! We had awaked in the morning to see from the car windows the people of Nebraska going out to their day's work in the fields, and here in the evening we sit and watch the Colorado folk coming home to their rest after the day's work is over. Truly this steam is a Latter-Day apocalypse and this America a land of magnificent distances.

I found out on this trip that my fellow-travellers (and the fact holds good nearly all over America) took the greatest interest in British India, and finding that I had spent so many years there, they plied me with questions. On some journeys it would be the political aspect of our government of Hindostan that interested, at others the commercial or the social. But going through Colorado, one of the haunts of the " grizzly " and the " mountain lion," I had to detail my experiences of sport in India. Above all, *the tiger* interested them. It is the only animal in the world that may be said to give the grizzly a point or two. And there are some even who deny this; but I, who have shot the tiger, and never seen a grizzly, naturally concede the first place in perilous courage to Stripes, the raja of the jungle. In one particular aspect, at any rate, the tiger is supreme among quadrupeds. It has the splendid audacity to make man his regular food.

Now, it is generally supposed that the " man-eater " is a specially formidable variety of the species ; that it is only the boldest, strongest, and fiercest of the tigers that preys on man. But the very reverse is of course the truth.

When hale and strong the tiger avoids the vicinity of men, finding abundant food in the herds of deer and other wild animals that share his jungles. But when strength and speed of limb begin to fail, the brute has to look for easier prey than the courageous bison or wind-footed antelope, and so skulks among the ravines and waste patches of woodland that are to be found about nearly every village. Then when twilight obscures the scene, he creeps out noiseless as a shadow, and lies in ambush in a crop of standing grain or bhair-tree brake, and watches the country folk go by from the fields in twos and threes, driving their plough cattle before them. After a while, there comes sauntering past alone, a man or a woman who has lagged behind the company ; yet not so far behind but that the friends ahead can hear the scream which tells of the tiger's leap, though too far for help to be of use. During four years 350 human beings and 24,000 head of cattle were killed by these animals in one district in Bombay, while many single tigers have been known to destroy over a hundred people before they were shot. One in the Mandla district caused the desertion of thirteen villages and threw out of cultivation two hundred and fifty square miles of country ; while another, only one of many similar cases, was credited with the appalling total of eighty human victims per annum ! The yearly loss in cattle and by decrease of cultivation through the ravages of these fearful beasts has been estimated at ten million pounds sterling !

No wonder, then, that even these doughty grizzly-slayers of the Rockies respect the tiger's name.

CHAPTER III.

IN LEADVILLE.

The South Park line—Oscar Wilde on sunflowers as food—In a
wash-hand basin—Anti-Vigilance Committees—Leadville the city
of the carbonates—"Busted" millionaires—The philosophy of
thick boots—Colorado miners—National competition in lions—
Abuse of the terms "gentleman" and "lady"—Up at the mines
—Under the pine-trees.

STARTING from Denver for Leadville in the evening, it
seemed as if we were fated to see nothing of the very
interesting country through which the South Park line
runs. At first there is nothing to look at but open prairie
land sprinkled with the homesteads of agricultural pioneers,
but as the moon got up there was gradually revealed
a stately succession of mountain ridges, and in about
two hours we found ourselves threading the spurs of the
Sangre di Christi range and following the Platte River up
toward its sources. Crossing and recrossing the cañon, with
one side silvered, and the other thrown into the blackest
shadow by the moon, and the noisy stream tumbling along
beside us in its hurry to get down to the lazy levels of the
great Nebraska Valley, I saw glimpses of scenery that
can never be forgotten. It was fantastic in the extreme;
for apart from the jugglery of moonlight, in itself so wonderful always, the ideas of relative distance and size, even
of shape, were upset and ridiculed by the snowy peaks
that here and there thrust themselves up into the sky and by

the patches and streaks of snow that concealed and altered the contour of the nearer rocks in the most puzzling manner imaginable. And all this time the little train—for the line is narrow-gauge—kept twisting and wriggling in and out as if it were in collusion with the hills, and playing into their hands to disconcert the traveller.

I have seen at different times great curiosities of engineering, as in travelling over the Ghâts in Western India, where everything is stupendous and at times even terrific, where danger seems perpetual and disaster often inevitable. In passing by train from Colombo to Kandy in Ceylon, and crossing Sensation Rock, the railway cars actually hang over the precipice, so that when you look out of the window the track on which you are running is invisible, and you can drop an orange plumb down the face·of this appalling cliff on to the tops of the palm-trees, which look like little round bushes in the valley down below. From Durban to Pietermaritzburg again, on the line along which, when it was first opened, the engine-driver brought out from England refused to take his train, declaring it to be too dangerous, but along which, nevertheless, the British troops going up to Zululand were all safely carried. The South Park line, however, can compare with these, and must be accepted as one of the acknowledged triumphs of railway enterprise. For much of its length the rocks had to be fought inch by inch, and they died hard. The result to-day is a very picturesque and interesting ride, with a surprise in every mile and beauty all the way.

On the way to the "City of the Carbonates," I heard much of Leadville ways and life. That very morning the energetic police of the town had arrested two young ladies for parading the sunflower and the lily too conspicuously. One had donned a sunflower for a hat, the other walked along

holding a tall lily in her hand.   The Leadville youth had
gathered in disorderly procession behind the æsthetic pair.
So the police arrested the fair causes of the disturbance.

I told Oscar Wilde of this a few days later.   " Poor sweet
things ! " said he ; " martyrs in the cause of the Beautiful."
He was on his way to Salt Lake City at the time, and I told
him how the Mormon capital was par excellence " the city
of sunflowers," and assured him that the poet's feeding on
" gilliflowers rare " was not, after all, too violent a stretch of
imagination, as whole tribes of Indians (and Longfellow
himself has said that every Indian is a poem, which is very
nearly the same thing as a poet) feed on the sunflower. The
Apostle of Art Decoration was delighted.

" Poor sweet things ! " said he ; " feed on sunflowers !
How charming !   If I could only have stayed and dined
with them !   But how delightful to be able to go back to
England and say that I have actually been in a country
where whole tribes of men *live on sunflowers !* The precious-
ness of it ! "

It is a fact, probably new to some of my readers, that the
wild sunflower is the characteristic weed of Utah, and that
the seeds of the plant supply the undiscriminating Red Man
with an oil-cake which may agreeably vary a diet of grass-
hoppers and rattlesnakes, but has not intrinsically any flavour
to recommend it.   So South Kensington must not rush
away with the idea that the noble savage who has the Crow
for his " totem," feeds upon the *blossoms* of the vegetable
they worship.   It is the prosaic oil-cake that the Pi-ute eats.

But all I heard got mixed up eventually into a general
idea that every man in the place who had not committed
a murder was a millionaire, and all those who had not
lost their lives had lost a fortune.   The mines, too, got
gradually sorted up into two kinds—those that had   five

million now in sight, sir," or those whose "bottoms had fallen out." But one fact that pleased me particularly was the "Anti-Vigilance" Committee of Leadville. Every one knows that a "Vigilance Committee" consists of a certain number of volunteer guardians of the peace, who call (with a rope) upon strangers visiting their neighbourhood and offer them the choice of being hanged at once for the offences they purpose committing or of going elsewhere to commit them. The strangers, as it transpires in the morning, sometimes choose one course and sometimes the other. This is all very right and proper, and conduces to a general good understanding. But in Leadville, the citizens started *an anti-vigilance committee* and so the Vigilance Committee sent in their resignations to themselves— and accepted them. I do not think I ever heard of a fact so appalling in its significance. But the humour of it is that the Anti-Vigilance Committee managed somehow to keep the peace in Leadville as it had never been kept before.

It reminded me of an incident of the Afghan war. A certain tribe of hill-men persisted in killing the couriers who carried the post from one British camp to the other, and the generals were nearly at their wits' end for means of communication, when the murderers sent in word offering to carry the post themselves—and did so, faithfully !

It was in Leadville also that lived the barber who, going forth one night, was met by two men who told him peremptorily to take his hands out of his pockets, as they intended to take out all the rest. But he had nothing in his pockets except two Derringers, so he pulled his hands out and shot the two men dead where they stood. Next morning the citizens of Leadville placed the barber in a triumphal chair, and carried him round the town as a bright example to the public, presented him with a gold watch and chain as a testimonial of their esteem for his courage—and then escorted him the first stage out of the town, advising him never to return.

But this was in the Leadville of the very remote past—1880 or thereabouts—and not in the Carbonate City of the present, 1882. The town is now as quiet as such a town can be, a wonderfully busy place and a picturesque one.

And while my companions talked I sat in the wash-hand basin and smoked. Why the wash-hand basin? Because there was nowhere else to sit. The "smoking-car" of this particular train happened to be also the gentlemen's lavatory, a commodious snuggery measuring about eight feet by five. And as there were only eight smokers on board we were not so crowded as we should have been if there had been eighteen, and then, you see, we made more room still by two of the eight staying away. For the rest, two of us sat in the wash-hand basins, one on a stool between our legs, another on a stool with his knees against the gentlemen opposite, and the balance stood. We were an example of tight packing even to the proverbial sardine. But I found the water-tap at the edge of the basin an inconvenient circumstance. I would venture to suggest to American railway companies that for the comfort of smokers when sitting in the basins they should place these taps a little farther back.

I suppose I ought to give some mining statistics about Leadville. But the very fact that I shall be neglecting an obvious duty if I omit all statistics, nearly decides me to omit them. The deliberate neglect of an obvious duty is, however, a luxury which only the very virtuous can indulge in ; and to compromise therefore with the situation, I would state that the mining output of Leadville is to-day about eleven times as great as it was two years ago, and that five years ago there was no output at all. That is to say, this town of Leadville, with a population, floating and permanent together, of some 40,000 souls, and yielding from its mines about a thousand dollars per head of the total population, was five years ago a camp of a few hundred miners, as a rule so disappointed with the prospect of the place that another year of the *status quo* would have seen Leadville deserted. But the secret of the carbonates being "ore-iferous" was discovered, and Tabor, like the fossil of some antediluvian giant, was gradually revealed by the pick of the miner, in all his Plutocratic bulk. A few years ago he was selling peanuts at the corner of a street. To-day he moves about, king of Denver, with Leadville for an appanage. His potentiality in cheques increases yearly by another cipher added to the total, and drags at each remove a lengthening chain of wealth. Why do men go on accumulating money when they are already masters of enough? Surely it is better to be rich than a pauper? But in Colorado this is not the general opinion. Men there prefer to be ruined rather than be merely rich. And the result is that you could hardly throw a boot out of the hotel window without hitting an ex-millionaire. Not that I would advise anybody to go throwing boots promiscuously out of hotel windows in Leadville. You would run a good chance of following your boots.

"Do you see that man there, paring his boot with a knife?" asked my companion.

"Yes," said I, "I see him; there is a good deal of him to see."

"Well," said he, "that's So-and-so. He sold so-and-so for $400,000 about a year ago. But he busted last Fall. And if you get into conversation with him, he'll be glad to borrow a dollar from you."

"Then I shall not get into conversation with him," I replied.

"And do you see that old fellow on the other side, leaning against the hitching post, outside the Post Office?"

"Well," said I, "they seem to be mostly leaning against the hitching-post, but I presume you mean the gentleman in the middle."

"Yes," was the reply. "That's So-and-so. He struck the so-and-so, got $80,000 for his share about six weeks ago—and is busted."

And so on *ad infinitum.* The problem was a very puzzling one to me at first—why do such men make fortunes if they take the first opportunity of throwing them away? But the solution, I fancy, is this—that these men do not care for money. It is to them what knowledge is to the philosopher, a means of acquiring more—worthless in itself, but, as leading to larger results, worthy of all eagerness in its pursuit. They do not put Wealth before themselves as an accumulation of current coins, capable of purchasing everything that makes life materially pleasant. They contemplate it merely in the bulk. Much in the same way a whaler never thinks of the number of candles in the spermaceti into which he has struck a harpoon. He looks at his quarry only as a "ten barrel" or a "fifteen barrel" whale, as the case may be. He does not content himself with the illuminating potentialities of the creature he pursues. He is only anxious as to how it will barrel off, and the barrels might be pork, or potatoes, or anything else. So with the man who goes out mine-hunting. He harpoons a lode, lays open so many "*millions*" of ore, sells it to a company for a "*million*" or two, and straightway goes and "busts" for so many "*millions.*" It does not seem to concern such a one that a "million" of dollars is so many guineas, or roubles, or napoleons, or mohurs, and so forth, and that if he goes on to the end of his life, he can never achieve more than *money*. His arithmetic goes mad, and he begins computing from the wrong end of the line. Ten thousands of dollars make one 50-cent piece, two 50-cent pieces make one quarter, five quarters make one nickel, five nickels make one cent, and "quite a lot" of cents make one fortune. So at it he goes again, trying to foot up a satisfactory balance with thousands for units—and "busts" before he gets to the end of the sum.

Leadville itself as I first saw it, ringed in with snow-covered hills, a bright sun shining and a slight snow falling, remains in my memory as one of the prettiest scenes in my experience. In Switzerland even it could hold its own, and triumph. I wandered about its streets and into its shops and saloons, curious to see some of those men of whom I had heard so much; but whatever may have been their exercises with bowie-knife and pistol at a later hour of the day, I was never more agreeably disappointed than by the manners and bearing of the Leadville miners early in the morning.

There is nothing gives a man so much self-reliance as having thick boots on. This fact I have evolved out of my own consciousness, for when I was out in the Colonies I often tried to analyze a certain sense of "independence" which I found taking possession of me. The climate no doubt was exceptionally invigorating, and I was a great deal on horseback. But I had been subjected to the same conditions elsewhere without experiencing the same results. And after a great deal of severe mental inquiry, I decided that it was—my thick boots! And I was right. No man can feel properly capable of taking care of himself in slippers. In patent-leather boots he is little better, and in what are called "summer walking-shoes" he still finds himself fastidious about puddles, and at a disadvantage with every man he meets who does not mind a rough road. But once you begin to thicken the sole, self-reliance commences to increase, and by the time your boots are as solid as those of a Colorado miner you should find yourself his equal in "independence." And some of their boots are prodigious. The soles are over an inch thick, project in front of the toes perhaps half an inch, and form a ledge, as it were, all round the foot. What a luxury with such boots it must be to kick a man!

The rest of the costume was often in keeping with the shoe leather, and in every case where the wearers did not belong to the shops and offices of the town, there was a general attention to strength of material and personal comfort, at a sacrifice of appearance, which was refreshing and unconventional. They are a fine set, indeed, this miscellaneous congregation of nationalities which men call "Colorado diggers." There is hardly a stupid face among them, and certainly not a cowardly one. And then compare them with the population of their native places—the savages of the East of London, the outer barbarians of Scandinavia, the degraded peasantry of Western Ireland! The contrast is astonishing. Left in Europe they might have guttered along in helpless poverty relieved only by intervals of crime, till old age found them in a workhouse. But here they can insist on every one pretending to think them "as good as himself" (such is, I believe, the formula of this preposterous hypocrisy), and, at any rate, may hope for sudden wealth. Above all, a man here does not go about barefooted, like so many of his family "at home," or in ragged shoe-leather, like so many more of them; but stands, and it may even be sleeps, in boots of unimpeachable solidity. So he goes down the street as if it were his own, planting his feet firmly at every step, and, not having to trouble himself about the condition of the footway, keeps his head erect. Depend upon it, thick boots are one of the secrets of " independence " of character.

But Leadville, this wonderful town that in four years sprang up from 300 to 30,000 inhabitants, is not entirely a city of miners. On the day that I was there larger numbers than usual were in the streets, in consequence of an election then in progress holding out promises of unusual entertainment. Besides these there is, of course, the permanent population of commerce and ordinary business; and I was struck here, as I had not been before since I left Boston, with the natural phenomenon of a race reverting to an old type. Boston reminded me at times of some old English cathedral city. Leadville was like some thriving provincial town. The men would not have looked out of place in the street, say, of Reading, while the women, in their quiet and somewhat old-fashioned style of dressing, reminded me very curiously of rural England. Indeed, I do not think my anticipations have ever been so completely upset as in Leadville. All the way from New York I have been told to wait " till I got to Colorado " before I ventured to speak of rough life, and Leadville itself was sometimes particularized to me as the Ultima Thule of civilization, the vanishing-point of refinement.

But not only is Leadville not " rough;" it is even flirting with the refinements of life. It has an opera-house, a good drive for evening recreation, and a florist's shop. There were not many plants in it, it is true, but they were nearly all of them of the pleasant old English kinds— geraniums, pansies, pinks, and mignonette. Two other shops interested me, one stocked with mineral specimens—

malachite, agate, amethyst, quartz, blood-stone, onyx, and
an infinite variety of pieces of ore, gold, silver, lead, iron,
copper, bismuth, and sulphur—with which pretty settings
are made, of a quaint grotto-work kind, for clocks and ink-
stands. The other a naturalist's shop, in which, besides
fossils, exquisite leaves in stone and petrified tree-fragments,
I found the commencement of a zoological collection—the
lynx with its comfortable snow-coat on, and the grey mountain wolf not less cozily dressed ; squirrels, black and grey,
" the creatures that sit in the shade of their tails," and the
"friends of Hiawatha," with various birds—the sage hen and
the prairie chicken, the magpie (very like the English bird),
and the " lark,"—a very inadequate substitute indeed for the
bird that " at Heaven's gate sings," that has been sanctified
to all time by Shelley, and the idol of the poets of the Old
World—and heads of large game, horned and antlered, and
the skin of a " lion." It is a curious fact that every country
should thus insist on having *a lion.* For the real African
animal himself I entertain only a very qualified respect. For
some of his substitutes, the panther of Sumatra and the Far
East, the (now extinct) cat of Australia, and the puma of the
United States, that respect is even more moderate in degree.
" The American lion " is, in fact, about as much like the
original article as the American " muffin " is like the
seductive but saddening thing from which it takes its name.
The puma, which is its proper name, is the least imposing
of all the larger cats. It cannot compare even with the
jaguar, and would not be recognized by the true lion, or by
the tiger, as being a kinsman. It is just as true of lions as
it is of Glenfield starch—" when you ask for it, *see that you
get it.*" I admit that it is very creditable to America that
in the great competition of nations she should insist on not
being left behind even in the matter of lions, but surely it

would be more becoming to her vast resources and her undeniable enterprise if she imported some of the genuine breed, instead of, as at present, putting up with such a shabby compromise as the puma.

This tendency to exaggeration in terms has I know been very frequently commented upon. But I don't remember having heard it suggested that this grandiosity must in the long-run have a detrimental effect upon national advancement. Presuming for instance that an American understands the real meaning of the word "city," what gross and ridiculous notions of self-importance second-class villages must acquire by hearing themselves spoken of as "cities." Or supposing that one understands the real meaning of the word "lady," how comes it that an ill-bred, ill-mannered chambermaid is always spoken of as a "lady"? If the name is only given in courtesy, why not call them "princesses" at once and rescue the nobler word from its present miserable degradation?

I was in the Chicago Hotel and a coloured porter was unstrapping my luggage. I rang the bell for a message boy, and on another black servant appearing I gave him a written note to take down to the manager. But in that insolent manner so very prevalent among the blacker hotel servants in America, he said : "*That other gentleman will take it down.*" "Other gentleman!" I gasped out in astonishment ; "there IS only *one* gentleman in this room, and two negro servants. And if," I continued, forgetting that I was in America, and rising from my chair, "you are not off as fast as you can go, I'll— " But the "gentleman" fled so precipitately with my message that I got no further.

Now could anything be more preposterous than this poor creature's attempt to vindicate his right to the flattering title conferred upon him by the Boots, and which he in turn conferred upon the Barman, until everybody in the hotel, from the Manager downwards, was involved in an absurd entanglement of mutual compliments? It may of course be laughed at as a popular humour. But a stranger like myself is perpetually recognizing the mischief which this absurd want of moral courage and self-respect in the upper classes is working in the country. Nor have Americans any grounds whatever to suppose that this sense of " courtesy " is peculiar to them. It is common to every race in the world, *and most conspicuous in the lowest.* The Kaffirs of Africa and the Red Indians address each other with titles almost as fulsome as " gentleman," while in India, the home of courtesy and good breeding, the natives of the higher castes address the very lowest by the title of *Maharaj* (" great prince "). It is accepted by the recipient exactly in the spirit in which it is meant. He understands that the higher classes do not wish to offend him by calling him by his real name, and his Oriental good taste tells him that any intermediate appellation might be misconstrued. So he calls himself, as he is called, by the highest title in the land. There is no danger here of any mistake. Every one knows that the misfortune of birth or other " circumstances beyond his control " have made him a menial. But no one tells him so. He is " *Maharaj.*"

For myself, I adopted the plan of addressing every negro servant as a " Sultan." It was not abusive and sounded well. He did not know what it meant any more than he knows the meaning of " gentleman," but I saved my self-respect by not pretending to put him on an equality with myself.

At Leadville the hotel servants are white men, and the result is civility. But I was in the humour at Leadville to be pleased with everything. The day was divine, the landscape enchanting, and the men with their rough riding-costumes, strange, home-made-looking horses, Mexican saddles (which I now for the first time saw in general use) and preposterous "stirrups," interested me immensely. Of course I went up to a mine, and, of course, went down it. And what struck me most during the expedition? Well, the sound of the wind in the pine-trees.

It was a delightful walk—away up out of the town, with its suburbs of mimic pinewood "chalets" and rough log-huts, and the hills all round sloping back from the plateau so finely, patched and powdered with snow-drifts, fringed and crowned with pine-trees, here darkened with a forest of them, there dotted with single trees, and over all, the Swiss magic of sunlight and shadow; away up the hill-side, through a wilderness of broken bottles and battered meat cans, a very paradise of rag-pickers, among which are scattered the tiny homes of the miners. Women were busy chopping wood and bringing in water. Children were romping in parties. But the men, their husbands and fathers, were all "up at the mines" at work, invisible, in the bowels of the mountain; keeping the kobolds company, and throwing up as they went great hillocks of rubbish behind them like some gigantic species of mole, or burrowing armadillo of the old glyptodon type. And so on, up the shingle-strewn hillside thickly studded with charred tree-stumps, desolation itself—a veritable graveyard of dead pine-trees. Above us, on the crest of the mountain, the forest was still standing, and long before we reached them we heard the wind-haunted trees of Pan telling their griefs to the hills. It is a wonderful music, this of the pine-trees, for it has fascinated every people among whom they grow, from the bear-goblin haunts of Asiatic Kurdistan through the elf-plagued forests of Germany to the spirit-land of the Canadian Indians. It is indeed a mystery, this voice in

E

the tree-tops, with all the tones of an organ—the vox-humana
stop wonderful—and in addition all the sounds of nature,
from the sonorous diapason of the ocean to the whisperings
of the reed-beds by the river. When I came upon them in
Leadville the pines were rehearsing, I think, for a storm that
was coming.   Lower down the slope, the trees were standing as quiet as possible, and in the town itself at the bottom
of the hill the smoke was rising straight. But up here, at the
top, under the pine-trees, the first act of a tempest was in
full rehearsal.   And all this time wandering about, I had
not seen one single living soul.   There stood the sheds
built over the mines.   But no one was about.   At the door
of one of them was a cart with its horses.   But no driver.
This extraordinary absence of life gave the hill-top a strange
solemnity—and though I knew that under my feet the earth
was alive with human beings, and though every now and
then a little pipe sticking out of a shed would suddenly
snort and give about fifty little angry puffs at the rate of a
thousand a minute, the utter solitude was so fascinating that
I understood at once why pine-covered mountains, especially
where mines are worked, should all the world over be such
favourite sites in legend and ballad for the homes of elfin
and goblin folk.

   The afternoon was passing before I set out homeward and
I could hardly get along, so often did I turn round to look
back at the views behind me.   And in front, and on either
side, were the hills, with their hidden hoards of silver and
lead, watching the town, whence they know the miners will
some day issue to attack them, and on their slopes lay
mustered the shattered battalions of their pines, here looking as if invading the town, into which their skirmishers,
dotted about among the houses, had already fought their
way ; there, as if they were retreating up the hillside with

their ranks closed against the houses that pursued them, or straggling away up the slopes and over the crest in all the disorder of defeat.

And so, down on to the level of the plateau again, with its traffic and animation and all the busy life of a hardworking town.

CHAPTER IV.

FROM LEADVILLE TO SALT LAKE CITY.

What is the conductor of a Pullman Car ?—Cannibalism fatal to lasting
friendships—Starving Peter to feed Paul—Connexion between
Irish cookery and Parnellism—Americans not smokers—In Denver
—"The Queen City of the Plains"—Over the Rockies—Pride in
a cow, and what came of it—Sage-brush—Would ostriches pay n
the West ?—Echo Cañon—The Mormons' fortifications—Great
Salt Lake in sight.

WHAT is the "conductor" of a Pullman car? Is he a
private gentleman travelling for his pleasure, a duke in
disguise, or is he a servant of the company placed on the
cars to see to the comfort, &c., of the company's customers?
I should like to know, for sometimes I have been puzzled
to find out. The porter is an admirable institution, when
he is amenable to reason, and I have been fortunate enough
to find myself often entrusted to perfectly rational specimens.
The experiences of travellers have, as I know from their
books, been sometimes very different from mine—ladies,
especially, complaining—but for myself I consider the Union
Pacific admirably manned.

But it is a great misfortune that the company do not run
hotel cars. I was told that the reason why we were made
over helplessly to such caterers as those at North Platte and
Sterling for our food was, that the custom of passengers is
almost the only source of revenue the "eating-houses"
along the line can depend upon. Without the custom of

passengers they would expire— atrophise—become deceased. What I want to know is *why they should not expire.* I, as a traveller, see no reason whatever, no necessity, for their being kept alive at a cost of so much suffering to the company's customers. Let them decease, or else establish a claim to public support. During a long railway journey the system is temporarily deranged and appetites are irregular, so that some people *can* not eat when they have the opportunity, and when they *could* eat, do not get it. Some day, no doubt, a horrible cannibalic outrage on the cars will awaken the directors to the peril of carrying starving passengers, and the luxury of the hotel-car will be instituted.

Not that I could censure the poor men of the South Seas or Central Africa for eating each other. There seems to me something a trifle admirable in this economy of their food. But cannibalism must, in the very nature of it, be deterrent to the formation of lasting friendships between strangers. So long as two men look upon each other as possible side dishes, there can be no permanent cordiality between them. Mutual confidence, the great charm of sincere friendship, must be wanting. You could never be altogether at your ease in a company which discussed the best stuffing for you.

Meanwhile, the custom of carrying their own provisions is increasing in favour among passengers, so that, hotel cars or not, these Barmecide "eating-houses" may yet expire from inanition. The waiting (done by girls) is, I ought to say, admirable—but then so it was at Sancho Panza's supper and at Duke Humphrey's dinner-table. And yet the hungry went empty away.

Between Cheyenne and Ogden the commissariat is distinctly better, and the unprovided traveller triumphs mildly over the more careful who have carried their own provisions. But, striking a balance on the whole journey, there is no doubt that the comfort of the trip, some sixty odd hours, from Omaha to Ogden, is materially increased by starting with a private stock of food. Bitter herbs without indigestion is better than a stalled ox with dyspepsia.

An old Roman epicure gravely expressed his opinion that Africa could never be a progressive country, inasmuch as its shrimps were so small. And I think I may venture to say that if the cookery in the central States does not improve, the country must gradually drift backwards into barbarism. For there is a most intimate connexion between cookery and civilization.

It is the duty of the historian, and not the task of the traveller, to trace national catastrophes to their real causes —often to be found concealed under much adventitious matter, and when found often surprising from their insignificance—-and I leave it, therefore, to others to specify the particular feature of Irish cookery that tends to create a disinclination to paying rent.

That the agitated demeanour of the after-dinner speakers during Irish tenant-right meetings was due solely to the infuriating and ferocious course of food to which they had just submitted, is as certain as that the extraordinary class of noises, cavernous and hollow-sounding, produced by their applausive audiences was owing to the fact that they had not dined at all. In the West of Ireland (where I travelled with those "experts in constitutional treason" who were then organizing the "No Rent" agitation), the agitators and conspirators had no time for long dinners, as the mobs outside were as impatient as hunger, so they sat down, invariably, to everything at once—mutton, bacon, sausages, turkey and ham, with relays of hot potatoes every two minutes. While one conspirator was addressing the peasantry, the upper half of his body thrust out of the lower half of the window, and only his legs in the dining-room, the rest were eating against time, and as soon as the speaker's legs were seen to get up on tiptoe, which they always did for the peroration, the next to speak had to rise from his food. The result was of course incoherent violence. But a closer analysis is required to detect the causes of Irish dislike to rent.

That it would be eventually found that potatoes and patriotism have an occult affinity I have no doubt; but, as I have said above, such research more properly belongs to the province of the historian. The Spartan stirring his black broth with a spear revealed his nature at once, and the single act of the Scythians, using their beefsteaks for saddles until they wanted to eat them, gives at a glance their character to the nation.

At any rate, it is as old as Athenæus that "to cookery we owe well-ordered States;" for States result from the congregation of individuals in towns, and towns are the sum of agglomerated households, and households, it is notorious, never combine except for the sociable consumption of food. So long as, in the Dark Ages, every man cooked for himself, or, in the primitive days of cannibalism, helped himself to a piece of a raw neighbour, there could be no friendly heartiness at meals; but, as soon as cooks appeared, men met fearlessly round a common board, towns grew up round the dinner-table, and, as Athenæus remarks, well-ordered States grew up round the towns. But if we were to judge of the prospects of the people who live, say, about Green River or North Platte, by the character of the food (as supplied to travellers) the opinion could not be very complimentary or encouraging.

It is a prevalent idea in England that Americans smoke prodigiously, even as compared with "the average Britisher." Now, in America there is very little smoking. You may perhaps think I am wrong. A great many Americans, I allow, buy cigars in the most reckless fashion. But (apart from the fact that cigars are not necessarily tobacco) I find that as a rule they throw away more than they smoke. Speaking roughly, then, I should say so-called "smokers" in this country might be divided into three classes : those who buy cigars because they cost money ; those who buy them because cigars give them a decent excuse for spitting ; and those who buy them under the delusion that the friend who is with them smokes, and that hospitality or courtesy requires that they should humour his infatuation. Of the trifling residue, the men who smoke because, as they put it, "they like it," it is not worth while to speak. Now, one of the results of this general aversion to tobacco is that when a foreigner addicted to the weed comes over and tries to smoke, he is hunted about so, that (as I have often done myself) he longs to be in his coffin, if only to get a quiet corner for a pipe. In hotels they hunt you down, floor by floor, till they get you on to a level with the street, and then from room to room till they get you out on to the pavement. There is nowhere where you can read and smoke—or write and smoke—or have a quiet chat with a friend over a pipe —or in fact *smoke* at all, in the respectable, civilized, Christian sense of the word. Of course, if you like, you can " smoke " in the public hall of the hotel. But I would just as soon sit out on the kerbstone at the corner of the street as among a crowd of men holding cigars in their mouths and shouting business. Out on the kerbstone I should at any rate find the saving grace of passing female society. In private houses again, smokers are consigned to the knuckle end of the domicile and the waste corners thereof, as if they snatched a fearful joy from some secret fetish rites, or had to go apart into privacy to indulge in a little surreptitious cannibalism. In the streets, friends do not like you to smoke when with them, and there are very few public conveyances in which tobacco is comfortably possible.

In trains there is a most conspicuous neglect of smokers. I found, for instance, on my journey from New York to Chicago, that the only place I could smoke in was the end compartment of the fourth car from my own. That is to say, let it be as stormy and dark as it may, you have to pass from one car to the other half the length of the train, and when you do get to "the smoking compartment" you find it is only intended to hold *five* passengers. I confess I am surprised that these palace cars, otherwise so agreeable, should be such hovel cars for smokers. Nor, by the way, seeing that the company specially notifies that the passage from one car to the other is "dangerous" while the train is in motion, do I think it fair that smokers should be encouraged, and indeed compelled, to run bodily risks in order to arrive at their tobacco. Some day no doubt there will be Pullman smoking cars, and when there are—I will find something else to grumble at.

Imagine then my astonishment when arriving at the Windsor Hotel at Denver, I was shown into a bonâ-fide smoking-room, with cosy chairs, well carpeted, with a writing table properly furnished, all the newspapers of the day, and a roaring fire in an open fireplace ! Here at last was civilization. Here was a room where a man might sit with self-respect, and enjoy his pipe over a newspaper, smoke while he wrote a letter, foregather over tobacco with a friend in a quiet corner ! No noise of loquacious strangers, no mob of outsiders to make the room as common as the street, no fusillade of expectoration, no stove to desiccate you—above all, no coloured "gentleman" to come in and say, "Smoke nut 'lard here, sar !" I was delighted. But my curiosity, at such an aberration into intelligence, led me to confide in the manager.

"How is it," I asked, "you have got what no other hotel in America that I have stayed in has got—a comfortable smoking-room after the English style?"

"*Guess*," said he, "*because an English company built this hotel!*"

And I went upstairs, at peace with myself and all English companies.

The first view of Denver is very prepossessing, and further acquaintance begets better liking. Indeed on going into the streets of "the Queen City of the Plains" I was astonished. The buildings are of brick or stone, its roads are good and level, and well planted with shade-trees, its suburbs are orderly rows of pretty villas, adorned with lawn, and shrubs, and flowers. Though one of the very youngest towns of the West, it has already an air of solidity and permanence which is very striking, while on such a day as I saw it, it is also one of the very cleanest and airiest. And the snow-capped hills are in sight all round.

Particularly notable in Denver are its railway station— and yet, with all its size, it is found too small for the rapidly increasing requirements of the district—and the Tabor Opera-House. This is really a beautiful building inside, with its lavish upholstery, its charming "ladies' rooms,' and smoking-rooms, its variety of handsome stone, its carved cherry-wood fittings, its perfectly sumptuous boxes. The stage is nearly as large as that at Her Majesty's, quite as large as any in New York, while in general appointments and in novelty of ornaments, it has very few rivals in all Europe. In one point, the beauty of the mise-en-scène from the gallery, the Denver house certainly stands quite alone, for whereas in all other theatres or opera-houses, "the gods" find themselves up in the attics, as it were, with only white-washed walls about them, and the sides of the stage shut out from view, here they are in handsomely furnished galleries, with a clear view of the whole stage over the tops of the pagoda-roofed boxes—these curious "pepper-box" roofs being themselves a handsome ornament to the scene. By having only a limited number of "stalls" on the level, sloping the "pit" up to the "grand tier," and making the stage nearly occupy the whole width of the house, everybody in the building gets an equally good view of the stage. It is indeed an opera-house to be proud of; and Denver *is* proud of it.

There is an idea sometimes mooted that Denver has been run on too fast; that it has "seen its day," and may be as suddenly deserted as it has been peopled. But there is absolutely no chance of this whatever. Colorado is as yet only in its cradle, and the older it gets the more substantial will Denver become, for this city—and very soon it will be almost worthy of that name—is the Paris of "the Centennial State," the ultimate ambition of the moderately successful miner. It is not a place to make your money in and leave. But having made your money, to go to and live in. For a man or woman must be very fastidious indeed who cannot be content to settle down in this, one of the prettiest and healthiest towns I have ever visited. Denver accordingly is attracting to it, year by year, a larger number of that class of citizens upon which alone the permanent prosperity of a town can depend, the men of moderate capital, satisfied with a fair return from sound investments, who put their money into local concerns, and make the place their "home."

I left Denver in the early morning. Outside the station were standing five trains all waiting to be off, and one by one their doleful bells began to toll, and one by one they

sneaked away. Ours was the last to be off; but at length
we too got our signal: that is to say, the porter picked up
the stool which is placed on the platform for the convenience
of short-legged passengers stepping into the cars—and without a word we crept off, as if the train was going to a
funeral, or was ashamed of something it had done. This
silent, casual departure of trains is a perpetually recurring
surprise to me. Would it be contrary to republican principles to ring a bell for the warning of passengers? One
result, however, of this surreptitious method of making off,
is that no one is ever left behind. Such is the perversity of
human nature! In England people are being perpetually
"left behind" because they think such a catastrophe to be
impossible. In America they are never left behind, because
they are always certain they will be.

At first the country threatened a repetition of the old
prairie, made more dismal than ever by our recent experiences of the Switzerland of Colorado. But the scene
gradually picked up a feature here and there as we went
along, and knowing that we were climbing up "the
Rockies," we had always present with us the pleasures of
hope. But if you wish to see the Rocky Mountains so as
to respect them, do not travel over them in a train. They
are a fraud, so far as they can be seen from a car window.
But in minor points of interest they abound. Curious
boulders, of immense size and wonderful shapes, lie strewn
about the ground, all water-worn by the torrents of a long-
ago age, and some of them pierced with holes—the work of
primeval shell-fish. Beds of river gravel cover the slopes,
and on every side were abundant vestiges of deluges, themselves antediluvian. And then we came upon isolated cliffs
of red sandstone, with kranzes running along their faces—
exactly the same kranzes as the Zulus made such good use

of during the war—and showing in their irregular bases how old-world torrents had washed away the clay and softer materials that had once no doubt joined these isolated cliffs together into a chain of hills, and had left the sandstone heart of each hill bare and alone. And so on, up over "the Divide" into Wyoming, still a paradise for the rifle and the rod, past Cheyenne, a town of many shattered hopes, and out into the region of snow again.

Our engine was perpetually screaming to the cattle to get off the track, a series of short, sharp screams that ought to have sufficed to have warned even cattle to get out of the way. As a rule they recognized the advisability of leaving the rails, but one wretched cow, whether she was deaf, or whether she was stupid, or whether, like Cole's dog, she was too proud to move, I cannot say, but in spite of the screams of the engine she held her ground and got the worst of the collision. The cow-catcher struck her, and as we passed her, the poor beast lay in the blood-mottled snow-drift at the bottom of the bank, still breathing, but almost dead. As for the train, the cow might have been only a fly.

And so we went on climbing—herds of cattle grazing on the slopes, and in the splendid "parks" which lay stretched out beneath us wherever the hills stood far apart—with frequent snow-sheds interrupting all conversation or reading with their tunnel-like intervals, till we reached the Red Granite Cañon, with great masses of that splendid stone fairly mobbing the narrow course of a mountain stream, and beyond them snow—snow—snow, stretching away to the sky-line without a break. And then Sherman, the highest point of the mountains upon the whole line—only some 8000 feet though, all told—with a half-constructed monument to Oakes Ames crowning the summit. When finished, this massive cone of solid granite blocks will be sixty feet high.   And then on to the Laramie Plains, with some wonderful reaches of grazing-ground, and almost fabulous records of ranching profits,   And here is Laramie itself, that will some day be a city, for timber and minerals and stock will all combine to enrich it.   But to-day it is desolate enough, muffled up in winter, with snowbirds in great flights flecking the white ground.   And so out again into the snow wilderness,   here and there cattle snuffing about on the desolate hill-sides, and snow-sheds—timber-covered ways to prevent the snow drifting on to the track—becoming more frequent, and the white desolation growing every mile more utter.   And the moon got up to confuse the horizon of land with the background of the sky.   And so to sleep, with dreams of the Arctic regions, and possibilities, the dreariest in the world, of being snowed up on the line.

Awakening with snow still all round us, and snow falling heavily as we reach Green River.   And then out into a country, prodigiously rich, I was told, in petroleum, but in which I could only see that sage-brush was again asserting its claims to be seen above the snow-drift, and that wonderful arrangements in red stone thrust themselves up from the hill crests.   Terraces reminding me of miniature table-mountains such as South Africa affects ; sharply scarped pinnacles jutting from the ridges like the Mauritius peaks ; plateaux with isolated piles of boulders ; upright blocks shaped into the semblance of chimneys ; crests broken into battlements, and—most striking mimicry of all snow wildernesses—a reproduction in natural rock of the great fortress of Deeg, in India.   With snow instead of water, the imitation of that vast buttressed pile was singularly exact, and if there had been only a brazen sun overhead and a coppery sky flecked with circling kites, the counterfeit would have been perfect. But Deeg would crumble to pieces with astonishment if snow were to fall near it, while here there was enough to content a polar bear.

What a pity sage brush—the "three-toothed artemisia" of science—has no commercial value. Fortunes would be cheap if it had. But I heard at Leadville that a local chemist had treated the plant after the manner of cinchona, and extracted from its bark a febrifuge with which he was about to astonish the medical world and bankrupt quinine. That it has a valuable principle in cases of fever, its use by the Indians goes a little way to prove, while its medicinal properties are very generally vouched for by its being used in the West as an application for the cure of toothache, as a poultice for swellings, and a lotion ("sage oil") for erysipelas, rheumatism, and other ailments. Some day, perhaps, a fortune will be made out of it, but at present its chief value seems to be as a moral discipline to the settler and as covert for the sage-hen.

Would not the ostrich thrive upon some of these pro-digious tracts of unalterable land? Can all America not match the African karoo shrub, which the camel-sparrow loves? Ostrich farming has some special recommendations, especially for "the sons of gentlemen" and others dis-inclined for arduous labour, who have not much of either money or brains to start with. Is it not a matter of common notoriety that when pursued this fowl buries its head in the sand, and thus, of course, falls an easy prey to the intending farmer? If, on the other hand, he does not want the whole of the bird, he has only to stand by and pluck its feathers out, which, having its head buried, it cannot, of course perceive. (These feathers fetch a high price in the market.) Supposing, however, that the adventurous emigrant wishes to undertake ostrich farming bonâ fide, he has merely to pull the birds out from the sand, and drive them into an enclosure—which he will, of course, have previously made —and sit on the gate and watch them lay their eggs. When they lay eggs, ostriches—this is also notorious—bury them in the sand and desert them, and the gentleman's son on the fence can then go and pick them out of the sand. (Ostriches' eggs fetch five pounds apiece.) These birds, moreover, cost very little for feeding, as they prefer pebbles. They can, therefore, be profitably cultivated on the sea beach. But I would remind intending farmers that ostriches are very nimble on their feet. It is also notorious that they have a shrewd way of kicking. A kick from an ostrich will break a cab-horse in two. The intending farmer, therefore, when he has compelled the foolish bird to bury its head in the sand and is plucking out its tail feathers, should stand well clear of the legs. This is a practical hint.

We dined at Evanston, neat-handed abigails, as usual, handing round dishes fearfully and wonderfully made out of old satchels and seasoned with varnish. There is a Chinese quarter here, with its curious congregation of celestial hovels all plastered over with, apparently, the labels of tea-chests. I should think the Chinese were all self-made men. At any rate they do not seem to me to have been made by any one who knew how to do it properly.

However, we had not much time to look at them, for cows on the track and one thing and another had made us rather late ; so we were very soon off again, the travellers, after their hurried and indigestible meal, feeling very much like the jumping frog, after he couldn't jump, by reason of quail shot.

The snow had been gradually disappearing, and as we approached Echo Cañon we found ourselves gliding into scenes that in summer are very beautiful indeed, with their turf and willow-fringed streams and abundant vegetation. And then, by gradual instalments of rock, each grander than the next, the great cañon came upon us. What a superb defile this is ! It moves along like some majestic poem in a series of incomparable stanzas. There is nothing like it in the Himalayas that I know of, nor in the Suleiman range. In the Bolan Pass, on the Afghan frontier, there are intervals of equal sublimity; and even as a whole it may compare with it. But taken all for all—its length (some thirty miles), its astonishing diversity of contour, its beauty as well as its grandeur—I confess the Echo Cañon is one of the masterpieces of Nature. I can speak of course only of what I have seen. I do not doubt that the Grand Cañon in Arizona, which is said to throw all the wonders of Colorado and the marvels of Yellowstone or Yosemite into the shade, would dwarf the highway to Utah, but within my experience the Echo is almost incomparable. It would be very diffi-cult to convey any idea of this glorious confusion of crags. But imagine some vast city of Cyclopean architecture built on the crest and face of gigantic cliffs of ruddy stone. Imagine, then, that ages of rain had washed away all the minor buildings, leaving only the battlements of the city, the steeples of its churches, its causeways and buttresses, and the stacks of its tallest chimneys still standing where they had been built. If you can imagine this, you can imagine anything, even Echo Cañon—but I must confess that my attempt at description does not recall the scene to me in the least.

However, I passed through it and, up on the crest of a very awkward cliff for troops to scale under fire, had pointed out to me the stone-works which the Mormons built when they went out in 1857 to stop the advance of the Federal army.

 "highway to utah"

F

And there is no doubt of it that the passage of that defile, even with such rough defences as the Saints had thrown up, would have cost the army very dear. For these stone-works, like the Afghans' *sunghums*, and intended, of course for cover against small arms only, were carried along the crest of the cliffs for some miles, and each group was connected with the next by a covered way, while in the bed of the stream below, ditches had been dug (some six feet deep and twenty wide), right across from cliff to cliff, and a dam constructed just beyond the first ditch which in an hour or two would have converted the whole cañon for a mile or so into a level sheet of water. On this dam the Mormon guns were masked, and though, of course, the Federal artillery would soon have knocked them off into the water, a few rounds at such a range and raking the army—clubbed as it would probably have been at the ditches—must have proved terribly effective. This position, moreover, though it could be easily turned by a force diverging to the right *before* it entered the cañon, could hardly be turned by one that had already entered it. And to attempt to storm those heights, with men of the calibre of the Transvaal Dutchmen holding them, would have been splendid heroism—or worse.

And then Weber Cañon, with its repetitions of castellated cliffs, and its mimicry of buttress and barbican, bastion and demilune, tower and turret, and moat and keep, and all the other feudal appurtenances of the fortalice that were so dear to the author of "Kenilworth," with pine-trees climbing up the slopes all aslant, and undergrowth that in summer is full of charms. The stream has become a river, and fine meadows and corn-land lie all along its bank ; large herds of cattle and companies of horses graze on the hill slopes, and wild life is abundant. Birds are flying about the valley under the supervision of buzzards that float in the air, half-mountain high, and among the willowed nooks parties of moor-hens enjoy life. And so into Ogden.

Night was closing in fast, and soon the country was in darkness. Between Ogden and the City of the Saints lay a two hours' gap of dulness, and then on a sudden I saw out in front of me a thin white line lying under the hills that shut in the valley.

"That, sir? That is Salt Lake."

CHAPTER V.

THE CITY OF THE HONEY-BEE.

Zion—Deseret—A City of Two Peoples—"Work" the watchword of
Mormonism—A few facts to the credit of the Saints—The text of
the Edmunds Bill—In the Mormon Tabernacle—The closing
scene of the Conference.

I HAVE described in my time many cities, both of the east
and west ; but the City of the Saints puzzles me.   It is the
young rival of Mecca, the Zion of the Mormons, the
Latter-Day Jerusalem.   It is also the City of the Honey-bee,
"Deseret," and the City of the Sunflower—an encampment
as of pastoral tribes, the tented capital of some Hyksos,
"Shepherd Kings"—the rural seat of a modern patriarchal
democracy ; the place of the tabernacle of an ancient
prophet-ruled Theocracy—the point round which great
future perplexities for America are gathering fast ; a political storm-centre—"a land fresh, as it were, from the hands
of God ;" a beautifnl Goshen of tranquillity in the midst of
a troublous Egypt—a city of mystery, that seems to the
ignorant some Alamut or "Vulture's Nest" of an Assassin
sect ; the eyrie of an "Old Man of the Mountains :"—to
the well-informed the Benares of a sternly pious people ; the
templed city of an exacting God—a place of pilgrimage in
the land of promise, the home of the "Lion of Judah," and
the rallying-point in the last days of the Lost Tribes, the
Lamanites, the Red Indians—the capital of a Territory in
which the people, though "Americans," refuse to make

haste to get rich ; to dig out the gold and silver which they know abounds in their mountains ; to enter the world's markets as competitors in the race of commerce—a people content with solid comfort ; that will not tolerate either a beggar or a millionaire within their borders, but insist on a uniform standard of substantial well-being, and devote all the surplus to "building up of Zion," to the emigration of the foreign poor and the erection of splendid places of ceremonial worship—a Territory in which the towns are all filled thick with tre es and the air is sweet with the fragrance of fruit and flowers, and the voices of birds and bees as if the land was still their wild birthright ; in which meadows with herds of cattle and horses are gradually overspreading deserts hitherto the wild pashalik of the tyrant sage-brush—a land, alternately, of populous champaign and of desolate sand waste, with, as its capital, a City of Two Peoples between whom there is a bitterness of animosity, such as, in far-off Persia, even Sunni and Shea hardly know.

Indeed, there are so many sides to Salt Lake City, and so much that might be said of each, that I should perhaps have shirked this part of my experiences altogether were I not conscious of possessing, at any rate, *one* advantage over all my "Gentile" predecessors who have written of this Mecca of the West. For it was my good fortune to be entertained as a guest in the household of a prominent Mormon Apostle, a polygamist, and in this way to have had opportunities for the frankest conversation with many of the leading Mormons of the territory. My candidly avowed antipathy to polygamy made no difference anywhere I went, for they extended to me the same confidence that they would have done to any Gentile who cared to know the real facts.

In the ordinary way, I should begin by describing the City itself. But even then, so subtle is the charm of this place—Oriental in its general appearance, English in its details—that I should hesitate to attempt description. Its quaint disregard of that "fine appearance" which makes your "live" towns so commonplace; its extravagance in streets condoned by ample shade-trees; its sluices gurgling along by the side-walks; its astonishing quiet; the simple, neighbourly life of the citizens—all these, and much more combine to invest Salt Lake City with the mystery that is in itself a charm.

Speaking merely as a traveller, and classifying the towns which I have seen, I would place the Mormon Zion in the same *genus* as Benares on the Ganges and Shikarpoor in Sinde, for it attracts the visitor by interests that are in great part intellectual. The mind and eye are captivated together. It is a fascination of the imagination as well as of the senses. For the capital of Utah is not one of Nature's favourites. She has hemmed it in with majestic mountains, but they are barren and severe. She has spread the levels of a great lake, but its waters are bitter, Marah. There is none of the tender grace of English landscape, none of the fierce splendour of the tropics; and yet, in spite of Nature, the valley is already beautiful, and in the years to come may be another Palmyra. As yet, however, it is the day of small things. Many of the houses are still of adobe, and they overlook the trees planted to shade them. Wild flowers still grow alongside the track of the tram-cars, and wild birds perch to whistle on the telephone wires in the business thoroughfares.

But the future is full of promise, for the prosperity of the city is based upon the most solid of all foundations, agricultural wealth, and it is inhabited by a people whose religion is work. For it is a fact about Mormonism which I have not yet seen insisted upon, that the first duty it teaches is *work*, and that it inculcates industry as one of the supreme virtues.

The result is that there are no pauper Mormons, for there are no idle ones. In the daytime there are no loafers in the streets, for every man is afield or at his work, and soon after nine at night the whole city seems to be gone to bed. A few strangers of course are hanging about the saloon doors, but the pervading stillness and the emptiness of the streets is dispiriting to rowdyism, and so the Gentile damns the place as being "dull." But the truth is that the Mormons are too busy during the day for idleness to find companionship at night, and too sober in their pleasures for gaslight vices to attract them.

As a natural corollary to this life of hard work, it follows that the Mormons are in a large measure indifferent to the affairs of the world outside themselves. Minding their own business keeps them from meddling with that of others. They are, indeed, taught this from the pulpit. For it is the regular formula of the Tabernacle that the people should go about their daily work, attend to that, and leave everything else alone. They are never to forget that they are "building up Zion," that their day is coming in good time, but that meanwhile they must *work* "and never bother about what other people may be doing." In this way Salt Lake City has become a City of Two Peoples, and though Mormon and Gentile may be stirred up together sometimes, they do not mingle any more than oil and water.

There are no paupers among the Mormons, and 95 per cent. of them live in their own houses on their own land ; there is no "caste" of priesthood, such as the world supposes, inasmuch as every intelligent man is a priest, and liable at any moment to be called upon to undertake the duties of the priests of other churches—but without any pay.

Last winter there was a census taken of the Utah Penitentiary and the Salt Lake City and county prisons with the following result:—In Salt Lake City there are about 75 Mormons to 25 non-Mormons: in Salt Lake county there are about 80 Mormons to 20 non-Mormons. Yet in the city prison there were 29 convicts, all non-Mormons; in the county prison there were 6 convicts all non-Mormons. The jailer stated that the county convicts for the five years past were all anti-Mormons except *three!*

In Utah the proportion of Mormons to all others is as 83 to 17. In the Utah Penitentiary at the date of the census there were 51 prisoners, only 5 of whom were Mormons, and 2 of the 5 were in prison for polygamy, so that the 17 per cent. "outsiders" had 46 convicts in the penitentiary, while the 83 per cent. Mormons had but 5!

Out of the 200 saloon, billiard, bowling alley and pool-table keepers not over a dozen even profess to be Mormons. All of the bagnios and other disreputable concerns in the territory are run and sustained by non-Mormons. Ninety-eight per cent. of the gamblers in Utah are of the same element. Ninety-five per cent. of the Utah lawyers are Gentiles, and 98 per cent. of all the litigation there is of outside growth and promotion. Of the 250 towns and villages in Utah, over 200 have no "gaudy sepulchre of departed virtue," and these two hundred and odd towns are almost exclusively Mormon in population. Of the suicides committed in Utah ninety odd per cent. are non-Mormon, and of the Utah homicides and infanticides over 80 per cent. are perpetrated by the 17 per cent. of "outsiders."

The arrests made in Salt Lake City from January 1, 1881, to December 8, 1881, were classified as follows :—

Men	.	.	.	.	.	. 782
Women	.	.	.	.	.	. 200
Boys	.	.	.	.	.	. 38

Total 1020

Mormons—Men and boys	.	163	
Mormons—Women .	.	. 6	—169
Anti-Mormon—Men and boys	.	657	
Anti-Mormon—Women	.	. 194	—851

Total 1020

A number of the Mormon arrests were for chicken, cow, and water *trespass*, petty larceny, &c. The arrests of non-Mormons were 80 per cent. for prostitution, gambling, exposing of person, drunkenness, unlawful dram-selling, assault and battery, attempt to kill, &c.

Now, if the 75 per cent. Mormon population of Salt Lake City were as lawless and corrupt as the record shows the 25 per cent. non-Mormons to be, there would have been 2443 arrests made from their ranks during the year 1881, instead of 169 ; while if the 25 per cent. non-Mormon population were as law-abiding and moral as the 75 per cent. Mormons, instead of 851 non-Mormon arrests during the year, there would have been but 56 !

These are the kind of statistics that non-Mormons in Salt Lake City hate having published. But the world ought to know them, if only to put to shame the so-called " Christian " community of Utah, that is never tired of libelling, personally and even by name, the men and women whom Mormons have learned to respect from a lifetime's experience of the integrity of their conduct and the purity of their lives—the so-called "Christian" community that is afraid to hear itself contrasted with these same Mormons, lest the shocking balance of crime and immorality against themselves should be publicly known. But there is no appeal from these statistics. They are incontrovertible.

The time at which I arrived in Utah was a very critical one for the Latter-Day Saints. The States, exasperated into activity by sectarian agitation—and by the intrigues of a few Gentiles resident in Utah who were financially interested in the transfer of the Territorial Treasury from Mormon hands to their own—had just determined, once more, to extirpate polygamy, and the final passage of the long-dreaded "Edmunds Bill" had marked down Mormons as a proscribed people, and had indicted the whole community for a common offence.

The following is the text of this remarkable bill :—

"*Be it enacted by the Senate and House of Representatives of the United States of America in Congress assembled,* That section 5352 of the Revised Statutes of the United States be, and the same is hereby, amended so as to read as follows, namely :

"Every person who has a husband or wife living who, in a territory or other place over which the United States have exclusive jurisdiction, hereafter marries another, whether married or single, and any man who hereafter simultaneously, or on the same day, marries more than one woman, in a territory or other place over which the United States have exclusive jurisdiction, is guilty of polygamy, and shall be punished by a fine of not more than $500 and by imprisonment for a term of not more than five years; but this section shall not extend to any person by reason of any former marriage whose husband or wife by such marriage shall have been absent for five successive years, and is not known to such person to be living, and is believed by such person to be dead, nor to any person by reason of any former marriage which shall have been dissolved by a valid decree of a competent court, nor to any person by reason of any former marriage which shall have been pronounced void by a valid decree of a competent court, on the ground of nullity of the marriage contract.

"SEC. 2—That the foregoing provisions shall not affect the prosecution or punishment of any offence already committed against the section amended by the first section of this act.

"SEC. 3—That if any male person, in a territory or other place over which the United States have exclusive jurisdiction, hereafter cohabits with more than one woman, he shall be deemed guilty of a misdemeanour, and on conviction thereof, shall be punished by a fine of not more than $300, or by imprisonment for not more than six months, or by both said punishments, in the discretion of the court.

"SEC. 4—That counts for any or all of the offences named in sections one and two of this act may be joined in the same information or indictment.

"SEC. 5—That in any prosecution for bigamy, polygamy, or unlawful cohabitation, under any statute of the United States, it shall be sufficient cause of challenge to any person drawn or summoned as a juryman or talesman, first, that he is or has been living in the practice of bigamy, polygamy or unlawful cohabitation with more than one woman, or that he is or has been guilty of an offence punishable by either of the foregoing sections, or by section 5352 of the Revised Statutes of the United States, or the Act of July 1st, 1862, entitled, 'An Act to punish and prevent the practice of polygamy in the territories of the United States and other places, and disapproving and annulling certain Acts of the Legislative Assembly of the Territory of Utah;' or second, that he believes it right for a man to have more than one living and undivorced wife at the same time, or to live in the practice of cohabiting with more than one woman; and any person appearing or offered as a juror or talesman, and challenged on either of the foregoing grounds, may be questioned on his oath as to the existence of any such cause of challenge, and other evidence may be introduced bearing upon the question raised by such challenge; and this question shall be tried by the court. But as to the first ground of challenge before mentioned, the person challenged shall not be bound to answer if he shall say upon his oath that he declines on the ground that his answer may tend to criminate himself; and if he shall answer as to said first ground, his answer shall not be given in evidence in any criminal prosecution against him for any offence named in sections one or three of this Act; but if he declines to answer on any ground, he shall be rejected as incompetent.

"SEC. 6—That the President is hereby authorized to grant amnesty to such classes of offenders, guilty before the passage of this act of bigamy, polygamy, or unlawful cohabitation, on such conditions and under such limitations as he shall think proper; but no such amnesty shall have effect unless the conditions thereof shall be complied with.

"SEC. 7—That the issue of bigamous or polygamous marriages, known as Mormon marriages, in cases in which such marriages have been solemnized according to the ceremonies of the Mormon sect, in any territory of the United States, and such issue shall have been born before the 1st January, A.D. 1883, are hereby legitimated.

"SEC. 8—That no polygamist, bigamist, or any person cohabiting with more than one woman, and no woman cohabiting with any of the persons described as aforesaid in this section, in-any territory or other place over which the United States have exclusive jurisdiction, shall be entitled to vote at any election held in any such territory or other place, or be eligible for election or appointment to or be entitled to hold any office or place of public trust, honour, or emolument in, under, or for any such territory or place, or under the United States.

Polygamists could not vote

" Sec. 9—That all the registration and election offices of every description in the Territory of Utah are hereby declared vacant, and each and every duty relating to the registration of voters, the conduct of elections, the receiving or rejection of votes, and the canvassing and returning of the same, and the issuing of certificates or other evidence of election in said territory, shall, until other provision be made by the Legislative Assembly of said territory as is hereinafter by this section provided, be performed under the existing laws of the United States and of said territory by proper persons, who shall be appointed to execute such offices and perform such duties by a board of five persons, to be appointed by the President, by and with the advice and consent of the Senate, not more than three of whom shall be members of one political party, a majority of whom shall be a quorum. The canvass and return of all the votes at elections in said territory for members of the Legislative Assembly thereof shall also be returned to said board, which shall canvass all such returns and issue certificates of election to those persons who, being eligible for such election, shall appear to have been lawfully elected, which certificates shall be the only evidence of the right of such persons to sit in such Assembly, provided said board of five persons shall not exclude any persons otherwise eligible to vote from the polls, on account of any opinion such person may entertain on the subject of bigamy or polygamy; nor shall they refuse to count any such vote on account of the opinion of the person casting it on the subject of bigamy or polygamy; but each house of such Assembly, after its organization, shall have power to decide upon the elections and qualifications of its members.'

The day also on which I arrived in Salt Lake City was itself a memorable one, for it was the closing day of the fifty second annual conference of the Church of Jesus Christ of Latter-Day Saints—notable, beyond other conferences, as a public expression of the opinions of the leaders of the Mormon Church, at a crisis of great importance. The whole hierarchy of Utah took part in the proceedings, and it was fitly closed by an address from President Taylor himself, evoking such a demonstration of fervid and yet dignified enthusiasm as I have never seen equalled.

My telegram to the *New York World* on that occasion may still stand as my description of the scene.

" Acquainted though I am with displays of Oriental fanaticism and Western revivalism, I set this Mormon enthusiasm on one side as being altogether of a different character, for it not only astonishes by its fervour, but commands respect by its sincere sobriety. The congregation of the Saints assembled in the Tabernacle, numbering, by my own careful computation, eleven thousand odd, and composed in almost exactly equal parts of the two sexes, reminded me of the Puritan gatherings of the past as I imagined them, and of my personal experiences of the Transvaal Boers as I know them. There was no rant, no affectation, no straining after theatrical effect. The very simplicity of this great gathering of country-folk was striking in the extreme, and significant from first to last of a power that should hardly be trifled with by sentimental legislation. I have read, I can assert, everything of importance that has ever been written about the Mormons, but a single glance at these thousands of hardy men fresh from their work at the plough —at the rough vehicles they had come in, ranged along the street leading to the Tabernacle, at their horses, with the mud of the fields still upon them—convinced me that I knew nothing whatever of this interesting people. Of the advice given at this Conference it is easy to speak briefly, for all counselled alike. In his opening address, President Taylor said,—

"'The antagonism we now experience here has always existed, but we have also come out of our troubles strengthened. I say to you, be calm, for the Lord God Omnipotent reigneth, and He will take care of us.'

"Every succeeding speaker repeated the same advice, and the outcome of the five days' Conference may therefore be said to have been an exhortation to the Saints 'to pay no attention whatever to outside matters, but to live their religion, leave the direction of affairs to their priesthood, and the result in the hands of God.'

"Bishops Sharp and Cluff challenged the Union to show more conspicuous examples of loyalty than those that 'brighten the records of Utah;' Bishop Hatch referred to a 'Revolutionary' ancestry; and Apostle Brigham Young (a son of the late President) alluded to the advocacy in certain quarters of warlike measures with which he was not himself in sympathy. 'I am not,' he said, 'altogether belligerent, and am not advocating warlike measures, but I do want to advocate our standing true and steadfast all the time. If I am to be persecuted for living my religion, why, I am to be persecuted. That is all. Dodging the issue will not change it. I have read the bill passed to injure us, but am satisfied that everything will come out all right, that the designs of our enemies will be frustrated, and confusion will come upon them.' Apostle Woodruff reminded the enemies of the Church that it 'costs a great deal to shed the blood of God's people;' and Apostle Lorenzo Snow said,—'I do not have any fear or trouble about fiery ordeals, but if any do come we should all be ready for them.'

"These and other references to possible trouble seem to show that the leaders of the Church consider the state of the public mind such as to make these allusions necessary. But loyalty to the Constitution was the text of every address, and even as regards the Edmunds Bill itself, Apostle Lorenzo Snow said,—'There is something good in it, for it legalizes every issue from plural marriages up to January 1, 1883. No person a few years ago could have ever expected such an act of Congress. But it has passed, and been signed by the President.' The expressions of the speakers with regard to polygamy were at times very explicit. The President yesterday said,—'Some of our kind friends have suggested that we cast our wives off, but our feelings are averse to that. We are bound to them for time and eternity—we have covenanted before high heaven to remain bound to them. And I declare, in the name of Israel's God, that we will keep the covenant, and I ask all to say to this Amen.' (Here, like the sound of a great sea-wave breaking in a cave, a vast *Amen* arose from the concourse.) 'We may have to shelter behind a hedge while the storm is passing over, but let us be true to ourselves, our wives, our families, and our God, and all will be well.' Again to-day he exhorted the Saints 'to keep within the law, but at the same time to live their religion and be true to their wives, and the principles of their Church.' Several other speakers touched upon the fact of plurality being an integral doctrine of Mormonism, and not to be interfered with without committing an outrage against their religion. Retaliation was never suggested, unless the advice given to the congregation to make all their purchases at Mormon shops may be accepted as a tendency towards Boycotting. But the Church was exhorted to stand firm, to allow persecution to run its course, and above all, to be 'manly in their fidelity to their wives.' Nor could anything exceed the impressiveness of the response which the people gave instantaneously to the appeal of their President for the support of their voices. The great Tabernacle was filled with waves of sound as the 'Amens' of the congregation burst out. The shout of men going into battle was not more stirring than the closing words of this memorable conference spoken as if by one vast voice : 'Hosannah ! for the Lord God Omnipotent reigneth ; He is with us now and will be for ever. Amen ! ' "

CHAPTER VI.

LEGISLATION AGAINST PLURALITY.

A people under a ban—What the Mormon men think of the Anti-Polygamy Bill—And what the Mormon women say of polygamy—Puzzling confidences—Practical plurality a very dull affair—But theoretically a hedge hog problem—Matrimonial eccentricities—The fashionable milliner fatal to plurality—Absurdity of comparing Moslem polygamy with Mormon plurality—Are the women of Utah happy?—Their enthusiasm for Women's Rights.

UTAH, therefore, at the time of my visit was "a proclaimed district"—to use the Anglo-Indian phrase for tracts suspected of infanticide—and every Mormon within it had a share in the disgrace thrust upon it. Nor was the triumph of the Gentile concealed at the result. The Mormons, therefore, were consolidated, in the first instance, by the equal pressure of the new law upon all sections of the church alike ; in the next by the openly expressed exultation of the Gentiles. I wrote at the time : "They feel that they are under a common ban. The children have read the Bill or have had its purport explained to them, and it is well known even among the Gentiles how keen the grief was in every household when the news that the Bill had passed reached Utah. Wives still shed bitter tears over the act of Congress which breaks up their happy homes, and robs them and their children of the protecting presence of a husband and father. The Bill was aimed to put a stop to a supposed self-indulgence of the men. But the Mormons have never thought of it in this light at all. They see in it only an attempt to punish their wives. And it is this alleged cruelty to their wives and children that has stubborned the Mormon men.

Meanwhile the Mormons affect a contemptuous disregard of the Commission and all its works. I have spoken to many, some of them leaders of local opinion, and everywhere I find the same amused indifference to it expressed. "We have too many real troubles," they say, "to go manufacturing imaginary ones. We must live our religion in the present and leave the future to God."

"But," I would say, "this is *not* a question of the future. All children born after the 1st of January, 1883, will be illegitimate—and in these matters Nature is generally very punctual. Now, are you going to break the law or going to keep it?"

Some would answer "neither," and some "both," but all would agree that there was no necessity for worrying themselves about evils which may never befall, and that the Edmunds Bill, with all its malignity and cunning, was "a stupid blunder," an "impossible" enactment, "an absurdity." So the questioning would probably end in laughter.

" But in spite of this expressed indifference to the working of the Bill, there can be little doubt that the more responsible Mormons have already made up their minds as to the course they will take. 'The people' will follow them of course, and forecasting the future, therefore, I anticipate that a small minority will break down under the pressure, and will return their plural wives to their parents, with such provision as they can make for their future support.

" Of the remainder, that is to say the bulk of the Mormons, I believe, indeed I feel convinced, that they will simply ignore the Bill so long as it ignores them, and that when it is put in force against them, they will accept the penalty without complaint. In some cases the onus of proving guilt will no doubt be made heavier by 'passive resistance,' and where the whole family is solid in throwing obstacles in the way of espionage, conviction will necessarily be very difficult. As a case in point may be cited the instance of the Mormon in Salt Lake City, who married a second wife and successfully defied both the law and the public to fix his relationship to the lady in question and her children. She herself was content with saying that her children were honourable in birth, and that the wedding-ring on her finger was a fact and not a fiction. But who her husband was neither the law nor the press could find out for two years, and only then by the confession of the sinner himself."

I was sitting one day with two Mormon ladies, plural wives, and the conversation turned upon marriage.

"But," said I, "now that you have experienced the disadvantages of plurality, shall you advise your daughters to follow your example?"

"No," said both promptly, "I shall not advise them one way or the other. They must make their own choice, just as I did."

"Choice, I am afraid, is hardly a choice though. Plurality, I fear, is too nearly a religious duty to leave much option with girls."

"Nonsense," said the elder of the two, "I was just as free to choose my husband as you were to choose your wife. I married for love."

"And do you really believe," broke in the other, "that any woman in the world would marry a man she did not like from a sense of *religious duty !*"

"Yes," said I, regardless of the fair speaker's scorn, "I thought plenty of women had done so. More than that, thousands have renounced marriage with men whom they loved and taken the veil, for Heaven's sake."

"Very true," was the reply, "a woman may renounce marriage and become a nun as a religious duty. But the same motive would never have persuaded that woman to marry against her inclinations. There is all the difference in the world between the two. Any woman will tell you that."

"Then you mean to say," I persisted, "that you and your friends consider that you are voluntary agents when you go into plurality? that you do so entirely of your own accord and of your own free choice?"

"Certainly I do," was the reply. "You may not believe us, of course, but that I cannot help. All I can say to you is, that if I had the last seven years of my life to live over again, I should do exactly what I did seven years ago."

"And what was that?" I asked.

"Refuse to marry a Gentile, to please my friends, and marry a polygamist to please myself. I had two offers from unmarried men, either of which my family were very anxious I should accept. But I did not care for either. But when my husband, who had already two wives, proposed to me, I accepted him, in spite of my friends' protests. And I would marry him again if the choice came over again."

"Then yours must surely be exceptional cases, for I cannot bring myself to believe that those who have been 'first' wives would ever consent to their husband's re-marriage, if their past could be recalled."

"But I *was* his first wife," said the elder lady, "and my husband's second wife was his first love. And if my past were recalled as you put it, I would give my consent just as willingly as I did twelve years ago. Perhaps," said she, laughing, "you will call mine an 'exceptional' case too.

But if you go through the Mormons individually, I am afraid you will find that the 'exceptional' cases are very large."

"And how about the minority?" I asked, "the wives whose hearts have been broken by plurality?"

"Well," was the reply, "there are plenty of unhappy wives. But this is surely not peculiar to polygamy, is it? There are plenty of women who find they have made a mistake. But is it not the same in monogamy? And yet, though our poor women can get divorces with no trouble, and at an expense of only ten dollars, and are certain of a competence after divorce, and of re-marriage if they choose, they do not do it. There is no greater disgrace attaching to divorce here than in Europe. Indeed allowances are made for the special trials of plurality, and mere unhappiness is in itself quite sufficient for a woman to get a divorce. Yet divorce is very rare indeed, not one-tenth as common as in Massachusetts, for instance."

"There are bad men amongst us just as there are everywhere," continued the other lady, "and a bad Mormon is the worst man there can be. But we are not the only people that have bad husbands among them."

And so it went on. I was met at every point by assurances as sincere as tone of voice and language could make them appear. Eventually I scrambled out of the subject as best I could, covering my retreat with the remark,—

"Well, my only justification in saying that I do not believe you, is this, that if I said I did, *no one would believe me.*"

Of this much, however, I am convinced, that whatever may have been true thirty years ago—and there has not been a single trustworthy book written about Mormonism since 1862—it is not true to-day that the Church interferes with the domestic relations of the people. When there is a

divorce the Church takes care that the man does not turn
his wife adrift without provision. But as far as I have been
able to learn, the authorities do not meddle in any other way
between man and woman, so long, of course, as neither is a
scandal to the community. When a scandal arises the
Church takes prompt notice of it, and the offender, if incor-
rigible, is next heard of as "apostatizing," or, in other
words, being turned out of Mormonism as unfit to live in
it. But once married into polygamy, religion is all-power-
ful in reconciling women to the sacrifices they have to
make, precisely, I suppose, in the same way that religion
reconciles the nun to the sacrifices which her Church accepts
from her.

Practical Plurality, then, is a very dull affair. I was disappointed in it. I had expected to see men with long whips,
sitting on fences, swearing at their gangs of wives at work in
the fields. I expected every now and then to hear of drunken
saints beating seven or eight wives all at once, and perhaps
even to have seen the unusual spectacle of a house full of
women and children rushing screaming into the street with one
intoxicated husband and father in pursuit. Everywhere else
in the world wife-beating is a pastime more or less indulged
in *coram publico*. In London, at any rate, men so arrange
their chastisements that you can hear the screams from the
street and see the wife run out of the front door on to the
pavement. In Salt Lake City therefore, it seemed only
reasonable to suppose that the amount of the screaming would
be in proportion to the number of the wives, and that eventually ill-used families would be seen pouring simultaneously
out of several doors, and scattering over the premises with
hideous ululation. Where are the aged apostles who have
so often been described as going about in their swallow-tail
coats courting each other's daughters? Where are the "girl-

expectation of Mormon by America

hunting elders" and "ogling bishops"? Where are the families of one man and ten wives to be found taking the air together that pictures have so often shown us? Of course there are anomalies, and very objectionable they are. Thus one young man has married his half-aunt, another his half-sister, and three sisters have wedded the same man; but these instances are all "historical," so to speak, and have been so often trotted out by anti-Mormon book-makers, that they are hardly worth repeating. Nor does it appear to me to be of any force to begin raking to-day into the old suspicions as to what Mormons dead and gone used to do.

What is polygamy like *to-day*? That is the question. Polygamy to-day, then, has settled down into the most matter-of-fact system that is possible for such exceptional domestic arrangements. In the first place, it is not compulsory, and some of the leading saints are monogamous. About one-fourth of married Mormons are polygamous, and of these something less than three per cent. are under forty years of age. The bill of 1862 making polygamy penal effected little or no difference in the annual average of plural marriages, but since 1877 there has been a very sensible decrease.

These facts, then, seem to prove first that polygamy, though accepted as a doctrine of the Church, is not generally acted upon—and why? For the best of reasons. Either that the men cannot afford to keep up more than one establishment, or that they are too happy with one wife to care to marry a second, or that the first wife refuses to allow any increase of the household—all of which reasons show that polygamy is controlled by prudential and domestic considerations, and is not the indiscriminate "debauchery" that so many of the public believe it to be. It is also evident that the younger Mormons are not so active in marrying as the elder men were at their age, for ten years ago the proportion of polygamous Mormons under forty years of age was much greater, which *may* mean that the inaction of Congress was gradually working towards the end which the action of '62 thwarted. By legislating against polygamy, plural marriages increased—1863 to 1866 being as busy years in the Endowment House as any that ever preceded them—while by letting polygamy severely alone they have been decreasing.

Polygamy in fact, by the relaxation of the régime, now that Brigham Young's personal government has ceased, has taken its place as an ordinary civil institution, entailing serious responsibilities upon those who choose to enter into it, and not carrying with it such promises of temporal advantage as at one time were reserved for the plurally wedded. There is not the same enthusiasm about it that there was, owing probably to the diffusion among the people of a better sense of the position of women and of the opinions of the world with regard to polygamy. Under the administration of President Taylor there has been a marked disinclination in the Church to interfere with the domestic relations of the community, except, as I have said before, when reprimand or punishment seemed to be called for ; and it is reasonable therefore to argue that the material decline in the number of plural marriages between 1878 and 1882 would have continued, the proportion of young enthusiasts have gone on decreasing and, as the elders died out, the total of polygamists become annually less. Such, I would contend, is the reasonable inference from the facts I have given.

Polygamy, as a problem, reminds me of a hedgehog. But as the hedgehog may not be familiar to my American readers, let me explain. The hedgehog, then, is a small animal with a very elastic skin, closely set all over with strong sharp spines. A rural life is all its joy. In habits and character it assimilates somewhat to the Mormon peasant, being inoffensive, useful, industrious, prolific, and largely frugivorous. But when hunted it is otherwise. For the hedgehog, if closely pursued, takes hold of its ears with its hind paws and, tucking its nose into the middle of its stomach, rolls itself into a perfect ball. The spines then stand out straight and in every direction equally. Nor, thus defended, does the hedgehog shun the public eye. On the contrary, it lies out in the full sunlight, in the middle of the sidewalk or the dusty high-road, a challenge to the inquisitive attention of every passing dog. And you can no more keep a dog from going out of its way to reconnoitre the queer-looking object than you can keep needles away from loadstones. They do not all behave in the same way to it, though. The mutton-headed dogs sit down by it and contemplate it vacantly, and go away after a bit in a kind of brown study. The silly ones smell it too close, and go off down the road in a streak of dust and yelp. The experienced dogs sniff at it and trot on. "Only that hedgehog again!" they say. The malicious prick their noses and lose their temper, and then prick their noses worse and lose their tempers more. The puppy barks at it remotely, receding every time by the recoil of its own bark, till it barks itself backwards into the opposite ditch. But the hedgehog lies perfectly still, as round and as spiny as ever, in the middle of the high-road. All the dogs are much the same to it. Some roll it a little one way, and some roll it a little the other. It gets dusty or it gets wet. But there it lies as inscrutable, puzzling, and odious to passing dogs as ever. By-and-by when it is dark, and everybody has got tired of poking it and sniffing it and wondering at it, the hedgehog will quietly unroll itself and creep away to some secluded spot betwixt orchard and corn-field, ar ' remote from the highways of men and their dogs.

I am particularl· led to this moralizing because a Mormon has just been enumerating, at my request, some of the more extraordinary anomalies that he knows of in recent polygamy. I took notes of a few, and they seem to me sufficiently puzzling to justify a place in these pages.

A young and very pretty girl, in " the upper ten " of Mormonism, married a young man of her own class, but stipulated before marriage that he should marry a second wife as soon as he could afford to do so.

A young couple were engaged, but quarrelled, and the lover out of pique married another lady. Two years later his first love, having refused other offers in the mean time, married him as his second wife.

A man having married a second wife to please himself, married a third to please his first. " She was getting old, she said, and wanted a younger woman to help her about the house."

A couple about to be married made an agreement between themselves that the husband should not marry again unless it was one of the relatives of the first wife. The ladies selected have refused, and the husband remains true to his promise.

The belle of the settlement, a Gentile, refused monogamist offers of marriage, and married a Mormon who had two wives already.

A girl, distracted between her love for her suitor and her love for her mother, compromised in her affections by stipulating that he should marry both her mother and herself, which he did.

A girl, a Gentile, bitterly opposed at first to polygamy,

married a polygamist at the solicitation of his first wife, her great friend.

Two girls were great friends, and one of them, getting engaged to a man (by no means of prepossessing appearance), persuaded her friend to get engaged to him too, and he married them both on the same day.

These are enough. Moreover, they are not isolated cases, and I believe I am right in saying that I can give a second instance, of recent date, of nearly all of them. Nor are these anonymous fictions like the "victims" of anti-Mormon writers. I have names for each of them. One of them tells me she could name "scores" of the same kind.

It appears to me, therefore, that the women of Utah have shaken somewhat the modern theories of the conjugal relation, and—with all one's innate aversion to a system which is capable of such odious abnormalisms—a most interesting and baffling problem for study. It is, as I said, a regular hedgehog of a problem. If you could only catch hold of it by the nose or the tail, you could scrunch it up easily. But it has spines all over. It is at once provocative and unapproachable.

I remember once in India giving a tame monkey a lump of sugar inside a corked bottle. The monkey was of an inquiring kind, and it nearly killed it. Sometimes, in an impulse of disgust, it would throw the bottle away, out of its own reach, and then be distracted till it was given back to it. At others it would sit with a countenance of the most intense dejection, contemplating the bottled sugar, and then, as if pulling itself together for another effort at solution, would sternly take up the problem afresh, and gaze into it. It would tilt it up one way and try to drink the sugar through the cork, and then, suddenly reversing it, try to catch it as it fell out at the bottom. Under the impression that it could capture it by a surprise it kept rapping its teeth against the glass in futile bites, and, warming to the pursuit of the revolving lump, used to tie itself into regular knots round the bottle. Fits of the most ludicrous melancholy would alternate with these spasms of furious speculation, and how the matter would have ended it is impossible to say. But the monkey one night got loose and took the bottle with it. And it has always been a delight to me to think that whole forestfuls of monkeys have by this time puzzled themselves into fits over the great Problem of Bottled Sugar. What profound theories those long-tailed philosophers must have evolved! What polemical acrimony that bottle must have provoked! And what a Confucius the original monkey must have become! A single morning with such a Sanhedrim discussing such a matter would surely have satiated even a Swift with satire.

Taking then polygamy to be the bottle, and the Gentile to be the monkey, it appears to me that the only alternatives in solution are these: Either smash the whole thing up altogether, or else fall back upon that easy-going old doctrine of wise men, that "morality" is after all a matter of mere geography.

An Oriental legend shows us Allah sitting in casual conversation with a man. A cockroach comes along, and Allah stamps on it. "What did you do that for?" asks the human, looking at the ruined insect. "Because I am God Almighty," was the reply.

Now, polygamy can be smashed flat if the States choose to show their power to do so. But no man who takes a part in that demolition must suppose that in so doing he will be accepted by the community as rescuing them from degradation. If left alone, polygamy will die out. Mormons deny this, but I feel sure that they know they are wrong when they deny it, for nothing but a perpetual miracle of loaves and fishes will make polygamy and families of forty possible when population and food-supply come to talk the position over seriously between them. The expense of plurality will before long prohibit plurality.

"The fashionable milliner" is the most formidable adversary that the system has yet encountered. A twenty-dollar bonnet is a staggering argument against it. When women were contented with sunshades, and made them for themselves, the husband of many wives could afford to be lavish, and to indulge his household in a diversity of headgear. But that old serpent, the fashionable milliner, has got over the garden wall, and Lilith[1] and Eve are no longer content with primitive garments of home manufacture.

No. Polygamy will before long be impossible, except to the rich; and in an agricultural community, restricted in area, and further restricted by the scarcity of water, there can never be many rich men. As it is, the *cost* of plurality was on several occasions referred to by Mormons whom I met during my tour, and I know one man who has for three years postponed his second marriage, as he does not consider that his means justify it; while I fancy it will not be disputed by any one who has inquired into polygamy that, as a general rule, prudential considerations control the system. Polygamy, then, I sincerely believe, carries

---

[1] By the way, it is curious that it should be charged against the Mormons that they have made Adam a polygamist. It is not a Mormon invention at all. For, as is well known, legends far older than Moses' writings declare that Eve married into plurality, and that Lilith was the "first wife" of our great progenitor.

its own antidote with it, and if left alone will rapidly cure itself. In the mean time the community that practises it does not consider itself " degraded," and those who take part in smashing it up must not think it does.

The Mormons are a peasant people, with many of the faults of peasant life, but with many of the best human virtues as well. They are conspicuously industrious, honest, and sober.

There is, of course, nothing whatever in common between Oriental polygamy and Mormon plurality. The main object, and the main result of the two systems are so widely diverse, that it is hardly necessary even to refer to the hundred other points of difference which make comparison between the two utterly absurd.

Yet the comparison is often made in order to prove the Mormons "degraded," and it is a great pity that such superficial and stupid arguments should be used when far more effective ones are at hand. Polygamy, though difficult to handle, is very vulnerable. The hedgehog, after all, will have to unroll some time or another. But to assault polygamy because the Mormons are "Turks" or "debauched Mahometans," or the other things which silly people call them, is monstrous.

The women have complicated the problem by multiplying instances of eccentric "affection." But with it all they persist in believing that they have retained a most exalted estimate of womanly honour. The men, again, have inextricably entangled all recognized ideas of matrimonial responsibilities. Yet they have not lost any of the manliness which characterizes the pioneers of the West.

Their social anomalies are deplorable, but they are not desperate. Education and the influx of outsiders must infallibly do their work, and any attempt to rob these men

and women of the fruits of their astonishing industry and
of the peaceful enjoyment of the soil which they have
conquered for the United States from the most warlike
tribes among the Indians, and from the most malignant
type of desert, is not only not statesmanship, but it is not
humanity.

Are the women of Utah happy? No; not in the
monogamous acceptation of the word "happy." In polygamy the highest happiness of woman is contentment.
But on the other hand her greatest unhappiness is only
discontent. She has not the opportunity on the one hand
of rising to the raptures of perfect love. On the other, she
is spared the bitter, killing anguish of "jealousy" and of
infidelity.

But contentment is not happiness. It is its negative,
and often has its source in mere resignation to sorrow.
It is the lame sister of happiness, the deaf-mute in the
family of joy. It lives neither in the background nor
foreground of enjoyment, but always in the middle distance.
Tender in all things, it never becomes real happiness by
concentration; having to fill no deep heart-pools, it trickles
over vast surfaces. It goes through life smiling but seldom
laughing. Now, in many philosophies we are taught that
this same contentment is the perfect form of happiness.
But humanity is always at war with philosophy. And I for
one will never believe that perpetual placidity is the highest
experience of natures which are capable of suffering the
raptures of joy and of grief. I had rather live humanly,
travelling alternately over sunlit hills and gloomy valleys,
than exist philosophically on the level prairies of monotonous contentment. Holding, then, the opinion that it is
a nobler life to have sounded the deeps and measured the
heights of human emotions than to have floated in shallows

continually, I contend that polygamy is wrong in itself and a cardinal crime against the possibilities of a woman's heart. A plural wife can never know the utmost happiness possible for a woman.   They confess this.   And by this confession the practice stands damned.

Physically, Mormon plurality appears to me to promise much of the success which Plato dreamed of, and Utah about the best nursery for his soldiers that he could have found.   Look at the urchins that go clattering about the roads, perched two together on the bare backs of horses, and only a bit of rope by way of bridle.   Look at the rosy, demure little girls that will be their wives some day. Take note of their fathers' daily lives, healthy outdoor work.   Go into their homes and see the mothers at *their* work.   For in Utah servants get sometimes as much as six dollars a week (and their board and lodging as well of course), and most households therefore go without this expensive luxury.   And then as you walk home through one of their rural towns along the tree-shaded streets, with water purling along beside you as you walk, and the clear breeze from the hills blowing the perfume of flowers across your path in gusts, with the cottage homes, half smothered in blossoming fruit-trees, on either hand, and a perpetual succession of gardens,—then, I say, come back and sit down, if you can, to call this people "licentious," "impure," "degraded."

The Mormons themselves refuse to believe that polygamy is the real objection against them, and it will be found impossible to convince them that the Edmunds bill is really what it purports to be, a crusade against their domestic arrangements only.   There are some among them who thoroughly understand the "political" aspect of the case, and are aware that "the reorganization of Utah" would give

very enviable pickings to the friends of the Commission.
Others, have made up their minds that behind this generous
anti-polygamy sentiment is mean sectarian envy, and that
this is only one more of those amiable efforts of narrow Christians to crush a detested and flourishing sect.

Jealousy, in fact, is the Mormons' explanation of the
Edmunds bill. The Gentiles, they say, are hankering after
the good things of Utah, and hope by one cry after another
to persecute the Mormons out of them. But it is far more
curious that the jealousy of their own sex should be
suggested by Mormon women as the cause of *their* partici-
pation in the clamour against polygamy. Yet so it is ; the
Gentile women are, they say, "jealous" of a community
where every woman has a husband ! It is a perplexing
suggestion, and so thoroughly reverses all rational course of
argument, that I wish it had never been seriously put forward. Imagine the ladies of the Eastern States who have
made themselves conspicuous in this campaign, who have
fought and bled to rescue their poor sisters from slavery, to
free them from the grasp of Mormon Bluebeards—imagine, I
say, these ladies being told by the sisters for whom they are
fighting, that they ought to be ashamed of themselves for
being *envious* of the women in polygamy : Instead of being
thanked for helping to strike the fetters of plurality off their
suffering sisters, they are met with the retort that they ought
to try being wives and mothers themselves before they come
worrying those who have tried it and are content ! They
are requested not to meddle with "what they don't understand," and are threatened with a counter-crusade against
the polyandry of Washington, New York, and other cities !
But even more staggering is the fact that Mormon women
base their indignation against their persecuting saviours on
woman's rights, the very ground upon which those saviours
have based their crusade ! The advocates of woman's rights

are a very strong party in Utah ; and their publications use the very same arguments that strong-minded women have made so terrible to newspaper editors in Europe, and members of Parliament. Thus the *Woman's Exponent*— with "The Rights of the Women of All Nations" for its motto—publishes continually signed letters in which plural wives affirm their contentment with their lot, and in one of its issues is a leading article, headed " True Charity," and signed Mary Ellen Kimball, in which the women of Mormondom are reminded that they ought to pray for poor benighted Mr. Edmunds and all who think like him ! Then follows a letter from a Gentile, addressed to " the truthful, pure-hearted, intelligent, Christian women " of Utah, and after this an article, " Hints on Marriage," signed " Lillie Freeze." But for a sentence or two it might be an article by a Gentile in a Gentile " lady's paper," for it speaks of " courtship " and " lovers," and has the quotation, " two souls with but a single thought, two hearts that beat as one," and all the other orthodox pretty things about true love and married bliss. Yet the writer is speaking of polygamy ! In the middle of this article written " for love's sweet sake," and as womanly and pure as ever words written by woman, comes this paragraph :—

" In proportion as the power of evil increases, a disregard for the sacred institution of marriage also increases among the youth, and contempt for the marriage obligation increases among the married until this most sacred relationship will be overwhelmed by disunion and strife, and only among the despised Latter-Day Saints will the true foundation of social happiness and prosperity be found upon the earth ; but in order to realize this state we must be guided by principles more perfect than those which have wrought such dissolution. God has revealed a plan for establishing a new order of society which will elevate and benefit all mankind who embrace it. The nations that fight against it are working out their own destruction, for their house is built upon the sand, and one of the corner-stones in the doomed structure is already loosened through their disregard and dishonour of the institution of marriage."

Now what is to be done with women who not only declare they are happy in polygamy, but persist in trying to improve their monogamous sisters? How is the missionary going to begin, for instance, with Lillie Freeze?

If the Commission deals leniently with them, they will offer only a passive resistance to the law. But if there is any appearance of outrage, General Sherman may have some work to do, and it will be work more worthy of disciplined troops than mere Indian fighting. There would be abundance of that too, but the Mormons are themselves sufficient to test the calibre of any troops in the world. For they are orderly, solid in their adherence to the Church, and trained during their youth and early manhood to a rough, mountain-frontier life. They are in fact very superior " Boers," and Utah is a very superior Transvaal, strategically. Mormonism is not the wind-and-rain inflated pumpkin the world at a distance believes; it is good firm pumpkin to the very core. Nor are the Indians a picturesque fiction. They are an ugly reality, and under proper guidance a very formidable one. In the mean time there is no talk of war, and the Sword of Laban is lying quietly in its sheath. For one thing, the commission has given no " cause " for war; for another, the present hierarchy of the Church are men of peace.

Such, then, as I view it, is the position in Utah at the present time. Mormonism has taken up, in the phrase of diplomatic history, "an attitude of observation," and the future is " in the hands of the Lord God of Israel."

CHAPTER VII.

SUA SI BONA NÔRINT.

A Special Correspondent's lot—Hypothecated wits—The Daughters of Zion—Their modest demeanour—Under the banner of Woman's Rights—The discoverer discovered—Turning the tables—"By Jove, sir, you *shall* have mustard with your beefsteak ! "

IT has been my good fortune to see many countries, and my ill-luck to have had to maintain, during all my travels, an appearance of intelligence. Though I have been over much of Europe, over all of India and its adjoining countries, Afghanistan, Beloochistan, Burmah, and Ceylon, in the north and west and south of Africa, and in various out-of-the-way islands in miscellaneous oceans, I have never visited one of them purely "for pleasure." I have always been "representing" other people. My eyes and ears have been hypothecated, so to speak—my intelligence been in pledge. When I was sent out to watch wars, there was a tacit agreement that I should be shot at, so that I might let other people know what it felt like. When run away with by a camel in a desert that had no "other end" to it, I accepted my position simply as material for a letter for which my employers had duly paid. They tried to drown me in a mill-stream ; that was a good half-column. Two Afridis sat down by me when I had sprained my knee by my horse falling, and waited for me to faint that they might cut my throat. But they overdid

it, for they looked so like vultures that I *couldn't* faint.
But it made several very harrowing paragraphs. I have
been sent to sea to get into cyclones in the Bay of Biscay,
and hurricanes in the Mozambique Channel, that I might
describe lucidly the sea-going properties of the vessels
under test. I have been sent to a King to ask him for
information that it was known beforehand he would not
give, and commissioned to follow Irish agitators all over
Ireland, in the hope that I might be able to say more
about them than they knew themselves. It has been my
duty to walk about inquisitively after Zulus, and to run
away judiciously with Zulus after me. Sometimes I have
taken long shots at Afghans, and sometimes they have
taken short ones at me. In short, I have been deputed
at one time and another to do many things which I should
never have done "for pleasure," and many which, for
pleasure, I should like to do again. But wherever I have
been sent I have had to go about, seeing as much as I
could and asking about all I couldn't see, and have become, professionally, accustomed to collecting evidence,
sifting it on the spot, and forming my own conclusions.
In a way, therefore, a Special Correspondent becomes of
necessity an expert at getting at facts. He finds that
everything he is commissioned to investigate has at least
two sides to it, and that many things have two *right* sides.
There are plenty of people always willing to mislead him,
and he has to pick and choose. He arrives unprejudiced,
and speaks according to the knowledge he acquires.
Sometimes he is brought up to the hill with a definite
commission to curse, but like Balaam, the son of Barak,
he begins blessing; or he is sent out to bless, and falls to
cursing. Until he arrives on the spot it is impossible for
him to say which he will do. But, whatever he does, the

Special Correspondent writes with the responsibility of a large public. It is impossible to write flippantly with all the world for critics.

Now, the demeanour of women in Utah, as compared with say Brighton or Washington, is modesty itself, and the children are just such healthy, pretty, vigorous children as one sees in the country, or by the seaside in England— and, in my opinion, nowhere else. Utah-born girls, the offspring of plural wives, have figures that would make Paris envious, and they carry themselves with almost Oriental dignity. But remember, Salt Lake City is a city of rustics. They do not affect " gentility," and are careful to explain at every opportunity that the stranger must not be shocked at their homely ways and speech. There is an easiness of manner therefore which is unconventional, but it is only a blockhead who could mistake this natural gaiety of the country for anything other than it is. There is nothing, then, so far as I have seen, in the manners of Salt Lake City to make me suspect the existence of that " licentiousness " of which so much has been written ; but there is a great deal on the contrary to convince me of a perfectly exceptional reserve and self-respect. I know, too, from medical assurance, that Utah has also the practical argument of healthy nurseries to oppose to the theories of those who attack its domestic relations on physiological grounds.

But the " Woman's Rights " aspect of polygamy is one that has never been theorized on at all. It deserves, however, special consideration by those who think that they are " elevating" Mormon women by trying to suppress polygamy. It possesses also a general interest for all. For the plural wives of Salt Lake City are not by any means " waiting for salvation " at the hands of the men and women of the East. Unconscious of having fetters on, they evince no enthusiasm for their noisy deliverers.

On the contrary, they consider their interference as a slur upon their own intelligence, and an encroachment upon those very rights about which monogamist females are making so much clamour. They look upon themselves as the *leaders* in the movement for the emancipation of their sex, and how, then, can they be expected to accept emancipation at the hands of those whom they are trying to elevate? Thinking themselves in the van of freedom, are they to be grateful for the guidance of stragglers in the rear? They laugh at such sympathy, just as the brave man might laugh at encouragement from a coward, or wealthy landowners at a pauper's exposition of the responsibilities of property. Can the deaf, they ask, tell musicians anything of the beauty of sounds, or need the artist care for the blind man's theory of colour?

Indeed, it has been in contemplation to evangelize the Eastern States, on this very subject of Woman's Rights! To send out from Utah exponents of the proper place of woman in society, and to teach the women of monogamy their duties to themselves and to each other! "Woman's true status "—I am quoting from their organ—" is that of companion to man, but so protected by law that she can act in an independent sphere if he abuse his position, and render union unendurable." They not only, therefore, claim all that women elsewhere claim, but they consider marriage the universal birthright of every female. First of all, they say, *be married*, and then in case of accidents have all other "rights" as well. But to start with, every woman must have a husband. She is hardly worth calling a woman if she is single. Other privileges ought to be hers lest marriage should prove disastrous. But in the first instance she should claim her right to be a wife. And everybody else should insist on that claim being recognized. The rest is very important to fall back upon, but union with man is her first step towards her proper sphere.

Now, could any position be imagined more ludicrous for the would-be saviours of Utah womanhood than this, that the slaves whom they talk of rescuing from their degradation should be striving to bring others *up* to their own standard? When Stanley was in Central Africa, he was often amused and sometimes not a little disgusted to find that instead of *his* discovering the Central Africans, the Central Africans insisted on "discovering" *him.* Though he went into villages in order to take notes of the savages, and to look at their belongings, the savages used to turn the tables on him by discussing him, and taking his clothes off to examine the curious colour, as they thought it, of his skin. So that what with shaking off his explorers, and hunting up the various articles they had abstracted for their unscientific scrutiny, his time used to be thoroughly wasted, and he used to come away crestfallen, and with the humiliating consciousness that it was the savages and not he that had gained information and been "improved" by his visit. They had "discovered" Stanley, not Stanley them. Something very like this will be the fate of those who come to Utah thinking that they will be received as shining lights from a better world. They will not find the women of Utah waiting with outstretched arms to grasp the hand that saves them. There will be no stampede of down-trodden females. On the contrary, the clarion of woman's rights will be sounded, and the intruding "champions" of that cause will find themselves attacked with their own weapons, and hoisted with their own petards. "With the sceptre of woman's rights the daughters of Zion will go down as apostles to evangelize the nation. 'Who is she that looketh forth as the morning, fair as the moon, clear as the sun, and terrible as an army with banners?' The Daughter of Zion!"

Mormon wives, then, are emphatically "woman's-rights women," a title which is everywhere recognized as indicating independence of character and an elevated sense of the claims of the sex, and as inferring exceptional freedom in action. And I venture to hold the opinion that it is only women who are conscious of freedom that can institute such movements as this in Utah, and only those who are enthusiastic in the cause, that can carry them on with the courage and industry so conspicuous in this community.

A Governor once went there specially instructed to release the women of Utah from their bondage, but he found none willing to be released! The franchise was then clamoured for in order to let the women of Utah "fight their oppressors at the polls," and the Mormon "tyrants" took the hint to give their wives votes, and the first use these misguided victims of plurality made of their new possession was to protest, 20,000 victims together, against the calumnies heaped upon the men of Utah "whom they honoured and loved." To-day it is an act of Congress that is to set free these worse-than-Indian-suttee-devotees, and whether they like it or not they are to be compelled to leave their husbands or take the alternative of sending their husbands to jail.

It reminds me of the story, "Sir, you *shall* have mustard with your beefsteak." A man sitting in a restaurant saw his neighbour eating his steak without mustard, and pushed the pot across to him. The stranger bowed his acknowledgment of the courtesy and went on eating, but without any mustard. But the other man's sense of propriety was outraged. "Beefsteak without mustard — monstrous," said he to himself; and again he pushed the condiment towards the stranger. "Thank you, sir," said the stranger, but without taking any, continued his meal as he preferred it, without mustard. But his well-wisher could not stand it any longer. He waited for a minute to see if the man would eat his beef in the orthodox manner, and then, his sense of the fitness of things overpowering him, he seized the mustard-pot and dabbing down a great splash of mustard on to the stranger's plate, burst out with, "By Jove, sir, you *shall* have mustard with your beefsteak!"

In the same way the monogamist reformers, having twice failed to persuade the wives of Utah to abandon their husbands by giving them facilities for doing so, are now going to take their husbands from them by the force of the law. "Sua si bona nôrint" is the excuse of the reformers to themselves for their philanthropy, and, like the old Inquisitors who burnt their victims to save them from heresy, they are going to make women wretched in order to make them happy. Says the *Woman's Exponent*: "If the women of Utah are slaves, their bonds are loving ones and dearly prized. They are to-day in the free and un-restricted exercise of more political and social rights than are the women of any other part of these United States. But they do not choose as a body to court the follies and vices which adorn the civilization of other cities, nor to barter principles of tried worth for the tinsel of senti-mentality or the gratification of passion."

It is of no use for "Mormon-eaters" to say that this is written "under direction," and that the women who write in this way are prompted by authority. Nor would they say it if they knew personally the women who write thus.

Moreover, Mormon-eaters are perpetually denouncing the "scandalous freedom" and "independence" extended to Mormon women and girls. And the two charges of excessive freedom and abject slavery seem to me totally incompatible.

I myself as a traveller can vouch for this: that one of my first impressions of Salt Lake City was this, that there was a thoroughly unconventional absence of restraint; just such freedom as one is familiar with in country neighbourhoods, where "every one knows every one else," and where the formalities of town etiquette are by general consent laid aside. And this also I can sincerely say: that I never ceased to be struck by the modest decorum of the women I meet out of doors. After all, self-respect is the true basis of woman's rights.

This aspect of the polygamy problem deserves, then, I think, considerable attention. An Act has been passed to compel some 20,000 women to leave their husbands, and the world looks upon these women as slaves about to be freed from tyrants. Yet they have said and done all that could possibly be expected of them, and even more than could have been expected, to assure the world that they have neither need nor desire for emancipation, as they honour their husbands, and prefer polygamy, with all its conditions, to the monogamy which brings with it infidelity at home and prostitution abroad. Again and again they have protested, in petitions to individuals and petitions to Congress, that "their bonds are loving ones and dearly prized." But the enthusiasm of reformers takes no heed of their protests. They are constantly declaring in public speeches and by public votes, in books and in newspapers —above all, in their daily conduct—that they consider themselves free and happy women, but the zeal of philanthropy will not be gainsaid, and so the women of Utah are, all else failing, to be saved from themselves. The "foul blot" of a servitude which the serfs aver does not exist is to be wiped out by declaring 20,000 wives mistresses, their households illegal, and their future children bastards!

"By Jove, sir, you *shall* have mustard with your beef-steak!"

CHAPTER VIII.

COULD THE MORMONS FIGHT?

An unfulfilled prophecy — Had Brigham Young been still alive?—
    The hierarchy of Mormonism—The fighting Apostle and his
    colleagues—Plurality a revelation—Rajpoot infanticide: how it
    was stamped out—Would the Mormons submit to the same pro-
    cess?—Their fighting capabilities — Boer and Mormon: an
    analogy between the Drakensberg and the Wasatch ranges—
    The Puritan fanaticism of the Saints—Awaiting the fulness of time
    and of prophecy.

"I SAY, as the Lord lives, we are bound to become a
sovereign State in the Union or an independent nation
by ourselves. I am still, and still will be Governor of
this Territory, to the constant chagrin of my enemies, and
twenty-six years shall not pass away before the Elders of
this Church will be as much thought of as kings on their
thrones." These were the words of Brigham Young on the
last day of August, 1856. And the Bill was passed in 1882.

Had Brigham Young been alive then, that prophecy
would assuredly have been fulfilled, for the coincidence of
recent legislation with the date he fixed, would have sufficed to convince him that the opportunity for a display of
the temporal power of his Church which he had foretold,
had arrived. Once before with similar exactness Brigham
Young fixed a momentous date.

He was standing in 1847 upon the site of the Temple,
when suddenly, as if under a momentary impulse, he turned

to those who were with him and said, "And now, if they will only let us alone *for ten years*, we will not ask them for any odds."

Exactly ten years later, to the very day, and almost to the very hour of the day, the news came of the despatch of a Federal army against Salt Lake City. Brigham Young called his people together—and what a nation they were compared to the fugitive crowd that had stood round him in 1847!—and simply reminding them of his words uttered ten years before, waited for their response. And as if they had only one voice among them all, the vast assemblage shouted, "*No odds.*"

And then and there he sent them into Echo Cañon— and the Federal army knows the rest.

Had he been alive to-day, that scene would probably have been repeated.

But Brigham Young is not alive. And his mantle has not fallen upon any of the Elders of the Church. They are men of caution, and the policy of Mormonism to-day is to temporize and to wait. All the States are " United " in earnest against them. Brigham Young always taught the people to reverence prophecy, but he taught them also to help to fulfil it. But nowadays Mormons are told to stand by and see how the Lord will work for them. And thus waiting, the Gentiles are gradually creeping up to them. Every year sees new influences at work to destroy the isolation of the Church, but the leaders originate no counteracting influences. Their defences are being sapped, but no counter-mines are run. As Gentile vigour grows aggressive, Mormonism seems to be contracting its frontiers. There is no Buonaparte mind to compel obedience. Mahomet is dead, and Ali, "the Lion of Allah," is dead, and the Caliphate is now in commission.

President Taylor is a self-reliant and courageous man, but for a ruler he listens too much to counsel. Though not afraid of responsibility, it does not sit upon him as one born to the ermine. Brigham Young was a natural king. President Taylor only suffices for an interregnum. Yet now, if ever, Mormonism needs a master-spirit. Nothing demoralizes like inaction. Men begin to look at things "from both sides," to compromise with convictions, to discredit enthusiasm. This is just what they are doing now. At one of the most eventful points of their history, they find the voices of the Tabernacle giving forth uncertain sounds. Their Urim and Thummim is dim; the Shekinah is flickering; their oracles stutter. They are told to obey the laws and yet to live their religion. In other words, to eat their cake and have it; to let go and hold tight—anything that is contradictory, irreconcilable, and impossible.

Meanwhile, wealth and interests in outside schemes have raised up in the Church a body of men of considerable temporal influence, who it is generally supposed "outside" are half-hearted. The Gentiles lay great stress on this. But no one should be deceived as to the real importance of this "half-heartedness." In the first place, a single word from President Taylor would extinguish the influence of these men politically and religously, at once and for ever. A single speech in the Tabernacle would reduce them to mere ciphers in Mormonism, and the Church would really, therefore, lose nothing more by their defection than the men themselves. But as a matter of fact they are *not* half-hearted. I know the men whom the outside world refers to personally, and I am certain therefore of my ground when I say that Mormonism will find them, in any hour of need, ready to throw all their temporal influence on to the side of the Church. The people need not be apprehensive, for there is no treason in their camp. There may be "Trimmers," but was there ever a movement that had no Trimmers?

The hierarchy in Utah stands as follows :—

President—John Taylor. *Counsellors to the President*—Joseph F. Smith, G. Q. Cannon. *Apostles*—Wilford Woodruff, Franklin Richards, C. C. Rich, Brigham Young, Moses Thatcher, M. Lyman, J. H. Smith, A. Carrington, Erastus Snow, Lorenzo Snow, S. P. Teasdel, and J. Grant. *Counsellors to the Apostles*—John W. Young, D. H. Wells.

Now in the present critical situation of affairs the personnel of this governing body is of some interest. President Taylor I have already spoken of. He is considered by all as a good head during an uneventful period, and that he is doing sound, practical work in a general administrative way is beyond doubt. But it is his misfortune to come immediately after Brigham Young. It is not often in history that an Aurungzebe follows an Akbar. But his counsellors, Apostles Cannon and Joseph Smith, are emphatically *strong* men. The former is a staunch Mormon, and a man of the world as well—perhaps the only Mormon who is—while the latter is "the fighting Apostle," a man of both brains and courage. Had he been ten years older he would probably have been President now. Of the remainder the men of conspicuous mark are Moses Thatcher, an admirable speaker and an able man, Merion Lyman, a very sound thinker and spirited in counsel, and D. H. Wells—perhaps the "strongest" unit in the whole hierarchy. He has made as much history as any man in the Church, and as one of its best soldiers and one of its shrewdest heads might have been expected to hold a higher rank than he does. He was one of the Counsellors of Brigham Young, but on the reconstruction of the governing body, accepted the position of Counsellor

I

to the Twelve. These five men, should the contingency for any decisive policy arise, will certainly lead the Mormon Church.

I was speaking one day to a Mormon, a husband of several wives, and was candidly explaining my aversion to that co-operative system of matrimony which the world calls "polygamy," but which the Saints prefer should be called "plurality." When I had finished, much to my own satisfaction (for I thought I had *proved* polygamy wrong), my companion knocked all my arguments, premises and conclusion together, into a cocked hat, by saying, —

"You are unprejudiced—I grant that; and you take higher ground for your condemnation of us than most do. But," said he, "you have never referred to the fact that we Mormons believe plurality to be *a revelation from God.* But we *do* believe it, and until that belief is overthrown angels from Heaven cannot convince us. You spoke of the power and authority of the United States. But what is that to the power and authority of God? The United States cannot do more than exterminate us for not abandoning plurality. But God can, and will, damn us to all eternity if we do abandon it."

Now what argument but force can avail against such an attitude as this? The better the Mormon, the harder he freezes to his religion—and part of his religion is polygamy —so important a part, indeed, that the whole future of the Saints is based upon it. The "Kingdom of God" is arranged with reference to it. The hopes of Mormons of glory and happiness in eternity depend upon it, and in this life men and women are perpetually exhorted to live up to it. It is pure nonsense therefore—so at least it seems to me— to request the Mormons to give up plurality, and keep the rest. You might just as well cut off all a man's limbs, and then tell him to get along "like a good and loyal citizen," with only a stomach.

Force of course will avail, in the end, just as it did in India when the Government determined to stamp out female infanticide among the Rajpoots. There, the procedure was from necessity inquisitorial (for the natives of the proscribed districts combined to prevent detection), but it was eventually effectual. It was simply this. Whenever a family was suspected of killing its female infants, a special staff of police was quartered upon the village in which that family lived, *at the expense of the village,* and maintained a constant personal watch over each of the suspected wives during the period immediately preceding childbirth. Nothing could have been so offensive to native sentiment as such procedure, but nothing else was of any use. In the end the suspects got wearied of the perpetual tyranny of supervision, and their neighbours wearied of paying for the police, and infanticide as a crime common to a whole community ceased after a few years to exist in India. Now if the worst came to the worst, something of the same kind is within the resources of the United States. Every polygamous family in the Territory might be brought under direct police supervision at the cost of their neighbours, and punishment rigidly follow every conviction. This would stamp out polygamy in time.

But it would be a long time, a very long time, and I would hesitate to affirm that Mormon endurance and submission would be equal to such a severe and such a protracted ordeal. There is nothing in their past history that leads me to look upon them as a people exceptionally tolerant of ill-usage.

The infanticidal families in India were, it is true, of a fighting caste and clan, but the suspected families were only a few hundreds in number. They could not, like the Mormons, rely upon a strength of twenty-five thousand adult males, an admirable strategic position, and the help, if necessary, of twenty thousand picked "warriors" from the surrounding Indian tribes ; and it is mere waste of words to say that the consciousness of strength has often got a great deal to do with influencing the action of men who are subjected to violence. And I doubt myself, looking to the recent history of England in Africa, and Russia in Central Asia, whether the United States, when they come to consider Mormon potentialities for resistance, will think it worth while to resort to violence in vindication of a sentiment. The war between the North and the South is not a case in point at all. There was more than a mere "sentiment" went to the bringing on of that war. Remember, I do not say that the Mormons entertain the idea of having to fight the United States. I only say that they would not be afraid to do it, in defence of their religion, if circumstances compelled it. And I am only arguing from nature when I say that those "circumstances" arrive at very different stages of suffering with different individuals. The worm, for instance, does not turn till it is trodden on. The grizzly bear turns if you sneeze at it. And I am only quoting history when I say that thirty thousand determined men, well armed, with their base of military supplies at their backs, could defend a position of great strategical strength for—well, a very considerable time against an army only ten times as numerous as themselves—especially if that army had to defend a thousand miles of communications against unlimited Indians.

It was my privilege when on the editorial staff of the *Daily Telegraph* in London to tell the country in the leading columns of that paper what I thought of the chances of success against the Boers of the Transvaal. I said that one Boer on his own mountains was worth five British soldiers, and that any army that went against those fanatical puritans with less than ten to one in numbers, would find "the sword of the Lord and of Gideon " too strong for them, and the Drakensberg range an impregnable frontier. As an Englishman I regret that my words were so miserably fulfilled, and England, after sacrificing a great number of men and officers, decided that it was not worth while "for a sentiment" to continue the war.

The points of resemblance between the Mormons and the Boers are rather curious.

The Boers of the Transvaal, though of the same stock as the great majority of the inhabitants of British Africa, were averse to the forms of government that had satisfied the rest. So they migrated, after some popular disturbances, and settled in another district where they hoped to enjoy the *imperium in imperio* on which they had set their longings. But British colonies again came up with them, and after a fight with the troops, the Boers again migrated, and with their long caravans of ox and mule waggons "trekked" away to the farthest inhabitable corner of the continent. Here for a considerable time they enjoyed the life they had sought for, established a capital, had their own governor, whipped or coaxed the surrounding native tribes into docility, and, after a fashion, throve. But yet once more the "thin red line " of British possession crept up to them, and the Boers, being now at bay, and having nowhere else to "trek " to, *fought.*

They were not exactly trained soldiers, but merely a territorial militia, accustomed, however, to warfare with native tribes, and, by the constant use of the rifle in hunting game, capital marksmen. So they declared war against Great

Britain, these three or four thousand Boers, and having worked themselves up into the belief that they were fighting for their religion, they unsheathed "the sword of the Lord and of Gideon," threatened to call in the natives, and holding their mountain passes, defied the British troops to force them. Nor without success. For every time the troops went at them, they beat them, giving chapter and verse out of the Bible for each whipping, and eventually concluded their extraordinary military operations by an honourable peace, and a long proclamation of pious thanksgiving "to the Lord God omnipotent." To-day, therefore, Queen Victoria is "suzerain" of the Transvaal, and the Boers govern themselves by a territorial government. To their neighbours they are known as very pious, simple, and stubborn people ; very shrewd in making a bargain ; very honest when it is made ; a pastoral and agricultural community, with strong objections to "Gentiles," who, by the way, are never tired of reviling them, especially with regard to alleged eccentricities in domestic relations.

Am I not right, then, in saying that the resemblance between the Boers and the Mormons is "curious"?

When I speak of the Mormons as being prepared to accept the worst that the commission under the Edmunds bill may do, it should be understood that this readiness to suffer does not arise from any misconception of their own strength. The Mormons are thoroughly aware of it ; indeed, the figures which I have given (25,000 adult males and 20,000 Indians) are not accepted by all of them as representing their full numbers. They fully understand also the capabilities of their position for defence, and are not backward to appreciate the advantages which the length of the Federal communications would give them for protracting a campaign.

Under the circumstances, therefore, the argument of a leading Mormon, that "if the United States really believe the people of Utah to be the desperate fanatics they call them, any action on their part that tends to exasperate such fanatics is foolhardy," may be accepted as quite seriously meant. For the Mormons, if bigoted about anything at all, are so on this point—*that they cannot be crushed.* As the elect of God, specially appointed by Him to prepare places of worship and keep up the fires of a religion which is very soon to consume all others, they cannot, they say, be moved until the final fulfilment of prophecy. The Jews have still to be gathered together, and "the nations from the north country" whose coming, according to the Bible, is to be so terrible, are to find the Mormons, "the children of Ephraim," ready prepared with such rites and such tabernacles that the "sons of Levi," the Jews, can perform their old worship, and, thus refreshed, continue their progress to the Holy Land. "And their prophets shall come in remembrance before the Lord, and they shall smite the rocks, and the ice shall flow down at their presence, and a highway shall be cast up in the midst of the great deep. And they shall come forth, and their enemies shall become a prey unto them, and the everlasting hills shall tremble at their presence." For this time, these men and women among whom I have lived are actually waiting!

Of course, we ordinary Christians, whose religion sits lightly upon us, cannot, without some effort, understand the stern faith with which the Mormons cling to their translations of Old Testament prophecy. Nor is it easy to credit the fierce earnestness with which, for instance, the Saints look forward to the accomplishment of the promise that they shall eventually possess Jackson County, Missouri. But if this spirit of intense superstition is not properly taken into account by those who try to make the Mormons alter their beliefs, they run the risk of under-estimating the seriousness of their attempt. If, on the other hand, it is properly taken into account, the difficulty of forcing this people to abandon their creeds will be at once seen to be very grave.

Except, perhaps, the Kurdish outbreak on the Persian frontier some three years ago, there has been no problem like the Mormon one presented to the consideration of modern Europe. In the case of the Kurds, two nations, Turkey and Persia, were within an ace of war, in consequence of the insurgents pretending that a point of religion was involved, and popular fanaticism very nearly slipping beyond the control of their respective governments.

When living at a distance from Salt Lake City, it is very difficult indeed to recognize the truth of the situation. Until I went there I always found that though in a general way the obstacles to a speedy settlement were admitted, yet that somehow or another there was always the afterthought that Mormonism was only an inflated imposture, and that it would collapse at the first touch of law. It was allowed on all hands that the position was a peculiar one, but it was hinted also that it was an absurd one. "No doubt," it was argued, "the Mormons are an obstinate set of men, but after all they have got common sense. When they see that everybody is against them, that polygamy is contrary to the spirit of the times, that all the future of Utah depends upon their abandonment of it, that resistance is worse than senseless," and so on, they will give in. Let opinion as to the "bigotry" of the Mormons or their capacity for mischief be what it might, there was always a qualifying addendum to the effect that "nothing would come of all this fuss." The Mormons, in fact, were supposed to be "bluffing," and it was taken for granted therefore that they had a weak hand.

But in Salt Lake City it is impossible to speak in this way. A Mormon—a man of absolute honesty of speech— in conversation on this subject declared to me that he *could* not abandon plurality without apostatizing, and rather than do it, he would burn his house and business premises down, go away to the Mexicans, *die*, if necessary. Now, that man may any day be put to the very test he spoke of. He will have to abandon polygamy, or else, if his adversaries are malicious, spend virtually the whole of his life in jail. Which will he do? And what will all the others of his way of thinking do? Will they defy the law, or will they try to break it down by its own weight— that is to say, load the files with such numbers of cases, and fill the prisons with such numbers of convicts that the machinery will clog and break down? The heroic alterna- tives of burning down their houses, going off to Mexico, and dying will not be offered them. Their choice will simply lie between monogamy (or celibacy) and prison, two very prosaic things—and one or the other they must accept. Such at any rate is the opinion of the world.

But the Mormons, as I have already shown, do not admit this simplicity in the solution at all. From the point of view of the law-makers, they allow that the option before them is very commonplace. But the law-makers, they say, have omitted to take into consideration certain facts which complicate the solution. For though, as I have said, the majority may be expected to accept such qualified martyrdom as is offered, and "await the Lord's time," yet there can be no doubt whatever that strict Mormons will not acquiesce in the suppression of their doctrines, and among so many who are strict is it reasonable to expect that there will be no violent advisers? Their teachers have perpetually taught them, and their leaders assured them that prophecy had found its fulfilment in the establishment of the Church in Utah. Here, and nowhere else, the Saints are to await " the fulness of time," when the whole world shall yield obedience to their government, and reverence to their religion. The Rocky Mountains, and no other, are "the mountains" of Holy Writ where " Zion " was to be built ; and they, the Mormons, are the remnant of Ephraim that are to welcome and pass on the returning Jews. How, then, can the Saints reconcile themselves to another exodus? Mexico, they say, would welcome them ; but if the richest lands in the world, and all the privileges they ask for were offered them, they could not stultify revelation and prophecy by accepting the offer. Moreover, they have been assured times without number that they should never be " driven " again, and times without number that their enemies " shall not prevail against them." To many, to most, this, of course, now points to some interposition of Divine Providence in their favour. The crisis may seem dangerous, and the opposition to them overwhelming. But they are convinced—it is no mere matter of opinion with them—that if they are only patient under persecution and keep on living their religion, the persecution will cease, and the triumph of their faith be fulfilled. Europe and America, they believe, are about to be involved in terrific disasters. Wars of unprecedented magnitude are to be waged, and natural catastrophes, unparalleled in history, are to occur. But, in the midst of all this shock of thrones, this convulsion of the elements, Zion on the Mountains is to be at peace and in prosperity. It will be the one still harbour in all the ocean of troubles, and to it, as to their final haven, all the elect of all the nations are to gather. The prudent, therefore, looking forward to this apocalypse of general ruin, counsel submission to the passing storm, endurance under legal penalties, and fidelity to their doctrine.

But all are not prudent. Every Gethsemane has its Peter. And from that memorable garden they draw a lesson. The Saviour, they say, meant fighting, but when he saw that resistance to such odds as came against him could have only ended in the massacre of his disciples, he went to prison.

That Brigham Young, if alive, would have decided upon a military demonstration, the sons of Zeruiah are very ready to believe, for they say that, even if the worst were to happen and they had eventually to capitulate under unreasonable odds, their position would be preferable to that which they hold to-day. To-day they lie, the whole community together, under the ban of civil disabilities, as a criminal class, at the mercy of police—a proscribed people. In the future, if compelled to surrender their arms, they would be in the position of prisoners on parole, under the honourable conditions of a military capitulation. The worst, therefore, that could happen would, they say, be better than what is.

Such, at any rate, they assert, would have been the argument of Brigham Young, and Gentiles even confess that if the late President were still at the head of the Church the temptation for " a great bluff " would be irresistible.

CHAPTER IX.

THE SAINTS AND THE RED MEN.

Prevalent errors as to the red man—Secret treaties—The policy of the Mormons towards Indians — A Christian heathen — Fighting-strength of Indians friendly to Mormons.

I HAPPENED some time ago to repeat, in the presence of two " Gentiles," a Mormon's remark that the Indians were more friendly towards the Saints than towards other Americans, and the comments of the two gentlemen in question exactly illustrated the two errors which I find are usually made on this subject.

One said: " Oh, yes, don't you know the Mormons have secret treaties with the Indians ? "

And the other: "And much good may they do them; these wretched Indians are a half-starved, cricket-eating set, not worth a cent."

Now, I confess that till I came to Utah I had an idea that the Utes were always " the Indians " that were meant when the friendly relations of the Mormons with the red men were referred to. About secret treaties I knew nothing, either one way or the other. But while I was there I took much pains to arrive at the whole truth—the President of the Church having very courteously placed the shelves of the Historian's office at my service—and I found no reference whatever, even in anti-Mormon literature, to any " secret treaty."

The Mormons themselves scorn the idea and give the following reasons : 1. No treaty made with a tribe of Indians could be kept secret. 2. There is no necessity for a treaty of any kind, as the dislike of the Indians to the United States is sufficiently hearty to make them friendly to the Territory if it came to a choice between the one or the other. 3. The conciliatory policy of the Church towards the Indians obviates all necessity for further measures of alliance.

And this I believe to be the fact. Indeed, I know that Mormons can go where Gentiles cannot, and that under a Mormon escort, lives are safe in an Indian camp that without it would be in great peril. I know further that on several occasions (and this is on official record) the expostulations of Mormons have prevented Indians from raiding—and I think this ought to be remembered when sinister constructions are put upon the friendliness of Saints towards the Indians.

From the very first, the Church has inculcated forbearance and conciliation towards the tribes, and even during the exodus from the Missouri River, harassed though they sometimes were by Indians, the Mormons, as a point of policy, always tried to avert a collision by condoning offences that were committed, instead of punishing them. If the red men came begging round their waggons they gave them food, and if they stole—and what Indian will not steal, seeing that theft is the road to honour among his people ?— the theft was overlooked. Very often, it is true, individual Mormons have avenged the loss of a horse or a cow by taking a red man's life, but this was always in direct opposition to the teachings of the Church, which pointed out that murder in the white man was a worse offence than theft in the red, and in opposition to the policy of the leaders, who have always insisted that it was " cheaper to feed than to fight " the Indians. In spite, however, of this treatment the tribes have again and again compelled the Mormons to take the field against them, but as a rule the extent of Mormon retaliation was to catch the plunderers, retake their stolen stock, hang the actual murderers (if murder had been committed) and let the remainder go after an amicable pow-wow. Strict justice was as nearly as possible always adhered to, and whenever their word was given, that word was kept sacred, even to their own loss.

Both these things, justice and truth, every Indian understands. They do not practise them, but they appreciate them. Just as among themselves they chivalrously undertake the support of the squaws and children of a conquered tribe, or as they never steal property that has been placed under the charge of one of their own tribe, so when dealing with white men, they have learned to expect fairness in reprisals and sincerity in speech. When they find themselves cheated, as they nearly always are by " Indian agents," they cherish a grudge, and when they suffer an unprovoked injury (as when emigrants shoot a passing red man just as they would shoot a passing coyote), they wreak their barbarous revenge upon the first victims they can find. From the Mormons they have always received honest treatment, comparative fairness in trade and strict truthfulness in engagements, while, taking men killed on both sides, it is a question whether the red men have not killed more Mormons than Mormons have red men.

During the war of 1865-67, I find, for instance, that all the recorded deaths muster eighty-seven on the Indian side and seventy-nine on the Mormon, while the latter, besides losing great numbers of cattle and horses, having vast quantities of produce destroyed and buildings burned down, had temporarily to abandon the counties of Piute and Sevier, as well as the settlements of Berrysville, Winsor, Upper and Lower Kanab, Shuesberg, Springdale and Northup, and many places in Kane County, also some settlements in Iron County, while the total cost of the war was over a million dollars—of which, by the way, the Government has not repaid a Territory a cent. During the twenty years preceding 1865 there had been numerous raids upon Mormon settlements, most of them due to the thoughtless barbarity of passing emigrants; but as a rule, the only revenge taken by the Mormons was expostulation, and the despatch cf missionaries to them with the Bible, and medicines and implements of agriculture.

The result to-day is exactly what Brigham Young foresaw. The Indians look upon the Mormons as suffering with themselves from the earth-hunger of "Gentiles," and feel a community in wrong with them, while they consider them different from all other white men in being fair in their acts and straightforward in their speech. In 1847 a chief of the Pottawatomies—then being juggled for the second time from a bad reservation to a worse—came into the camp of the Mormons—then for the second time flying from one of the most awful persecutions that ever disgraced any nation —and on leaving spoke as follows—(he spoke good French, by the way): "My Mormon brethren,—We have both suffered. We must help one another, and the Great Spirit will help us both. You may cut and use all the wood on our lands that you wish. You may live on any part of it that we are not actually occupying ourselves. Because one suffers, and does not deserve it, it is no reason he shall suffer always. We may live to see all well yet. However, if we do not, our children will. Good-bye."

Now, it strikes me that a Christian archbishop would find

it hard to alter the Red Indian's speech for the better. It is
one of the finest instances of untutored Christianity in
history, and contrasts so strangely with the hideous barbarities that make the history of Missouri so infamous, that I
can easily understand the sympathies of Mormons being
cast in with the Christian heathens they fled to, rather than
the heathen Christians they fled from. Nor from that day
to this, have the Mormons forgotten the hint the Pottawa-
tomie gave them, and on the ground of common suffering
and by the example of a mutual sympathy have kept up such
relations with the Indians, even under exasperation, that
the red man's lodge is now open to the Mormon when it is
closed to the Gentile.

What necessity, then, have the Mormons for secret treaties
with the Indians? None whatever. The Indians have
learned by the last half-century's experience that every
"treaty" made with them has only proved a fraud towards
their ruin, while during the same period they have learned
that the word of the Mormons, who never make treaties,
can be relied upon. So if the Saints were now to begin
making treaties, they would probably fall in the estimation
of the Indians to the level of the American Government,
and participate in the suspicion which the latter has so
industriously worked to secure, and has so thoroughly
secured.

The other error commonly made as to the Indians is to
underestimate their strength. Now the Navajoes alone
could bring into the field 10,000 fighting men ; and, besides
these, there are (specially friendly to the Mormons) the
Flatheads, the Shoshonees, the Blackfeet, the Bannocks,
part of the Sioux, and a few Apaches, with, of course, the
Utes of all kinds. The old instinct for the war-path is by
no means dead, as the recent troubles in the south of

Arizona give dismal proof; and a Mormon invitation would be quite sufficient to bring all "the Lamanites" together into the Wasatch Mountains.

That any such idea is ever entertained by Mormons I heartily repudiate. But I think it worth while to point out, that—if the influence of the Mormons on the Indians is considered of sufficient importance to base the charge of treasonable alliance upon it—it is quite illogical to sneer at that influence as making no difference in the case of difficulties arising. But as a point of fact, the Mormons have no other secret in their relations with the red men than that they treat them with consideration, and make allowances for their ethical obliquities; and further, as a point of fact also, these same tribes, "the Lamanites" of the Book of Mormon, "the Lost Tribes," are in themselves so formidable that under white leadership they would make a very serious accession of strength to any public enemy that should be able to enlist them.

K

CHAPTER X.

REPRESENTATIVE AND UNREPRESENTATIVE MORMONISM.

Mormonism and Mormonism—Salt Lake City not representative—The
miracles of water—How settlements grow—The town of Logan :
one of the Wonders of the West—The beauty of the valley—The
rural simplicity of life—Absence of liquor and crime—A police
force of one man—Temple mysteries—Illustrations of Mormon
degradation—Their settlement of the "local option" question.

SALT Lake City is not the whole of "Mormonism." In
the Eastern States there is a popular impression that it is.
But as a matter of fact, it hardly represents Mormonism at
all. The Gentile is too much there, and Main Street has
too many saloons. The city is divided into two parties,
bitterly antagonistic. Newspapers exchange daily abuse,
and sectarians thump upon their pulpit cushions at each
other every Sunday. Visitors on their travels, sight-seeing,
move about the streets in two-horse hacks, staring at the
houses that they pass as if some monsters lived in them.
A military camp stands sentry over the town, and soldiers
slouch about the doors of the bars.

All this, and a great deal more that is to be seen in
Salt Lake City, is foreign to the true character of a Mormon
settlement. Logan, for instance (which I describe later
on), is characteristic of Mormonism, and nowhere so
characteristic as in those very features in which it differs
from Salt Lake City. The Gentile does not take very

kindly to Logan, for there are no saloons to make the place a "live town," and no public animosities to give it what they call "spirit;" everybody knows his neighbour, and the sight-seeing fiend is unknown. The one and only newspaper hums on its way like some self-satisfied bumble bee ; the opposition preacher, with a congregation of eight women and five men, does not think it worth while, on behalf of such a shabby constituency, to appeal to Heaven every week for vengeance on the 200,000 who don't agree with him and his baker's dozen. There is no pomp and circumstance of war to remind the Saints of Federal surveillance, no brass cannon on the bench pointing at the town (as in Salt Lake City), no ragged uniforms at street corners. Everything is Mormon. The biggest shop is the Co-operative Store ; the biggest place of worship the Tabernacle ; the biggest man the President of the Stake. Everybody that meets, "Brothers" or "Sisters" each other in the streets, and after nightfall the only man abroad is the policeman, who as a rule retires early himself ; and no one takes precautions against thieves at night. It is a very curious study, this well-fed, neighbourly, primitive life among orchards and corn-fields, this bees-in-a-clover-field life, with every bee bumbling along in its own busy way, but all taking their honey back to the same hive. It is not a lofty life, nor "ideal" to my mind, but it *is* emphatically ideal, if that word means anything at all, and its outcome, where exotic influences are not at work, is contentment and immunity from crime, and an Old-World simplicity.

But Logan is not by any means a solitary illustration. For the Mormon settlements follow the line of the valleys that run north and south, and every one of them, where water is abundant, is a Logan in process of development.

For water is the philosopher's stone ; the fairy All-Good ; the First Cause ; the everything that men here strive after as the source of all that is desirable.   It is silver and gold, pearls and rubies, and virtuous women—which are " above rubies "—everything in fact that is precious.   It spirits up Arabian-Nights enchantments, and gives industry a talisman to work with.   Without it, the sage-brush laughs at man, and the horn of the jack-rabbit is exalted against him. With it, corn expels the weed, and the long-eared rodent is ploughed out of his possession.   Without it, greasewood and gophers divide the wilderness between them.   With it, homesteads spring up and gather the orchards around them.   Without it, the silence of the level desert is broken only by the coyote and the lark.   With it, comes the laughter of running brooks, the hum of busy markets, and the cheery voices of the mill-wheels by the stream.   Without it, the world seems a dreary failure.   With it, it brightens into infinite possibilities.   No wonder then that men prize it, exhaust ingenuity in obtaining it, quarrel about it.   I wonder they do not worship it.   Men have worshipped trees, and wind, and the sun, for far less cause.

Nothing indeed is so striking in all these Mormon settlements as the supreme importance of water.   It determines locations, regulates their proportions, and controls their prosperity.   Here are thousands of acres barren— though I hate using such a word for a country of such beautiful wild flowers—because there is no water.   There is a small nook bursting with farmsteads and trees, because there *is* water.   Men buy and sell water-claims as if they were mining stock " with millions in sight," and appraise each other's estates not by the stock that grazes on them, or the harvests gathered from them, but by the water-rights that go with them. Thus, a man in Arizona buys a forty-acre lot with a spring on it, and he speaks of it as 70,000 acres of "wheat." Another has acquired the right of the head-waters of a little mountain stream ; he is spoken of as owning "the finest ranch in the valley." Yet the one has not put a plough into the ground, the other has not a single head of cattle ! But each possessed the "open sesame" to untold riches, and in a country given over to this new form of hydromancy was already accounted wealthy.

Every stream in Utah might be a Pactolus, every pool a Bethesda. To compass, then, this miracle-working thing, the first energies of every settlement are directed in union. The Church comes forward if necessary to help, and every one contributes his labour. At first the stream where it leaves the cañon, and debouches upon the levels of the valley, is run off into canals to north and south and west (for all the streams run from the eastern range), and from these, like the legs of a centipede, minor channels run to each farmstead, and thence again are drawn off in numberless small aqueducts to flood the fields. The final process is simple enough, for each of the furrows by which the water is let in upon the field is in turn dammed up at the further end, and each surrounding patch is thus in turn submerged. But the settlement expands, and more ground is needed. So another canal taps the stream above the cañon mouth, the main channels again strike off, irrigating the section above the levels already in cultivation, and overlapping the original area at either end. And every time increasing population demands more room, the stream is taken off higher and higher up the cañon. The cost is often prodigious, but necessity cannot stop to haggle over arithmetic, and the Mormon settlements therefore have developed a system of irrigation which is certainly among the wonders of the West.

"Logan is the chief Mormon settlement in the Cache Valley, and is situated about eighty miles to the north of Salt Lake City. Population rather over 4000." Such is the ordinary formula of the guide book. But if I had to describe it in few words I should say this : " Logan is without any parallel, even among the wonders of Western America, for rapidity of growth, combined with solid prosperity and tranquillity. Population rather over 4000, every man owning his own farm. Police force, two men— partially occupied in agriculture on their own account. N.B.—No police on Sundays, or on meeting evenings, as the force are otherwise engaged."

And writing sincerely I must say that I have seen few things in America that have so profoundly impressed me as this Mormon settlement of Logan. It is not merely that the industry of men and women, penniless emigrants a few years ago, has made the valley surpassing in its beauty. That it has filled the great levels that stretch from mountain to mountain with delightful farmsteads, groves of orchard-trees, and the perpetual charm of crops. That it has brought down the river from its idleness in the cañons to busy itself in channels and countless waterways with the irrigation and culture of field and garden ; to lend its strength to the mills which saw up the pines that grow on its native mountains; to grind the corn for the 15,000 souls that live in the valley, and to help in a hundred ways to make men and women and children happy and comfortable, to beautify their homes, and reward their industry. All this is on the surface, and can be seen at once by any one.

But there is much more than mere fertility and beauty in Logan and its surroundings, for it is a town without crime, a town without drunkenness! With this knowledge one looks again over the wonderful place, and what a new significance every feature of the landscape now possesses! The clear streams, perpetually industrious in their loving care of lowland and meadow and orchard, and so cheery, too, in their incessant work, are a type of the men and women themselves; the placid cornfields lying in bright levels about the houses are not more tranquil than the lives of the people; the tree-crowded orchards and stack-filled yards are eloquent of universal plenty; the cattle loitering to the pasture contented, the foals all running about in the roads, while the waggons which their mothers are drawing stand at the shop door or field gate, strike the new-comer as delightfully significant of a simple country life, of mutual confidence, and universal security.

And yet I had not come there in the humour to be pleased, for I was not well. But the spirit of the place was too strong for me, and the whole day ran on by itself in a veritable idyll.

A hen conveying her new pride of chickens across the road, with a shepherd dog loftily approving the expedition in attendance; a foal looking into a house over a doorstep, with the family cat, outraged at the intrusion, bristling on the stoop; two children planting sprigs of peach blossoms in one of the roadside streams; a baby peeping through a garden wicket at a turkey-cock which was hectoring it on the sidewalk for the benefit of one solitary supercilious sparrow—such were the little vignettes of pretty nonsense that brightened my first walk in Logan. I was alone, so I walked where I pleased; took notice of the wild birds that make themselves as free in the streets

as if they were away up in the cañons; of the wild flowers
that still hold their own in the corners of lots, and by the
roadway; watched the men and women at their work in
garden and orchard, the boys driving the waggons to the
mill and the field, the girls busy with little duties of the
household, and "the little ones," just as industrious as all
the rest, playing at irrigation with their mimic canals, three
inches wide, old fruit-cans for buckets, and posies stuck
into the mud for orchards. I stopped to talk to a man
here and a woman there; helped to fetch down a kitten
out of an apple-tree, and, at the request of a boy, some
ten years old, I should say, opened a gate to let the team
he was driving, or rather being walked along with, go into
the lot.

It was a beautiful day, and all the trees were either in
full bloom or bright young leaf; and the conviction
gradually grew upon me that I had never, out of England,
seen a place so simple, so neighbourly, so quiet.

Later on I was driven through the town to the Temple.
The wide roads are all avenued with trees, and behind trees,
each in its own garden, or orchard, or lot of farm-land,
stands a ceaseless succession of cottage homes. Here and
there a "villa," but the great majority "cottages." Not the
dog-kennels in which the Irish peasantry are content to
grovel through life so long as they need not work and can
have their whisky. Not the hovels which in some parts of
rural England house the farm labourer and his unkempt
urchins. But cleanly, comfortable homes, some of adobe,
some of wood, with porticos and verandahs and other ornaments, six or eight or even ten rooms, with barns behind
for the cow and the horse and the poultry, bird-cages at the
doors, clean white curtains at the windows, and neatly
bedded flowers in the garden-plots. Hundred after hundred,

each in its own lot of amply watered ground, we passed the homes of these Mormon farmers, and it was a wonderful thing to me—so fresh from the old country, with its elegance and its squalor side by side; so lately from the "live" cities of Colorado, with their murrain of "busted" millionaires and hollow shells of speculative prosperity—this great township of an equal prosperity and a universal comfort. Every man I met in the street or saw in the fields owned the house which he lived in, and the ground that his railings bounded. Moreover they were his by right of purchase, the earnings of the work of his own two hands. No wonder, then, they demean themselves like men.

I was driving with the President of the "stake"—such is the name of the Church for the sub-divisions of its Territory —and the chief official, therefore, of Logan, when, in a narrow part of the road we met a down-trodden Mormon serf driving a loaded waggon in the opposite direction. The President pulled a little to one side, motioning the man to drive past. But the roadway thus left for him was rather rough and this degraded slave of the Church, knowing the rule of the road (that a loaded waggon has the right of way against all other vehicles), calmly pointed with his whip-handle to the side of the road, and said to his President, *" You drive there."* And the President did so, whereat the down-trodden one proceeded on his way in the best of the road.

Now this may be accepted as an instance of that abject servitude which, according to anti-Mormons, characterizes the followers of Mormonism. As another illustration of the same awe-stricken subjection may be here noted the fact, that whenever the President slackened pace, passersby, men and women, would come over to us, and shaking hands with the President, exchange small items of domestic,

neighbourly chat—the health of the family, convalescence
of a cow, and, speaking generally, discuss Tommy's measles.
Now, women would hardly waste a *despot's* time with intelligence of an infant's third tooth, or a man expatiate on the
miraculous recovery of a calf from a surfeit of damp lucerne.

I chanced also one day to be with an authority when
a man called in to apologize for not having repaid his
emigration money; and to me the incident was specially
interesting on this account, that very few writers on the
Mormons have escaped charging the Church with acting
dishonestly and usuriously towards its emigrants.   I have
read repeatedly that the emigrants, being once in debt, are
never able to get out of debt; that the Church prefers they
should not; that the indebtedness is held *in terrorem* over
them.   But the man before me was in exactly the same
position as every other man in Logan.   He had been brought
out from England at the expense of the Perpetual Emigration Fund (which is maintained partly by the "tithings,"
chiefly by voluntary donations), and though by his labour he
had been able to pay for a lot of ground and to build himself a house, to plant fruit-trees, buy a cow, and bring his
lot under cultivation, he had not been able to pay off any of
the loan of the Church.   It stood, therefore, against him at
the original sum.   But his delinquency distressed him, and
"having things comfortable about him," as he said, and
some time to spare, he came of his own accord to his
"Bishop," to ask if he could not *work off part of his debt.*
He could not see his way, he said to any ready money,
but he was anxious to repay the loan, and he came, therefore, to offer all he had—his labour.   Now, I cannot believe
that this man was abused.   I am sure he did not think he
was abused himself.   Here he was in Utah, comfortably
settled for life, and at no original expense to himself.   No

one had bothered him to pay up; no one had tacked on usurious interest. So he came, like an honest man, to make arrangements for satisfying a considerate creditor, but all he got in answer was, that "there was time enough to pay" and an exchange of opinions about a plough or a harrow or something. And he went off as crushed down with debt as ever. And he very nearly added to his debt on the way, by narrowly escaping treading on a presumptuous chicken which was reconnoitring the interior of the house from the door-mat.

To return to my drive. After seeing the town we drove up to the Temple. The Mormon "temples" must not be mistaken for their "tabernacles." The latter are the regular places of worship, open to the public. The former are buildings strictly dedicated to the rites of the Endowments, the meetings of the initiated brethren, and the ceremonial generally of the sacred Masonry of Mormonism. No one who has not taken his degrees in these mysteries has access to the temples, which are, or will be, very stately piles, constructed on architectural principles said by the Church to have been revealed to Joseph Smith piecemeal, as the progress of the first Temple (at Kirkland) necessitated, and said by the profane to be altogether contrary to all previously received principles. However this may be, the style is, from the outside, not so prepossessing as the cost of the buildings and the time spent upon them would have led one to expect. The walls are of such prodigious thickness, and the windows so narrow and comparatively small, that the buildings seem to be constructed for defence rather than for worship. But once within, the architecture proves itself admirable. The windows gave abundant light and the loftiness of the rooms imparts an airiness that is as surprising as pleasing, while the arrangement of staircases—leading, as

I suppose, from the rooms of one degree in the " Masonry "
to the next higher—and of the different rooms, all of considerable size, and some of very noble proportions indeed, is
singularly good.

I ought to say that this Temple at Logan is the only one
I have entered, and it is only because it is not completed.
This year the building will be finished—so it is hoped—and
the ceremony of dedication will then attract an enormous
crowd of Mormons. It is something over 90 feet in height
(not including ¡the towers, which are still wanting) and
measures 160 feet by 70. On the ground floor, judging
from what I know of the secret ritual of the Church, are the
reception-rooms of the candidates for the " endowments,"
various official rooms, and the font for baptism. The great
laver, 10 feet in diameter, will rest on the backs of twelve
oxen cast in iron (and modelled from a Devon ox bred by
Brigham Young) and will be descended to by flights of
steps, the oxen themselves standing in water half-knee-deep.
On the next floor are the apartments in which the allegorical
panorama of the " Creation " and the "Fall of Man" will be
represented. Here, too, will be the "Veil," the final degree
in what might be called, in Masonic phrase, " craft " or
" blue " Masonry, and, except for higher honorary grades,
the ultimate objective point of Mormon initiation. Above
these rooms is a vast hall, occupying the whole floor, in
which general assemblies of the initiated brethren and
" chapters " will be held. The whole forms a very imposing
pile of great solidity and some grandeur, built of a gloomy,
slate-coloured stone (to be eventually coloured a lighter
tint), and standing on a magnificent site, being raised above
the town upon an upper " bench" of the slope, and showing
out superbly against the monstrous mountain about a mile
behind it. The mountain, of course, dwarfs the Temple by

its proximity, but the position of the building was undoubtedly "an architectural inspiration," and gives the great
pile all the dominant eminence which Mormons claim for
their Church.

From the platform of the future tower the view is one
of the finest I have ever seen. The valley, reaching for
twenty miles in one direction, and thirty in the other,
with an average width of about ten miles, lies beneath
you, level in the centre, and gradually sloping on every
margin up to the mountains that bound it in. Immediately
underneath you, Logan spreads out its breadth of farm-land
and orchard and meadow, with the river—or rather two
rivers, for the Logan forks just after leaving the cañon—
and the canal, itself a pleasant stream, carrying verdure
and fertility into every nook and corner. To right and
left and in front, delightful villages—Hirum, Mendon,
Wellsville, Paradise, and the rest, all of them miniature
Logans—break the broad reaches of crop-land, with their
groves of fruit-trees, and avenues of willows and carob,
box-elder, poplar, and maple, while each of them seems
to be stretching out an arm to the other, and all of them
trying to join hands with Logan. For lines of homesteads
and groups of trees have straggled away from each pretty
village, and, dotted across the intervening meadows of
lucerne and fields of corn, form links between them all.
Behind them rise the mountains, still capped and streaked
with snow, but all bright with grass upon their slopes.
It was a delightful scene, and required but little imagination to see the 15,000 people of the valley grown into
150,000, and the whole of this splendid tract of land one
continuous Logan. And nothing can stop that day but an
earthquake or a chronic pestilence. For Cache Valley
depends for its prosperity upon something surer than

" wild-cat " speculations, or mines that have bottoms to fall out. The cumulative force of agricultural prosperity is illustrated here with remarkable significance, for the town, that for many years seemed absolutely stationary, has begun both to consolidate and to expand with a determination that will not be gainsaid.

The sudden success of a mining camp is volcanic in its ephemeral rapidity. The gradual growth of an agricultural town is like the solid accretion of a coral island. The mere lapse of time will make it increase in wealth, and with wealth it will annually grow more beautiful. Even as it is, I think this settlement of Mormon farmers one of the noblest of the pioneering triumphs of the Far West ; and in the midst of these breathless, feverish States where every one seems to be chasing some will-o'-the-wisp with a firefly light of gold, or of silver—where terrible crime is a familiar feature, where known murderers walk in the streets, and men carry deadly weapons, where every other man complains of the fortune he only missed making by an accident, or laments the fortune he made in three days, and lost in as many hours—it is surpassingly strange to step out suddenly upon this tranquil valley, and find oneself among its law-abiding men. It is exactly like stepping out of a mine shaft into the fresh pure air of daylight.

The Logan police force is a good-tempered-looking young man. There is another to help him, but if they had not something else to do they would either have to keep on arresting each other, in order to pass the time, or else combine to hunt gophers and chipmunks. As it is, they unite other functions of private advantage with their constabulary performances, and thus justify their existence. As one explanation of the absence of crime, there is not a single licence for liquor in the town.

Once upon a time there were three saloons in Logan. But one night a Gentile, passing through the town, shot the young Mormon who kept one of them, whereat the townsfolk lynched the murderer, and suppressed all the saloons. After a while licences were again issued, but a six months' experiment showed that the five arrests of the previous half-year had increased under the saloon system to fifty-six, so the town suppressed the licences again, and to-day you cannot buy any liquor in Logan. I am told, however, that an apostate, who is in business in the town, carries on a more or less clandestine distribution of strong drinks ; but any accident resulting therefrom, another murder, for instance, would probably put an end to his trade for ever, for it is not only the Mormon leaders, but the Mormon *people* that refuse to have drunkards among them.

These facts about Logan are a sufficient refutation of the calumny so often repeated by apostates and Gentiles, that the Mormons are not the sober people they profess to be. The rules now in force in Logan were once in force in Salt Lake City, but thanks to reforming Gentiles there are now plenty of saloons and drunkards in the latter. At one time there were none, but finding the sale of drink inevitable, the Church tried to regulate it by establishing its own shops, and forbidding it to be sold elsewhere. But the Federal judge refused the application. So the city raised the saloon licence to 3600 dollars per annum ! Yet, in spite of this enormous tax, two or three bars managed to thrive, and eventually numbers of other men, encouraged by the conduct of the courts, opened drinking-saloons, refused to pay the licence, and defied—and still defy—all efforts of the city to bring them under control. In Logan, however, these are still the days of no drink, and the days therefore of very little crime.

CHAPTER XI.

THROUGH THE MORMON SETTLEMENTS.

THE general resemblance between the populations of the various Mormon settlements is not more striking than the general resemblance between the settlements themselves.

Two nearly parallel ranges of the Rocky Mountains, forming together part of the Wasatch range, run north and south through the length of Utah, and enclose between them a long strip of more or less desolate-looking land. Spurs run out from these opposing ranges, and meeting, cut off this strip into "valleys" of various lengths, so that, travelling from north to south, I crossed in succession, in the line of four hundred miles or so, the Cache, Salt Lake, Utah, Juab, San Pete, and Sevier valleys (the last enclosing Marysvale, Circle Valley and Panguitch Valley), and having there turned the end of the Wasatch range, travelled into Long Valley, which runs nearly east and west across the Territory.

In the Cache and the Sevier valleys there are some noble expanses of natural meadow, but in all the rest the soil, where not cultivated, is densely overgrown with sage-brush, greasewood and rabbit-brush, and in no case except the Cache Valley (by far the finest section of the Territory) and Long Valley, is the water-supply sufficient to irrigate the whole area enclosed. The proportions under cultivation vary therefore according to the amount of the water, and the size of the settlements is of course in an almost regular ratio with the acreage under the plough. But all are exactly on the same pattern. Wide streets—varying from 80 to 160 feet in width—avenued on either side with cotton-wood, box-elder, poplar, and locust-trees, and usually with a runnel of water alongside each side-walk, intersect each other at right angles, the blocks thus formed measuring from four to ten acres. These blocks hold, it may be, as many as six houses, but, as a rule, three, two, or only one ; while the proportion of fruit and shade-trees to dwelling-houses ranges from a hundred to one to twenty to one. As the lots are not occupied in any regular succession, there are frequent gaps caused by empty blocks, while the streets towards the outer limits of the towns are still half overgrown with the original sage-brush. All the settlements therefore, resemble each other, except in size, very closely, and may be briefly described as groves of trees and fruit orchards with houses scattered about among them.

The settlements of the Church stretch in a line north and south throughout the whole length of the Territory, and on reaching the Rio Virgin, in the extreme south, follow the course of that river right across Utah to the eastern frontier. The soil throughout the line north and south appears to be of a nearly uniform character, as the same wild plants are to be found growing on it everywhere, and the sudden alternations of fertility and wilderness are due almost entirely to the abundance or absence of water.

Leaving Salt Lake City to go south, we pass through suburbs of orchard and garden, with nearly the whole town in panoramic review before us, and find ourselves in half an hour upon levels beyond the reach of the city channels, and where the sage-brush therefore still thrives in un-disturbed glory. Bitterns rise from the rushes, and flights of birds wheel above the patches of scrub. And so to the Morgan smelting camp, and then the Francklyn works, where the ore of the Horn Silver Mine is worked, and then the Germania, one of the oldest smelting establish-ments in the Territory, where innocent ore of all kinds is taken in and mashed up into various "bullions"—*irrita-menta malorum.* Two small stations, each of them six peach-trees and a shed, slip by, and then Sandy, a small mining camp of poor repute, shuffles past, and next Draper, an agricultural settlement that seems to have grown fruit-trees to its own suffocation.

The mountains have been meanwhile drawing gradually closer together, and here they join. Salt Lake Valley ends, and Utah Valley begins, and crossing a "divide" we find the levels of the Utah Lake before us, and the straggling suburbs of Lehi about us. These scattered cottages gradually thicken into a village towards the lake, and form a pleasant settlement of the orthodox Mormon type. The receipt for making one of these ought to be something as follows: Take half as much ground as you can irrigate, and plant it thickly with fruit-trees. Then cut it up into blocks by cutting roads through it at right angles; sprinkle cottages among the blocks, and plant shade-trees along both sides of the roads. Then take the other half of your ground and spread it out in fields around your settlement, sowing to taste.

The actual process is, of course, the above reversed.

A log hut and an apple-tree start together in a field of corn, and the rest grows round them. But my receipt looks the easier of the two.

Beyond Lehi, and all round it, cultivation spreads almost continuously—alternating delightfully with orchards and groves and meadows—to American Fork, a charming settlement, smothered, as usual, in fruit and shade-trees. The people here are very well-to-do, and they look it ; and their fields and herds of cattle have overflowed and joined those of Pleasant Grove—another large and prosperous Mormon settlement that lies further back, and right under the hills. It would be very difficult to imagine sweeter sites for such rural hamlets than these rich levels of incomparable soil stretching from the mountains to the lake, and watered by the cañon streams.

" Great Salt Lake " is, of course, *the* Utah Lake of the outside world. But " Utah Lake " proper, is the large sheet of fresh water which lies some thirty miles south of Salt Lake City, and gives its name to the valley which it helps to fertilize. All around it, except on the western shore, the Mormons have planted their villages, so that from Lehi you can look out on to the valley, and see at the feet of the encircling hills, and straggling down towards the lake, a semicircle of settlements that, but for the sterility of the mountain slopes on the west, might have formed a complete ring around it. But no springs rise on the western slopes, and the settlements of the valleys always lie, therefore, on the eastern side, unless some central stream gives facilities for irrigation on the western also.

Utah Lake is a lake of legends. In the old Indian days it was held in superstitious reverence as the abode of the wind spirits and the storm spirits, and as being haunted by monsters

of weird kind and great size.   Particular spots were too uncanny for the red men to pitch their lodges there ; and
even game had asylum, as in a city of refuge, if it chanced
to run in the direction of the haunted shore.   In later
times, too, the Utah Lake has borne an uncomfortable
reputation as the domain of strange water-apparitions, and
several men have recorded visions of aquatic monsters, for
which science as yet has found no name, but which, speaking
roughly, appear to have been imitations of that delightful
possibility, the sea serpent.   Science, I know, goes dead
against such gigantic worms, but this wonderful Western
country has astonishment in store for the scientific world.
If half I am told about the wondrous fossils of Arizona and
thereabouts be true, it may even be within American
resources to produce the kraken himself.   In the mean
time, as a contribution towards it, and a very tolerable
instalment, too, I would commend to notice the great
snake of the Utah Lake.   It has frightened men—and, far
better evidence than that, it has been seen by children
when playing on the shore.   I say " better," because
children are not likely to invent a plausible horror in order
to explain their sudden rushing away from a given spot
with terrified countenances and a consistent narrative—a
horror, too, which should coincide with the snake super-
stitions of the Pi-Ute Indians.   Have wise men from the
East ever heard of this fabled thing ?   Does the Smithso-
nian know of this terror of the lake—this freshwater kraken —
this new Mormon iniquity ?

Visitors have made the American Fork Cañon too well
known to need more than a reference here, but the Provo
Cañon, with its romantic waterfalls and varied scenery, is a
feature of the Utah Valley which may some day be equally
familiar to the sight-seeing world.   The botanist would

find here a field full of surprises, as the vegetation is of exceptional variety, and the flowers unusually profuse. Down this cañon tumbles the Provo River ; and as soon as it reaches the mouth—thinking to find the valley an interval of placid idleness before it attains the final Buddhistic bliss of absorption in the lake, the Nirvana of extinguished individuality—it is seized upon, and carried off to right and left by irrigation channels, and ruthlessly distributed over the slopes. And the result is seen, approaching Provo, in magnificent reaches of fertile land, acres of fruit-trees, and miles of crops.

Provo is almost Logan over again, for though it has the advantage over the northern settlement in population, it resembles it in appearance very closely. There is the same abundance of foliage, the same width of water-edged streets, the same variety of wooden and adobe houses, the same absence of crime and drunkenness, the same appearance of solid comfort. It has its mills and its woollen factory, its " co-op." and its lumber-yards. There is the same profusion of orchard and garden, the same all-pervading presence of cattle and teams. The daily life is the same too, a perpetual industry, for no sooner is breakfast over than the family scatters—the women to the dairy and household work, the handloom and the kitchen ; the men to the yard, the mill, and the field. One boy hitches up a team and is off in one direction ; another gets astride a barebacked horse and is off in another ; a third disappears inside a barn, and a fourth engages in conflict with a drove of calves. But whatever they are doing, they are all busy, from the old man pottering with the water channels in the garden to the little girls pairing off to school ; and the visitor finds himself the only idle person in the settlement.

From Provo—through its suburbs of foliage and glebe-land—past Springville, a sweet spot, lying back under the hills with a bright quick stream flowing through it and houses mobbed by trees. Here are flour-mills and one of the first woollen mills built in Utah. In the days of its building the Indians harried the valley, and young men tell how as children they used to lie awake at nights to listen to the red men as they swept whooping and yelling through the quiet streets of the little settlement; how the guns stood always ready against the wall, and the windows were barricaded every night with thick pine logs. What a difference now! Further on, but still looking on to the lake, is Spanish Fork (*née* Palmyra), where, digging a water channel the other day, the spade turned up an old copper image of the Virgin Mary, and some bones. This takes back the Mormon settlement of to-day to the long-ago time when Spanish missionaries preached of the Pope to the Piutes, and gave but little satisfaction to either man or beast, for their tonsured scalps were but scanty trophies and the coyote found their lean bodies but poor picking. Only fifteen years ago the Navajos came down into the valley through the cañon which the Denver and Rio Grande line now traverses, but the Mormons were better prepared than the Spanish missionaries, and hunted the Navajo soul out of the Indians, so that Spanish Fork is now the second largest settlement in the valley, and the Indians come there begging. They are all of the " tickaboo " and "*good* Injun" sort, the " how-how " mendicants of the period. All the inhabitants are farmers, and their settlement affords as good an illustration of the advantages of co-operation in stores, farm-work, mills—everything—as can well be adduced.

Co-operation, by the way, is an important feature of

Mormon life, and never, perhaps, so much on men's tongues and in their minds as at the present time. The whole community has been aroused by the consistent teaching of their leaders in their addresses at public "meetings," in their prayers in private households, to a sense of the "suicidal folly," as they call it, of making men wealthy (by their patronage) who use their power against the Saints; and the Mormons have set themselves very sincerely to work to trade only with themselves and to starve out the Gentiles. And it is very difficult indeed for an unprejudiced man not to sympathize in some measure with the Mormons. By their honesty they have made the name "Mormon" respected in trade all over America, and have attracted shopkeepers, who on this very honesty have thriven and become wealthy in Utah—and yet some of these men, knowing nothing of the people except that they are straightforward in their dealings and honourable in their engagements, join in the calumny that the Mormons are a "rascally," "double-dealing" set. For my own part, I think the Church should have starved out some of these slanderers long ago. Even now it would be a step in the right direction if the Church slipped a "fighting apostle" at the men who go on day after day saying and writing that which they know to be untrue, calling, for instance, virtuous, hard-working men and women "the villainous spawn of polygamy," and advocating the encouragement of prostitutes as a "reforming agency for Mormon youth"! Meanwhile "co-operation" as a religious duty is the doctrine of the day, and Gentile trade is already suffering in consequence. The movement is a very important one to the Territory, for if carried out on the proper principles of co-operation, the people will live more cheaply here than in any other State in America. As it is, many imported articles, thanks to co-operative competition, are cheaper here than further east, and when the boycotting is in full swing many more articles will also come down in price, as the Gentiles' profits will then be knocked off the cost to the purchaser. Every settlement, big and little, has its "co-op.," and the elders when on tour through the outlying hamlets lose no opportunity for encouraging the movement and extending it.

Passing Spanish Fork, and its outlying herds of horses, we see, following the curve of the lake, Salem, a little community of farmers settled around a spring; Payson, called Poteetnete in the old Indian days—after a chief who made life interesting, not to say exciting, for the early settlers—Springlake villa, where one family has grown up into a hamlet, and grown out of it, too, for they complain that they have not room enough and must go elsewhere; and Santaquin, a little settlement that has reached out its fields right across the valley to the opposite slope of the hills. This was the spot where Abraham Butterfield, the only inhabitant of the place at the time, won himself a name among the people by chasing off a band of armed Indians, who had surprised him at his solitary work in the fields, by waving his coat and calling out to imaginary friends in the distance to "Come on." The Indians were thoroughly fooled, and fled back up the country incontinently, while Abraham pursued them hotly, brandishing his old coat with the utmost ferocity, and vociferously rallying nobody to the bloody attack.

Here Mount Nebo, the highest elevation in the Territory was first pointed out to me—how tired I got of it before I had done !—and through fields of lucerne we passed from the Utah into the Juab Valley and an enormous wilderness of sage-brush. It is broken here and there by an infrequent patch of cultivation, and streaks of paling go straggling away across the grey desert. But without water it is a desperate section, and the pillars of dust moving across the level, and marking the track of the sheep that wandered grazing among the sage, reminded me of the sand-wastes of Beluchistan, where nothing can move a foot without raising a tell-tale puff of dust.

There, the traveller, looking out from his own cloud of sand, sees similar clouds creeping about all over the plain, judges from their size the number of camels or horses that may be stirring, and draws his own conclusions as to which may be peaceful caravans, and which robber-bands. By taking advantage of the wind, the desert banditti are able to advance to the attack, just as the devil-fish do on the sea-bottom, under cover of sand-clouds of their own stirring up ; and the first intimation which the traveller has of the character of those who are coming towards him, is the sudden flash of swords and glitter of spearheads that light up the edges of the advancing sand, just as lightning flits along the ragged skirts of a moving thunder-cloud.

But here there are no Murri or Bhoogti horsemen astir, and the Indians, Piutes or Navajos, have not acquired Beluchi tactics. These moving clouds here are raised by loitering sheep, formidable only to Don Quixote and the low-nesting ground-larks. They are close feeders, though, these sheep, and it is poor gleaning after them, so it is a rule throughout the Territory that on the hills where sheep graze, game need not be looked for.

An occasional ranch comes in sight, and along the old county road a waggon or two goes crawling by, and then we reach Mona, a pretty little rustic spot, but the civilizing radiance of corn-fields gradually dies away, and the relentless sage-brush supervenes, with here and there a lucid interval of ploughed ground in the midst of the demented desert. With water the whole valley would be superbly fertile, as we soon see, for there suddenly breaks in upon the monotony of the weed-growths a splendid succession of fields, long expanses of meadow-land, large groves of orchards, and the thriving settlement of Nephi.

Like all other prosperous places in Utah, it is almost entirely Mormon. There is one saloon, run by a Mormon, but patronized chiefly by the "outsiders"—for such is the name usually given to the "Gentiles" in the settlement—and no police. Local mills meet local requirements, and the "co-op." is the chief trading store of the place. There are no manufactures for export, but in grain and fruit there is a considerable trade. It is a quaint, straggling sort of place, and, like all these settlements, curiously primitive. The young men use the steps of the co-operative store as a lounge, and their ponies, burdened with huge Mexican saddles and stirrups that would do for dog-kennels, stand hitched to the palings all about. The train stops at the corner of the road to take up any passengers there may be. Deer are sometimes killed in the streets, and eagles still harry the chickens in the orchards. Wild-bird life is strangely abundant, and a flock of "canaries"—a very beautiful yellow siskin—had taken possession of my host's garden. "We *do* catch them sometimes," said his wife, "but they always starve themselves, and pine away till they are thin enough to get through the bars of the cage, and so we can never keep them." A neighbour who chanced in, was full of canary-lore, and I remember one incident that struck me as very pretty. He had caught a canary and caged it, but the bird refused to be tamed, and dashed itself about the cage in such a frantic way that out of sheer pity he let the wild thing go. A day or two later it came back, but with a mate, and when the cage was hung out the two birds went into captivity together, of their own free-will, and lived as happily as birds could live !

My host was a good illustration of what Mormonism can do for a man. In Yorkshire he was employed in a slaughtering-yard, and thought himself lucky if he earned twelve shillings a week. The Mormons found him, "converted" him, and emigrated him. He landed in Utah without a cent in his pocket, and in debt to the Church besides. But he found every one ready to help him, and was ready to help himself, so that to-day he is one of the most substantial men in Nephi, with a mill that cost him $10,000 to put up, a shop and a farm, a house and orchard and stock. His family, four daughters and a son, are all settled round him and thriving, thanks to the aid he gave them—"but," said he, "if the Mormons had not found me, I should still have been slaughtering in the old country, and glad, likely, to be still earning my twelve shillings a week." Another instance from the same settlement is that of a boy who, five years ago, was brought out here at the age of sixteen. His emigration was entirely paid for by the Church. Yet last year he sent home from his own pocket the necessary funds to bring out his mother and four brothers and sisters ! God speed these Mormons, then. They are doing both "the old country and the new" an immense good in thus transforming English paupers into American farmers—and thus exchanging the vices and squalor of English poverty for the temperance, piety, and comfort of these Utah homesteads. I am not blind to their faults. My aversion to polygamy is sincere, and I find also that the Mormons must share with all agricultural communities the blame of not sacrificing more of their own present prospects for the sake of their children's future, and neglecting their education, both in school and at home. But when I remember what classes of people these men and women are chiefly drawn from, and the utter poverty in which most of them arrive, I cannot, in sincerity, do otherwise than admire and respect the system which has fused such unpromising material of so many nationalities into one homogeneous whole.

For myself, I do not think I could live among the Mormons happily, for my lines have been cast so long in the centres of work and thought, that a bovine atmosphere of perpetual farms suffocates me. I am afraid I should take to *lowing*, and feed on lucerne. But this does not prejudice me against the men and women who are so unmistakably happy. They are uncultured, from the highest to the lowest. But the men of thirty and upwards remember these valleys when they were utter deserts, and the Indian was lord of the hills ! As little children they had to perform all the small duties about the house, the "chores," as they are called ; as lads they had to guard the stock on the hills ; as young men they were the pioneers of Utah. What else then could they be but ignorant—in the education of schools, I mean? Yet they are sober in their habits, conversation, and demeanour, frugal, industrious, hospitable, and God-fearing. As a people, their lives are a pattern to an immense number of mankind, and every emigrant, therefore, taken up out of the slums of manufacturing cities in the old countries, or from the hideous drudgery of European agriculture, and planted in these Utah valleys, is a benefit conferred by Mormonism upon two continents at once.

To return to Nephi. I went to a " meeting " in the

evening, and to describe one is to describe all. The old men and women sit in front—the women, as a rule, all together in the body of the room, and the men at the sides. How this custom originated no one could tell me; but it is probably a survival of habit from the old days when there was only room enough for the women to be seated, and the men stood round against the walls, and at the door. As larger buildings were erected, the women, as of old, took their accustomed seats together in the centre, and the men filled up the balance of the space. The oldest being hard of hearing and short of sight, would naturally, in an unconventional society, collect at the front of the audience. Looking at them all together, they are found to be exactly what one might expect—a congregation of hard-featured, bucolic faces, sun-tanned and deep-lined. Here and there among them is a bright mechanic's face, and here and there an unexpected refinement of intelligence. But taken in the mass, they are precisely such a congregation as fills nine-tenths of the rural places of worship all the world over. Conspicuously absent, however, is the typical American face, for the fathers and mothers among the Mormons are of every nationality, and the sons and daughters are a mixture of all. In the future this race should be a very fine one, for it is chiefly recruited from the hardier stocks, the English, Scotch, and Scandinavian, while their manner of life is pre-eminently fitted for making them stalwart in figure, and sound in constitution.

The meeting opens with prayer, in which the Almighty is asked for blessings upon the whole people, upon each class of it, upon their own place in particular, upon all the Church authorities, and upon all friends of the Mormons. But never, so far as I have heard, are intercessions made,

in the spirit of New Testament teaching, for the enemies
of the Church. References to the author of the Edmunds
Bill are often very pointed and vigorous. After the prayer
comes a hymn, sung often to a lively tune, and accompanied
by such instrumental music as the settlement can rely
upon, after which the elders address the people in succession. These addresses are curiously practical. They are
temporal rather than spiritual, and concern themselves
with history, official acts, personal reminiscences, and agricultural matter rather than points of mere doctrine. But
as a fact, temporal and spiritual considerations are too
closely blended in Mormonism to be disassociated. Thus
references to the Edmunds Bill take their place naturally
among exhortations to " live their religion," and to "build
up the kingdom " in spite of " persecution." Boycotting
Gentile tradesmen is similarly inculcated as showing a
pious fidelity to the interests of the Church. These are
the two chief topics of all addresses, but a passing reference
to a superior class of waggon, or a hope that every one
will make a point of voting in some coming election, is not
considered out of place, while personal matters, the health
of the speaker or his experiences in travel, are often thus
publicly commented upon. The result is, that the people
go away with some tangible facts in their heads, and subjects for ordinary conversation on their tongues, and not,
as from other kinds of religious meetings, with only generalities about their souls and the Ten Commandments. In
other countries the gabble of small-talk that immediately
overtakes a congregation let out of church sounds very incongruous with the last notes of the organ voluntary that
play them out of the House of God. But here the people
walking homeward are able to continue the conversation on
exactly the same lines as the addresses they have just

heard, to renew it the next day, to carry it about with them as conversation from place to place, and thus eventually to spread the "doctrine" of the elders over the whole district. A fact about waggon-buying sticks where whole sermons about salvation by faith would not.

CHAPTER XII.

FROM NEPHI TO MANTI.

English companies and their failures—A deplorable neglect of claret
    cup—Into the San Pete Valley—Reminiscences of the Indians—
    The forbearance of the red man—The great temple at Manti—
    Masonry and Mormon mysteries—In a tithing-house.

FROM Nephi, a narrow-guage line runs up the Salt Creek
Cañon, and away across a wilderness to a little mining settlement called Wales, inhabited by Welsh Mormons who work
at the adjacent coal-mines. The affair belongs to an
English company, and it is worth noting that " English
companies " are considered here to be very proper subjects
for jest. When nobody else in the world will undertake a
hopeless enterprise, an English company appears to be
always on hand to embark in it, and this fact displays a
confidence on the part of Americans in British credulity,
and a confidence on the part of the Britishers in American
honesty, which ought to be mutually instructive. Meanwhile this has nothing to do with these coal-mines in the
San Pete Valley, which, for all I know, may be very sound
concerns, and very profitable to the " English company " in
question. I hope it is. The train was rather a curious one,
though, for it stopped for passengers at the corner of the
street, and when we got " aboard," we found a baggage
car the only vehicle provided for us. A number of apostles

and elders were on Conference tour, and the party, therefore, was a large one ; so that, if the driver had been an enthusiastic anti-Mormon, he might have struck a severe blow at the Church by tilting us off the rails. The Salt Creek Cañon is not a prepossessing one, but there grew in it an abundance of borage, the handsome blue heads of flowers showing from among the undergrowth in large patches.

What a waste of borage! Often have I deplored over my claret in India the absence of this estimable vegetable, and here in Utah with a perfect jungle of borage all about me, I had no claret! I pointed out to the apostles with us that temperance in such a spot was flying in the face of providence, and urged them to plant vineyards in the neighbourhood. But they were not enthusiastic, and I relapsed into silent contemplation over the incredible ways of nature, that she should thus cast her pearls of borage before a community of teetotallers.

Traversing the cañon, we enter San Pete Valley, memorable for the Indian War of 1865-67, but in itself as desolate and uninteresting a tract of country as anything I have ever seen. Ugly bald hills and leprous sand-patches in the midst of sage-brush, combined to form a landscape of utter dreariness ; and the little settlements lying away under the hills on the far eastern edge of the valley—Fountain Green, Maroni, and Springtown—seemed to me more like penal settlements than voluntary locations. Yet I am told they are pretty enough, and certainly Mount Pleasant, the largest settlement in the San Pete country, looked as if it deserved its name. But it stands back well out of the desperate levels of the valley, and its abundant foliage tells of abundant water. A pair of eagles circled high up in the sky above us as we rattled along, expecting us apparently to die by the way, and hoping to be our under-

M

takers. A solitary coyote was pointed out to me, a lean and uncared-for person, that kept looking back over its shoulder as it trotted away, as if it had a lingering sort of notion that a defunct apostle might by chance be thrown overboard. It was a hungry and a thirsty looking country, and Wales, where we left our train, was a dismal spot. Here we found waggons waiting for us, and were soon on our way across the desert, passing a settlement-oasis now and again, and crossing the San Pete "river," which here sneaks along, a muddy, shallow stream, at the bottom of high, willow-fringed banks. And so to Fort Ephraim, a quaint little one-street sort of place that looks up to Manti, a few miles off, as a little boy looks up to his biggest brother, and to Salt Lake City as a cat might look up to a king.

In 1865-67, however, it was an important point. Several companies of the Mormon militia were mustered here, and held the mountains and passes on the east against the Indians, guarded the stock gathered here from the other small settlements that had been abandoned, and took part in the fights at Thistle Creek, Springtown, Fish Lake, Twelve Mile Creek Gravelly Ford, and the rest, where Black Hawk and his flying squadron of Navajos and Piutes showed themselves such plucky men. It is a pity, I think, that the history of that three years' campaign has never been sketched, for, as men talk of it, it must have abounded with stirring incident and romance. Besides, a well-written history of such a campaign, with the lessons it teaches, might be useful some day—for the fighting spirit of the Indians is not broken, and when another Black Hawk appears upon the scene, 1865 might easily be re-enacted, and Fort Ephraim once more be transformed from a farming hamlet to a military camp.

Yet I have often wondered at the apathy or the friendship of the Indians. Herds of cattle and horses and sheep
wander about among the mountains virtually unguarded.
Little villages full of grain, and each with its store well
stocked with sugar, and tobacco, and cloths, and knives,
and other things that the Indians prize, lie almost defence-
less at the mouths of cañons. Yet they have not been
molested for the last fifteen years. I confess that if I were
an Indian chief, I should not be able to resist the temptation of helping my tribe to an occasional surfeit of beef,
with the amusement thrown in of plundering a co-operative
store. But the Mormons say that the Indian is more honest
than a white man and, in illustration of this, are ready to
give innumerable instances of an otherwise inexplicable
chivalry. For one thing, though, the Mormons are looked
upon by the Indians in quite a different light to other
Americans, for they consider them to be victims, like themselves, of Federal dislike, while both as individuals and
a class they hold them in consideration as being superior
to Agents in fidelity to engagements. So that the compliment of honesty is mutually reciprocated. To illustrate
this aspect of the Mormon-Indian relations, some Indians
came the other day into a settlement, and engaged in a very
protracted pow-wow, the upshot of all their roundabout
palaver being this, that inasmuch as they, the Indians, had
given Utah to the Mormons, it was preposterous for the
Mormons to pay the Government for the land they took
up!

From Fort Ephraim to Manti the road lies chiefly through
unreclaimed land, but within a mile or two of the town the
irrigated suburbs of Manti break in upon the sage-brush,
and the Temple, which has been visible in the distance
half the day, grows out from the hills into definite details.

M 2

The site of this imposing structure certainly surprised me both for the fine originality of its conception, and the artistic sympathy with the surrounding scenery, which has directed its erection. The site originally was a rugged hill slope, but this has been cut out into three vast semicircular terraces, each of which is faced with a wall of rough hewn stone, seventeen feet in height. Ascending these by wide flights of steps, you find yourself on a fourth level, the hill top, which has been levelled into a spacious plateau, and on this, with its back set against the hill, stands the temple. The style of Mormon architecture, unfortunately, is heavy and unadorned, and in itself, therefore, this massive pile, 160 feet in length by 90 wide, and about 100 high, is not prepossessing, But when it is finished, and the terrace slopes are turfed, and the spaces planted out with trees, the view will undoubtedly be very fine, and the temple be a building that the Mormons may well be proud of. Looked at from the plain, with the stern hills behind it, the edifice is seen to be in thoroughly artistic harmony with the scene, while the enormous expenditure of labour upon its erection is a matter for astonishment. The plan of the building inside differs from those of the temples at Logan, St. George, and Salt Lake City, which again differ from each other, for it is a curious fact that the ritual of the secret ceremonies to which these buildings are chiefly devoted, is still under elaboration and imperfect, so that each temple in turn partially varies from its predecessor, to suit the latest alterations made in the Endowments and other rites celebrated within its walls. In my description of the Logan Temple, I gave a sketch of the purposes for which the various parts of the building were intended. That sketch, of course, cannot pretend to be exact, for only those Mormons who have " worked " through the degrees

can tell the whole truth; and as yet no one has divulged it. But with a general knowledge of the rites, and an intimate acquaintance with freemasonry, I have, I believe, put together the only reliable outline that has ever been published. The Manti temple will have the same arrangements of baptismal font and dressing-rooms on the ground floor, but as well as I could judge from the unfinished state of the building, the "endowments," in the course of which are symbolical representations of the Creation, Temptation and Fall, will be spread over two floors, the apartment for "baptism for the dead" occupying a place on the lower. The "sealing" is performed on the third. I have an objection to prying into matters which the Mormons are so earnest in keeping secret, but as a mason, the connexion between Masonry and Mormonism is too fascinating a subject for me to resist curiosity altogether.

As a settlement, Manti is pretty, well-ordered and prosperous. The universal vice of unbridged water-courses disfigures its roads just as it does those of every other place (Salt Lake City itself not excepted), and the irregularity in the order of occupation of lots gives it the same scattered appearance that many other settlements have. But the abundance of trees, the width of the streets, the perpetual presence of running water, the frequency and size of the orchards, and the general appearance of simple, rustic, comfort impart to Manti all the characteristic charm of the Mormon settlements. The orthodox grist and saw-mills, essential adjuncts of every outlying hamlet, find their usual place in the local economy; but to me the most interesting corner was the quaint tithing-house, a Dutch-barn kind of place, still surrounded by the high stone stockade which was built for the protection of the settlers during the Indian troubles fifteen years ago. Inside the tithing-house were two great bins half filled with wheat and oats, and a few bundles of wool. I had expected to find a miscellaneous confusion of articles of all kinds, but on inquiry discovered that the popular theory of Mormon tithing, "a tenth of everything,"—"even to the tenth of every egg that is laid," as a Gentile lady plaintively assured me, is not carried out in practice, the majority of Mormons allowing their tithings to run into arrears, and then paying them up in a lump in some one staple article, vegetable or animal, that happens to be easiest for them. The tenth of their eggs or their currant jam does not, therefore, as supposed, form part of the rigid annual tribute of these degraded serfs to their grasping masters. As a matter of fact, indeed, the payment of tithings is as nearly voluntary as the collection of a revenue necessary for carrying on a government can possibly be allowed to be. What it may have been once, is of no importance now. But to-day, so far from there being any undue coercion, I have amply assured myself that there is extreme consideration and indulgence, while the general prosperity of the territory justifies the leniency that prevails.

CHAPTER XIII.

FROM MANTI TO GLENWOOD.

Scandinavian Mormons—Danish öl—Among the orchards at Manti —On the way to Conference—Adam and Eve—The protoplasm of a settlement—Ham and eggs—At Mayfield—Our teamster's theory of the ground-hog—On the way to Glenwood—Volcanic phenomena and lizards—A suggestion for improving upon Nature —Primitive Art

"My hosts at Manti were Danes, and the wife brewed Danish öl." Such is the entry in my note-book, made, I remember, to remind me to say that the San Pete settlements are composed in great proportion of Danes and Scandinavians. These nationalities contribute more largely than any other—unless Great-Britishers are all called one nation—to the recruiting of Mormonism, and when they reach Utah maintain their individuality more conspicuously than any others. The Americans, Welsh, Scotch, English, Germans, and Swiss, merge very rapidly into one blend, but the Scandinavian type—and a very fine peasant type it is— is clearly marked in the settlements where the Hansens and the Jansens, Petersens, Christiansens, Nielsens, and Sorensens, most do congregate. By the way, some of these Norse names sound very curiously to the ear. "Ole Hagg" might be thought to be a nickname rather than anything else, and Lars Nasquist Brihl at best a joke. Their children are remarkably pretty, and the women models of thriftiness.

My hostess at Manti was a pattern. She made pies under an inspiration, and her chicken-pie was a distinct revelation. Her "beer" was certainly a beverage that a man might deny himself quite cheerfully, but to eat her preserves was like listening to beautiful parables, and her cream cheese gave the same gentle pleasure as the singing of thankful canticles.

In the garden was an arbour overrun with a wild grape-vine, and I took my pen and ink in there to write. All went well for a while. An amiable cat came and joined me, sitting in a comfortable cushion-sort of fashion on the corner of my blotting-pad. But while we sat there writing, the cat and I, there came a humming-bird into the arbour—a little miracle in feathers, with wings all emeralds and a throat of ruby. And it sat in the sunlight on a vine-twig that straggled out across the door, and began to preen its tiny feathers. I stopped writing to watch the beautiful thing. And so did the cat. For happening to look down at the table I saw the cat, with a fiendish expression of face and her eyes intent on the bird, gathering her hind legs together for a spring. To give the cat a smack on the head, and for the cat to vanish with an explosion of ill-temper, "was the work of an instant." The humming-bird flashed out into the garden, and I was left alone to mop up the ink which the startled cat had spilt. Then I went out and wandered across the garden, where English flowers, the sweet-william and columbine, pinks and wallflowers, pansies and iris, were growing, under the fruit-trees still bunched with blossoms, and out into the street. Friends asked me if I wasn't going to "the conference," but I had not the heart to go inside when the world out of doors was so inviting. There was a cool, green tint in the shade of the orchards, pleasant with the voices of birds and dreamy with the humming of bees. There was nobody else about, only children making posies of apple-blossoms and launching blue boats of iris-petals on the little roadside streams. Everybody was "at conference," and those that could not get into the building were grouped outside among the waggons of the country folk who had come from a distance. These conferences are held quarterly (so that the lives of the Apostles who preside at them are virtually spent in travelling) and at them everything is discussed, whether of spiritual or temporal interest and a general balance struck, financially and religiously. In character they resemble the ordinary meetings of the Mormons, being of exactly the same curious admixture of present farming and future salvation, business advice and pious exhortation.

Everybody who can do so, attends these meetings; and they fulfil, therefore, all the purposes of the Oriental *mela*. Farmers, stock-raisers, and dealers generally, meet from a distance and talk over business matters, open negotiations and settle bargains, exchange opinions and discuss prospects. Their wives and families, such of them as can get away from their homes, foregather and exchange their domestic news, while everybody lays in a fresh supply of spiritual refreshment for the coming three months, and hears the latest word of the Church as to the Edmunds Bill and Gentile tradesmen. The scene is as primitive and quaint as can be imagined, for in rural Utah life is still rough and hearty and simple. To the stranger, the greetings of family groups, with the strange flavour of the Commonwealth days, the wonderful Scriptural or apocryphal names, and the old-fashioned salutation, are full of picturesque interest, while the meetings of waggons filled with acquaintances from remote corners of the country, the confusion of European dialects —imagine hearing pure Welsh among the San Pete sage-brush !—the unconventional cordiality of greeting, are delightful both in an intellectual and artistic sense.

I have travelled much, and these social touches have always had a charm for me, let them be the demure reunions of Creoles *sous les filaos* in Mauritius ; or the French negroes chattering as they go to the baths in Bourbon ; the deep-drinking convivialities of the Planters' Club in Ceylon ; the grinning, prancing, rencontres of Kaffir and Kaffir, or the stolid collision of Boer waggons on the African *veldt ;* the stately meeting of camel-riding Beluchis on the sandy *put* of Khelat; the jingling ox-drawn ekkas foregathered to " bukh " under the tamarind-trees of Bengal; the reserved salutations of Hindoos as they squat by the roadside to discuss the invariable lawsuit and smoke the inevitable hubble-bubble; the noisy congregation of Somali boatmen before their huts on the sun-smitten shores of Aden ;—what a number of reminiscences I could string together of social traits in various parts of the world !   And these Mormon peasants, pioneers of the West, these hardy sons of hardy sires, will be as interesting to me in the future as any others, and my remembrance of them will be one of admiration for their unfashionable virtues of industry and temperance, and of gratitude for their simple courtesy and their cordial hospitality.

As we left Manti behind us, the waggons " coming into conference " got fewer and fewer, and soon we found ourselves out alone upon the broad levels of the valley, with nothing to keep us company but a low range of barren hills that did their best to break the monotony of the landscape. In places, the ground was white with desperate patches of " saleratus," the saline efflorescence with which agriculture in this Territory is for ever at war, and resembling in appearance, taste, and effects the " reh " of the Gangetic plains. Here, as in India, irrigation is the only known antidote, and once wash it out of the soil and get crops growing and the enemy retires. But as soon as cultivation ceases or irrigation slackens, the white infection creeps over the ground again, and if undisturbed for a year resumes possession. How unrelenting Nature is in her conflict with man!

We passed some warm springs a few miles from Manti, but the water though slightly saline is inodorous, and on the patches which they water I saw the wild flax growing as if it enjoyed the temperature and the soil. Then Six-Mile Creek, a pleasant little ravine, crossed by a rustic bridge, which gives water for a large tract of land, and so to Sterling, a settlement as yet in its cradle, and curiously illustrative of "the beginning of things" in rural Utah. One man and his one wife up on the hillside doing something to the water, one cock and one hen pecking together in monogamous sympathy, one dog sitting at the door of a one-roomed log-hut. Everything was in the Adam and Eve stage of society, and primeval. So Deucalion and Pyrrha had the earth to themselves, and the "rooster" stalked before his mate as if he was the first inventor of posterity. But much of this country is going to come under the plough in time, for there is water, and in the meantime, as giving promise of a future with some children in it, there is a school-house—an instance of forethought which gratified me.

The country now becomes undulating, remaining for the most part a sterile-looking waste of grease-wood, but having an almost continuous thread of cultivation running along the centre of the valley which, a few miles further on, suddenly widens into a great field of several thousand acres. On the other side of it we found Mayfield.

In Mayfield every one was gone to the Conference except a pretty girl, left to look after all the children of the village, and who resisted our entreaties for hospitality with a determination that would have been more becoming in an uglier person—and an old lady, left under the protection of a big blind dog and a little bobtailed calf. She received us with the honest courtesy universal in the Territory, showed us where to put our horses and where the lucerne was stacked, and apologized to us for having nothing better than eggs and ham to offer!

Fancy nothing *better* than eggs and ham! To my mind there is nothing in all travelling so delightful as these eggs-and-ham interruptions that do duty for meals. Not only is the viand itself so agreeable, but its odour when cooking creates an appetite.

What a moral there is here! We have all heard of the beauty of the lesson that those flowers teach us which give forth their sweetest fragrance when crushed. But I think the conduct of eggs and ham, that thus create an appetite in order to increase man's pleasure in their own consumption, is attended with circumstances of good taste that are unusually pleasing.

In our hostess's house at Mayfield I saw for the first time the ordinary floor-covering of the country through which we subsequently travelled—a "rag-carpet." It is probably common all over the world, but it was quite new to me. I discussed its composition one day with a mother and her daughter.

"This streak here is Jimmy's old pants, and that darker one is a military overcoat. This is daddy's plush vest. This bit of the pattern is—"

"No, mother, that's your old jacket-back; don't you remember?"—and so on all through the carpet.

Every stripe in it had an association, and the story of the whole was pretty nearly the story of their entire lives in the country.

" For it took us seven years to get together just this one strip of carpet. We folks haven't much, you see, that's fit to tear up."

I like the phrase " fit to tear up," and wonder *when*, in the opinion of this frugal people, anything *does* become suitable for destruction. But it is hardly destruction after all to turn old clothes into carpets, and the process is as simple as, in fact is identical with, ordinary hand-weaving. The cloth is simply shredded into very narrow strips, and each strip is treated in the loom just as if it were ordinary yarn, the result being, by a judicious alternation of tints, a very pleasant-looking and very durable floor-cloth. Rag-rugs are also made on a foundation of very coarse canvas by drawing very narrow shreds of rag through the spaces of the canvas, fastening them on the reverse side, and cutting them off to a uniform " pile " on the upper. In one cottage at Salina I remember seeing a rug of this kind in which the girl had drawn her own pattern and worked in the colours with a distinct appreciation of true artistic effect. An industrial exhibition for such products would, I have no doubt, bring to light a great many out-of-the-way handicrafts which these emigrant people have brought with them from the different parts of Europe, and with which they try to adorn their simple homes.

Our teamster from Mayfield to Glenwood, the next stage of my southward journey, was a very cautious person. He would not hurry his horses down hill—they were " belike " to stumble ; and he would not hurry them up hill—it "fretted " them. On the level intervals he stopped altogether, to " breathe " them. It transpired eventually that they were plough horses. I suspected it from the first. And from his driving I suspected that he was the plough-man. In other respects he was a very desirable teamster.

His remarks about Europe (he had once been to Chicago himself) were very entertaining, and his theory of "ground hogs" would have delighted Darwin. As far as I could follow him, *all* animals were of one species, the differences as to size and form being chiefly accidents of age or sex. This, at any rate, was my induction from his description of the "ground hog," which he said was a "kind of *squirrel*— like the prairie dog!" As he said, there were "quite a few" ground hogs, but they moved too fast among the brush for me to identify them. As far as I could tell, though, they were of the marmot kind, about nine inches long, with very short tails and round small ears. When they were at a safe distance they would stand up at full length on their hind legs, the colouring underneath being lighter than on the back. What are they? I have seen none in Utah except on these volcanic stretches of country between Salina and Monroe.

Much of Utah is volcanic, but here, beyond Salina, huge mounds of scoriæ, looking like heaps of slag from some gigantic furnace, are piled up in the centre of the level ground, while in other places circular depressions in the soil—sometimes fifty feet in diameter and lowest in the centre, with deep fissures defining the circumference—seem to mark the places whence the scoriæ had been drawn, and the earth had sunk in upon the cavities thus exhausted.

The two sides of the river (the Sevier) were in striking contrast. On this, the eastern, was desolation and stone heaps and burnt-up spaces with ant-hills and lizards.

Nothing makes a place look (to me at least) so hot as an abundance of lizards. They are associated in memory with dead, still heat, "the intolerable calor of Mambre," the sun-smitten cinder-heap that men call Aden, the stifling hillsides of Italy where the grapes lie blistering in the autumn sun, the desperate suburbs of Alexandria—what millions of scorched-looking lizards, detestable little salamanders, used to bask upon Cleopatra's Needles when they lay at full length among the sand !—the heat-cracked fields of India. I know very well that there are lizards and lizards ; that they might be divided—as the Hindoo divides everything, whether victuals or men's characters, medicines or the fates the gods send him—into "hot" and "cold" lizards. The salamander itself, according to the ancients, was icy cold. But this does not matter. All lizards make places *look* hot.

On the other side of the river, a favourite raiding-ground of "Mr. Indian," as the settlers pleasantly call him, lies Aurora, a settlement in the centre of a rich tract of red wheat soil with frequent growths of willow and buffalo-berry (or bull-berry or red-berry or "kichi-michi") marking the course of the Sevier.

But our road soon wound down by a "dug way" to the bottom-lands, and we found ourselves on level meadows clumped with shrubs and patched with corn-fields, and among scattered knots of grazing cattle and horses. Overhead circled several pairs of black hawks, a befitting reminder to the dwellers on these Thessalian fields, these Campanian pastures, that Scythian Piutes and Navajo Attilas might at any time swoop down upon them.

But the forbearance of the Indian in the matter of beef and mutton is inexplicable—and most inexplicable of all in the case of lamb, seeing that *mint* grows wild. This is a very pleasing illustration of the happiness of results when man and nature work cordially together. The lamb gambols about

among beds of mint ! What a becoming sense of the fitness
of things that would be that should surprise the innocent
thing in its fragrant pasture and serve up the two together !
"They were pleasant in their lives, and in death they were
not divided." And what a delightful field for similar efforts
such a spectacle opens up to the philosophic mind ! Here,
beyond Aurora, as we wind in and out among the brakes
of willow and rose-bush, we catch glimpses of the river, with
ducks riding placidly at anchor in the shadows of the foliage.
And not a pea in the neighbourhood ! Now, why not sow
green peas along the banks of the American rivers and
lakes ? How soothing to the weary traveller would be this
occasional relief of *canard aux petits pois !*

After an interval of pretty river scenery we found ourselves once more in a dismal, volcanic country with bald
hills and leprous sand-patches the only features of the
landscape, with lizards for flowers and an exasperating
heat-drizzle blurring the outlines of everything with its
quivering refraction. And then, after a few miles of this,
we are suddenly in the company of really majestic mountains,
some of them cedared to the peaks, others broken up into
splendid architectural designs of almost inconceivable
variety, richly tinted and fantastically grouped. How
wealthy this range must be in mineral ! In front of us,
above all the intervening hills, loomed out a monster
mountain, and turning one of its spurs we break all at once
upon the village of Glenwood — a beautiful cluster of foliage
with skirts of meadow-land spread out all about it — lying at
the foot of the huge slope.

Near Glenwood is an interesting little lake that I visited.
Its water is exquisitely clear and very slightly warm. Though
less than a foot deep in most places (it has one pool twelve
feet in depth), it never freezes, in spite of the intense cold at

this altitude. It is stocked with trout that do not grow to any size, but which do not on the other hand seem to diminish in numbers, although the consumption is considerable. The botany in the neighbourhood of the lake is very interesting, the larkspur, lupin, mimulus, violet, heart's-ease, ox-eye, and several other familiar plants of English gardens, growing wild, while a strongly tropical flavour is given to the vegetation by the superb footstools of cactus – imagine sixty-one brilliant scarlet blossoms on a cushion only fifteen inches across !—by the presence of a gorgeous oriole (the body a pure yellow freaked with black on the wings, and the head and neck a rich orange), and by a large butterfly of a clear flame-colour with the upper wings sharply hooked at the tips. Flower, bird, and insect were all in keeping with the Brazils or the Malayan Archipelago.

On a rock, close by the grist-mill, is the only specimen of the much-talked-of Indian " hieroglyphics" that I have seen. They *may* of course be hieroglyphics, but to me they look like the first attempts of some untutored savage youth to delineate in straight lines the human form divine. Or they *may* be only his attempts to delineate a cockroach.

CHAPTER XIV.

FROM GLENWOOD TO MONROE.

From Glenwood to Salina—Deceptiveness of appearances—An apostate Mormon's friendly testimony—Reminiscences of the Prophet
Joseph Smith—Rabbit-hunting in a waggon—Lost in the sage-
brush—A day at Monroe—Girls riding pillion—The Sunday
drum—Waiting for the right man : " And what if he *is* married ? "
—The truth about apostasy : not always voluntary.

SOON after leaving Glenwood, cultivation dies out, and for
twelve miles or so the rabbit-brush and grease-wood—the
"atriplex" of disagreeably scientific travellers, who always
speak of sage-brush as "artemisia," and disguise the gentle
chipmunk as "spermophilus"—divide the land between them.
The few flowers, and these all dwarfed varieties, attest the
poverty of the soil. The mountains, however, do their best
to redeem the landscape, and the scenery, as desolate
scenery, is very fine. The ranges that have on either hand
rolled along an unbroken series of monotonous contour, now
break up into every conceivable variety of form, mimicking
architecture or rather multiplying its types, and piling bluffs,
pierced with caves, upon terraces, and pinnacles upon
battlements. Causeways, like that in Echo Cañon, slant
down their slopes, and other vestiges of a terrific aqueous
action abound. Next to this riot of rock comes a long
series of low hills, grey, red, and yellow, utterly destitute of
vegetation, and so smooth that it looks as if the place were
a mountain-yard, where Nature made her mountains, and had

collected all her materials about her in separate convenient mounds before beginning to mix up and fuse. In places they were richly spangled with mica, giving an appearance of sparkling, trickling water to the barren slopes.

On the other side of the valley, the mountains, discountenancing such frivolities, had settled down into solid-bottomed masses of immense bulk, the largest mountains, in superficial acreage, I had seen all the journey, and densely cedared.

With Gunnison in sight across the valley, we reached Willow Creek, a pleasant diversion of water and foliage in the dreary landscape, and an eventful spot in the last Indian war, for among these willows here Black Hawk made a stand to dispute the Mormons' pursuit of their plundered stock, and held the creek, too, all the day. And so out on to the monotonous grease-wood levels again—an Indians' camp fire among the cedars, the only sign of a living thing—and over another " divide," and so into the Sevier Valley. The river is seen flowing along the central depression, with the Red-Mound settlement on the other side of the stream, and Salina on this side of it, lying on ahead.

Salina is one of those places it is very hard to catch. You see it first "about seven" miles off, and after travelling towards it for an hour and a half, find you have still " eight miles or so " to go. " Appearances are very deceptive in this country," as these people delight in saying to new-comers, and the following story is punctually told, at every opportunity, to illustrate it.

A couple of Britishers (*of course* " Britishers ") started off from their hotel " to walk over to that mountain there," just to get an appetite for breakfast. About dinner-time one of them gave up and came back, leaving his obstinate friend to hunt the mountain by himself. After dining, however, he took a couple of horses and rode out after his friend, and towards evening came up with him just as he was taking off his shoes and stockings by the side of a two-foot ditch.

" Hallo ! " said the horseman, " what on earth are you doing, Jack ? "

"*Doing !*" replied the other sulkily. " Can't you see ? I am taking off my boots to wade this infernal river."

" River ! " exclaimed his friend ; " what river ? That thing's only a two-foot ditch ! "

" Daresay," was the dogged response. " It *looks* only a two-foot ditch. But you can't trust anything in this beastly country. *Appearances are so deceptive.*"

But we caught Salina at last, for we managed to head it up into a *cul-de-sac* of the mountains, and overtook it about sundown. A few years ago the settlement was depopulated ; for Black Hawk made a swoop at it from his eyrie among the cedars on the overlooking hill, and after killing a few of the people, compelled the survivors to fly northward, where the militia was mustering for the defence of the valley. It was in this war that the Federal officer commanding the post at Salt Lake City, acting under the orders of General Sherman, refused to help the settlers, telling them in a telegram of twenty words to help themselves. The country, therefore, remembers with considerable bitterness that three years' campaign against a most formidable combination of Indians ; when they lost so many lives, when two counties had to be entirely abandoned, many scattered settlements broken up, and an immense loss in property and stock suffered.

At Salina I met an apostate Mormon who had deserted the religion because he had grown to disbelieve in it, but who had retained, nevertheless, all his respect for the leaders of the Church and the general body of Mormons. He is still a polygamist ; that is to say, having married two wives, he has continued to treat them honourably as wives. With me was an apostle, one of the most deservedly popular elders of the Church, and it was capital entertainment to hear the apostate and the apostle exchanging their jokes at each other's expense. I was shown at this house, by the way, an emigration loan receipt. The emigrant, his wife, and three children, had been brought out in the old waggon days at $50 a head. Some fifteen years later, when the man had become well-to-do and after he had apostatized, he repaid the $250, and some $50 extra as "interest." The loan ticket stipulated for "ten per cent. per annum," but as he said, it was "only Mormons who would have let him run on so long, and then have let him off so much of the interest."

My host was himself an interesting man, for he had been with the Saints ever since the stormy days of Kirtland, and had known Joseph Smith personally. "Ah, sir, he *was* a noble man!" said the old fellow. Among other out-of-the-way items which he told me about the founder of the faith, was his predilection for athletic exercises and games of all kinds; how he used to challenge strangers to wrestle, and be very wroth when, as happened once, the stranger threw him over the counter of a shop; and how he used to play base-ball with the boys in the streets of Nauvoo. This trait of Joseph Smith's character I have never seen noticed by his biographers, but it is quite noteworthy, as also, I think, is the extraordinary fascination which his personal appearance—for he was a very handsome man of the Sir Robert Peel type—seems to have exercised over his contemporaries. When speaking to them, I find that one and all will glance from the other aspects of his life to this—that he was "a *noble* man."

Rabbit-hunting across country in a two-horse waggon is

not a sport I shall often indulge in again.   The rabbit has
things too much its own way.   It does not seem to be a
suitable animal for pursuing in a vehicle.   It is too evasive.

Indeed, but for an accident, I should probably never have
indulged in it at all.   But it happened that on our way from
Salina to Monroe we lost our way.   Our teamster, for inscrutable reasons of his own, turned off from the main road
into a bye-track, which proved to have been made by some
one prospecting for clay, and the hole which he had excavated was its terminus.   I tried to think out his reason for
choosing this particular road, the least and most unpromis-
ing of the three that offered themselves to him.   It was
probably this.   Two out of the three roads, being wrong ones,
were *evils*.   One of these was larger than the other, and so
of the two evils he chose the less.   Q.E.D.

To get back into the road we struck across the sage-brush,
and in so doing started a jack-rabbit.   As it ran in the direction we wanted to go, we naturally followed it.   But the jack-
rabbit thought we were in murderous pursuit, and performed
prodigies of agility and strategy in order to escape us.   But
the one thing that it ought to have done, got out of our
road, it did not do.   We did not gain on the lively animal,
I confess, for it was all we could do to retain our seats, but
we gave it enough to prose about all the days of its life.
What stories the younger generation of jack-rabbits will
hear of " the old days " when desperate men used to come
out thousands of miles in two-horse waggons with canvas
hoods to try and catch their ancestors !   And what a hero
that particular jack-rabbit which we did *not* hunt will be !

The road southwards leads along hillsides, both up and
down, but on the whole gradually ascending, till the summit
of the spur is reached.   Here one of the most enchanting
landscapes possible is suddenly found spread out beneath you.

A vast expanse of green meadow-land with pools of blue water here and there, herds of horses grazing, flocks of wild fowl in the air, and on the right the settlement of Richfield among its trees and red-soiled corn-fields !

Crossing this we found that a spur, running down on it, divides it really into two, or rather conceals a second plain from sight. But in the second, sage-brush, " the damnable absinthe," that standard of desolation, waves rampant, and the telegraph wire that goes straddling across it seems as if it must have been laid solely for the convenience of larks. Every post has its lark, as punctually as its insulator, and every lark lets off its three delicious notes of song as we go by, just as if the birds were sentries passing on a " friend " from picket to picket. And here it was that we adventured with the jack-rabbit, much to our own discomfiture. But while we were casting about for our lost road, we came upon a desolate little building, all alone in the middle of the waste, which we had supposed to be a deserted ranch-house, and were surprised to find several waggons standing about. Just as we reached it, the owners of the waggons came out, and then we discovered that it was the " meeting-house " for the scattered ranches round, and seeing the several parties packing themselves into the different waggons re-membered (from a certain Sabbatical smartness of apparel) that it was Sunday. We were soon on our right road again, and passing the hamlets of Inverary and Elsinore on the right, came in sight of Monroe, and through a long prelude of cultivation reached that quaint little village just appa-rently at the fashionable hour for girls to go out riding with their beaux.

Couple after couple passed us, the girls riding pillion behind their sweethearts, and very well contented they all seemed to be, with their arms round the object of their

affections.   Except in France once or twice, I do not recol-
lect ever having seen this picturesque old custom in practice ; but judging from the superior placidity of *his* countenance and the merriment on *hers*, I should say it was an
enjoyable one, and perhaps worth reviving.

Another interesting feature of Sunday evening in Monroe
was the big drum.   It appeared that the arrival of the Apostle
who was with me had been expected, and that the people, who
are everywhere most curiously on the alert for spiritual refreshment, had agreed that if the Apostle on arriving felt equal
to holding a meeting, the big drum was to be beaten.   In
due course, therefore, a very little man disappeared inside
a building and shortly reappeared in custody of a very big
drum, which he proceeded to thump in a becoming Sabbatical manner.   But whether the drum or the association
of old band days overcame him, or whether the devil
entered into him or into the drum, it is certain that he soon
drifted into a funereal rendering of " Yankee Doodle."
He was conscious, moreover, of his lapse into weekday
profanity, and seemed to struggle against it by beating ponderous spondees.   But it was of no use.   Either the drum or
the devil was too big for him, and the solemn measure kept
breaking into patriotic but frivolous trochaics.   Attracted
by these proceedings, the youth of the neighbourhood had
collected, and their intelligent aversion to monopolists was
soon apparent by their detaching the little barnacle from his
drum and subjecting the resonant instrument to a most irregular bastinado.   They all had a go at it, both drumsticks
at once, and the result was of a very unusual character, as
neither of the performers could hear distinctly what was going
on on the other side of the drum, and each, therefore, worked
quite independently.   In the meanwhile some one had pro-
cured a concertina, and this, with a dog that had a fine

falsetto bark, constituted a very respectable "band" in point of noise. Thus equipped, the lads started off to beat up the village, and working with that enthusiasm which characterizes the self-imposed missions of youth, were very successful. Everybody came out to their doors to see what was going on, and having got so far, they then went on to the meeting. By twos and threes and occasional tens the whole village collected inside the meeting-house, or round the door unable to get in, and I must confess that looking round the room, I was surprised at the number of pretty peasant faces that Monroe can muster.

And here for the first time I became aware of a very significant fact, and one that well deserves notice, though I have never heard or seen it referred to—I mean the number of handsome marriageable girls who are unmarried in the Mormon settlements. Omitting other places, in each of which many well-grown, comely girls can be found unmarried, I saw in the hamlet of Monroe enough unwedded charms to make me think that either the resident polygamist had very bad taste or very bad luck. My host, a Mormon, was a widower (a complete widower I mean), and two *very* pretty girls, neighbours, looked after his household affairs for him. One was a blonde Scandinavian of Utah birth ; the other a dark-haired Scotch lassie emigrated three years ago—and each was just eighteen. (And in the Western country eighteen looks three-and-twenty.) I asked my host why he did not marry one of them, or both, and he told me that he had a family growing up, and that he had so often seen quarrels and separations result from the remarriage of fathers that he did not care to risk it.

And the Apostle, who was present, said, " Quite right."

Now please remember this was in polygamous Utah, in a secluded village, entirely Mormon, where, if anywhere, men and women might surely do as they pleased. In any monogamous society such a reason, followed by the approval of a Church dignitary, would not be worth commenting on, but here among Mormons it was significant enough.

I spoke to the girls, and asked them why they had not married.

" Because the right man has not come along yet," said one.

" But perhaps when the right man *does* come along he will be married already," I said.

" *And why should that make any difference ?* " was the reply.

In the meantime each of these shapely daughters of Eve had a " beau " who took her out riding behind him, escorted her home from meeting, and so forth. But neither of them had found " the right man."

Of Monroe, therefore, one of those very places, retired from civilization, " where the polygamous Mormon can carry on his beastly practices undetected, and therefore unpunished "—as the scandalous clique of Salt Lake City (utterly ignorant of Mormonism except what it can pick up from apostates) is so fond of alleging—I can positively state from personal knowledge that there are both men and women there who are guided in matters of marriage by the very same motives and principles that regulate the relation in monogamous society. Further, I can positively state the same of several other settlements, and judging from these, and from Salt Lake City, I can assure my readers that the standard of public morality among the Mormons of Utah is such as the Gentiles among them are either unable or unwilling to live up to.

In this connexion it is worth noting that public morality has in Utah one safeguard, over and above all those of other countries, namely, the strict surveillance of the Church. I have enjoyed while in Utah such exceptional advantages for arriving at the truth, as both Gentiles and Mormons say have never been extended to any former writer, and among other facts with which I have become acquainted is the silent scrutiny into personal character which the Church maintains.

Profanity, intemperance, immorality, and backbiting are taken quiet note of, and if persisted in against advice, are punished by a gradual withdrawal of "fellowship;" and result in what the Gentiles call "apostasy." Among the standing instructions of the teachers of the wards is this :—

"If persons professing to be members of the Church be guilty of allowing drunkenness, Sabbath-breaking, profanity, defrauding or backbiting, or any other kind of wickedness or unrighteous dealing, they should be visited and their wrong-doing pointed out to them in the spirit of brotherly kindness and meekness, and be exhorted to repent."

If they do not repent, they find the respect, then the friendship, and finally the association, of their co-religionists withheld from them, and thus tacitly ostracized by their own Church, they "apostatize" and carry their vices into the Gentile camp, and there assist to vilify those who have already pronounced them unfit to live with honest men or virtuous women.

CHAPTER XV.

AT MONROE.

"Schooling" in the Mormon districts—Innocence as to whisky, but connoisseurs in water—"What do you think of *that* water, sir?" —Gentile dependents on Mormon charity—The one-eyed rooster —Notice to All!

SITTING at the door next morning, I saw a very trimly-dressed damsel of twenty or thereabouts, coming briskly along under the trees, which there, as in every other Mormon settlement, shade the side-walk. She was the schoolmistress, I learned, and very soon her scholars began to pass along. I had thus an opportunity of observing the curious, happy-go-lucky style in which "schooling" is carried on, and I was sorry to see it, for Mormonism stands urgently in need of more education, and it is pure folly to spend half the revenue of the Territory annually in a school establishment, if the children and their parents are permitted to suppose that education is voluntary and a matter of individual whim. Some of the leading members of the Church are conspicuous defaulters in this matter, and do their families a gross wrong by setting "the chores" and education before them as being of equal importance. Even in the highest class of the community children go to school or stay away almost as they like, and provided a little boy or girl has the shrewdness to see that he or she can relieve the father or mother from trouble by being at home to run errands and do little jobs about the house, they can, I regret to think, regulate the amount of their own schooling as they please. I know very well that Utah compares very favourably, on paper, with the greater part of America, but I have compiled and examined too many educational statistics in my time to have any faith in them.

But in the matter of abstinence from strong drink and stimulants, the leaders of the Church set an admirable example, and I found it very difficult most of the time, and quite impossible part of it, to keep my whisky flask replenished.

My system of arriving at the truth as to the existence of spirit stores in any particular settlement, was to grumble and complain at having no whisky, and to exaggerate my regrets at the absence of beer. The courtesy of my hosts was thus challenged, and of the sincerity of the efforts made to gratify my barbaric tastes, I could have no doubt whatever. In most cases they were quite ignorant of even the cost of liquor, and on one occasion a man started off with a five-dollar piece I had given him to get me " five dollars' worth of whisky in this bottle," pointing to my flask. I explained to him that I only wanted the flask replenished, and that there would be change to bring back. He did not get any at all, however.

On one occasion the Bishop brought in, in evident triumph, two bottles of beer. On another I went clandestinely with a Mormon, after dark, and drank some whisky " as a friend," and not as a customer, with another Mormon, who " generally kept a bottle on hand " for secret consumption. That they would both have been ashamed for their neighbours to know what they were about, I am perfectly convinced. On a third occasion an official brought me half a pint of whisky, and the price was a dollar.

Now it is quite impossible for me, who have thus made personal experiment, to have any doubt as to the prevailing sobriety of these people. I put them repeatedly to the severest test that you can apply to a hospitable man, by asking point-blank for ardent spirits. Sometimes, in an off-hand way, I would give money and the flask to a lad, and ask him to " run across to the store and get me a little whisky or brandy." He would take both and meander round in an aimless sort of way. But I might almost as well have asked him to go and buy me a few birds-of-paradise or advance sheets of the " Encyclopædia Britannica." The father or a neighbour might perhaps suggest a "likely" place to get some stimulant, but, *as a rule*, the quest was unconditionally abandoned as hopeless.

The Elders of the Church set a strict example themselves, discouraging, by their own abstinence, indulgence even in tea and coffee. You are asked in a settlement whether you will have tea or coffee, just as in England you would be asked whether you would drink ale or claret. A strong man takes a cup of tea as a lady in Europe might take a glass of sherry, as justified by unusual exercise and fatigue. Being a Londoner, I entertain a most wholesome suspicion of water as a drink, and I reverence fresh milk. In rural Utah, milk being so abundant, the people think little of it, but they pride themselves on their water.

"What do you think of *that* water, sir?" was a question that puzzled me to answer at first, for I am not a connoisseur in drinking-water. If it had been a claret, I might have made a pretence of criticism. But *water!* Or if they had let me wash in it, I would have told them whether I thought it " hard " or " soft." But to pass an opinion on a particular tumbler of water, as if it were a special brand laid down by my host for his own drinking, completely puzzled

me. I can no more tell waters apart than I can tell Chinamen. Of course I can discriminate between the outcome of
the sea and of sulphur springs. But for the rest, it seems
to me that they only differ in their degrees of cleanliness, or,
as scientific men say, to "the properties which they hold in
solution," that is *mud*. And mud, I take it, is always pretty
much the same.

So at first when my host would suddenly turn to me with,
"What do you think of *that* water, sir?" I made the
mistake of supposing it might be one of the extraordinary
aqueous novelties for which this territory is so remarkable
—hot geyser water or petrifying water, or something else of
the kind— and would smack my lips critically and venture
on a suggestion of "lime," or "soda," or "alkali." But
my host was always certain to be down with, "Oh, no; I
assure you. That is reckoned the best water in the
county!"

I soon discovered, however, that the right thing to say
was that I preferred it, "on the whole," to the water *at the
last place*. This was invariably satisfactory—unless, of
course, there was a resident of "the last place" present,
when an argument would ensue. These people, in fact,
look upon their drinking-water just as on the continent they
look upon their vins ordinaires, or in England upon their
local brews, and to the last I could not help being delighted at the manner in which a jug of water and tumblers
were handed about among a party of fatigued and thirsty
travellers. I always took my share becomingly, but sometimes, I must confess, with silent forebodings.

For in some places there are springs which petrify, by
coating with lime, any substance they flow over, and I did
not anticipate with any gratification having my throat lined
with cement, or my stomach faced with building-stone.

"Who are those children ? " said I to my host at Munroe, pointing to two ragged little shoeless waifs that were standing in his yard and evidently waiting to be taken notice of. Instead of replying, my host turned towards them.

" Well, Jimmy," said he, " what is it to-day ? "

The wistful eyes looking out from under the tattered, broad-brimmed hats, brightened into intelligence.

"Another chicken for mother," said both together, promptly ; and then, as if suddenly overtaken by a sense of their audacity, the forlorn little lads dropped their eyes and stood there, holding each other's hands, as picturesque and pathetic a pair as any beggar children in Italy.   In the full sunlight, but half shaded by the immense brims of those wonderfully ancient hats, the urchins were irresistibly artistic, and if met with anywhere in the Riviera, would have been sure of that small-change tribute which the romantic tourist pays with such pleasant punctuality to the picturesque poverty of Southern childhood.   But this was in Utah.

And my host looked at them from under his tilted straw hat.   They stood in front of him as still as sculptors' models, but the fingers and toes kept exchanging little signals of nervous distress.

"All right.   Go and get one," said my host suddenly. " Take the young rooster that's blind of one eye."

He had to shout the last instructions in a rapid crescendo as the youngsters had sprung off together at the word " go," like twin shafts from those double-arrowed bows of the old Manchurian archers.   Three minutes later and a most woful scrawking heralded the approach of the captors and the captive.   The young rooster, though blind of one eye, saw quite enough of the situation to make him apprehensive, but the younger urchin had him tight under his arm, and, still under the exciting influences of the chase and capture, the boys stood once more before my host, with panting bodies, flushed cheeks, and tufts of yellow hair sprouting out through crevices of those wondrous old hats, which had evidently just seen service in the capture. And the rooster, feeling, perhaps, that he was now before the final court of appeal, scrawked as if machinery had got loose inside him and he couldn't stop it.

" How's your (*scraw-w-w-k*) mother ? "

" She's (*scraw·w-w-w-w-k*)—and she's (*scraw-w-w-k*) nothing to eat all yesterday." (*Scraw-w-k.*)

" Go on home, then."

And away down the middle of the road scudded the little fellows in a confusion of dust and scrawk.

"Who are those children ? " I asked again, thinking I had chanced on that unknown thing, a pauper Mormon.

"Oh," said my host, "he's a bad lot—an outsider—who came in here as a loafer, and deserted his wife. She's very ill and pretty nigh starving. Ay, she *would* starve, too, if her boys there didn't come round regular, begging of us. But loafers know very well that ' those —— Mormons ' won't let anybody go hungry. Ay, and they *act* as if they knew it, too."

In other settlements there are exactly such similar cases, but I would draw the attention of my readers—I wish I could draw the attention of the whole nation to it—to the following notice which stands to this day with all the force of a regular by-law in these Mormon settlements :—

" NOTICE TO ALL.

" If there are any persons in this city who are destitute of food, let them be who they may, if they will let their wants be known to me, privately or otherwise, I will see that they are furnished with food and lodging until they can provide for themselves. The bishops of every ward are to see that there are no persons going hungry.

"(Signed by the Presiding Bishop.)"

Now it may be mere "sentiment" on my part, but I confess that this "Notice to All," in the simplicity of its wording, in the nobility of its spirit, reads to me very beautifully. And what a contrast to turn from this text of a universal charity, that is no respecter of persons, to the infinite meanness of those who can write, and publish it to the world, of the whole community of Mormons as "the villainous spawn of polygamy!"

It is a recognized law among the Mormons that no tramp shall pass by one of their settlements hungry; if it is at nightfall, he is to be housed. Towards the Indians their policy is one of enlightened and Christian humanity. For their own people their charity commences from the first. Emigrated to this country by the voluntary donations which maintain the "Perpetual Emigration Fund," each new arrival is met with immediate care, and being passed on to his location, finds (as I have described in another chapter) a system of mutual kindliness prevailing which starts him in life. If sick, he is cared for. If he dies, his family is provided for. All this is fact. I have read it in no books, heard it from no hoodwinking elders. My informants are lads just arrived in Salt Lake City—within an hour or two of their arrival, in fact; young men just settling down in their first log hut in rural settlements: grown men now themselves engaged in the neighbourly duty of assisting new-comers.

I have met and talked to those men—Germans, Scandinavians, Britishers—in their own homes here in Utah, and

have positively assured myself of the fact I state, that
charity, unquestioning, simple-hearted charity, is one of the
secrets of the strength of this wonderful fabric of Mormonism. The Mormons are, more nearly than any other community in the world on such a scale, one family. Every
man knows all the rest of his neighbours with an intimacy
and a neighbourly interest that is the result of reciprocal
good services in the past. This is their bond of union.
In India there is "the village community" which moves,
though in another arc, on the same plane as the Mormon
settlement system. There, to touch one man's crop is to
inflame the whole clan with the sense of a common injury.
Here it is much the same. And as it is between the
different individuals in a settlement, so it is between the
different settlements in the territory. A brutal act, like
that eviction of the Mormon postmaster at Park City the
other day, disturbs the whole of Mormonism with apprehensions of impending violence. A libel directed at a man
or woman in Salt Lake City makes a hundred thousand
personal enemies in Utah. Now, with what petard will you
hoist such a rock?

Induce these Mormons to *hate* one another "for all the
world like Christians," as George Eliot said, and they can be
snapped as easily as the philosopher's faggots when once
they were unbundled. But in the meantime abuse of individuals or "persecution" of a class simply cements the
whole body together more firmly than ever. Mutual charity
is one of the bonds of Mormon union.

CHAPTER XVI.

JACOB HAMBLIN.

A Mormon missionary among the Indians—The story of Jacob
Hamblin's life—His spiritualism, the result of an intense faith—
His good work among the Lamanites—His belief in his own
miracles.

LEAVING Munroe, we find cultivation gradually disappearing,
and, after two or three miles, unmitigated brush supervenes.
A steep divide now thrusts itself across the road, and,
traversing near the summit a patch of pebbly ground which
seemed a very paradise for botanists, we descend again into
a wilderness of grease-wood, "the unspeakable Turk"
among vegetables. The mountains between which we pass
provide, however, a succession of fine views. They are of
that bulky, broad-based and slowly sloping type that is so
much more solemn and impressive than jagged, sharp-
pointed and precipitous formations.

A few miles more bring us to one of them, and for the
first time during the journey our road runs through the
thickly growing "cedars" which we have hitherto seen only
at a distance lying like dark clouds upon the hill-sides and
black drifts in the gulches. The wild flowers growing under
these "cedars" (and the pines which are sprinkled among
them) are of new varieties to me, and I enjoyed a five-mile
walk in this novel vegetation immensely. A few years ago,
though, "Mr. Indian" would have made himself too

interesting to travellers for men to go wandering about among the cedars picking posies. They would have found those "arrows tipped with jasper," which are so picturesque in Hiawatha, flying about instead of humming-birds tipped with emerald, and a tomahawk hurtling through the bushes would have been more likely to excite remark than the blue magpies which I saw looking after snails.

This district was, until very recently, a favourite hunting-ground of those Indians of whom old Jacob Hamblin was the Nestor—the guide, philosopher, friend, and victim. One day they would try "to fill his skin full of arrows;" on the next day they would be round him, asking him to make rain-medicine. They would talk Mormonism with him all day, and grunt approvingly; as soon as night fell they would steal his horse. He was always patching up peace between this tribe and that, yet every now and then they would catch him, have a great pow-wow over him, and being unable to decide whether he should be simply flayed or be roasted first over a charcoal fire, would let him go, with provisions and an escort for his home journey.

His life, indeed, was so wonderful—much more fascinating than any fiction—that I am not surprised at his believing, as he does, that he is under the special protection of Heaven, and, as he says, in a private covenant with the Almighty that "if he does not thirst for the blood of the Lamanites, his blood shall never be shed by them." He began life as a farmer near Chicago, but being baptized received at once "the immediate gift of the Holy Ghost," and at once entered upon a career of "miracles" and "prophecies" that when told in serious earnest are sufficient to stagger even Madame Blavatsky herself. He cured his neighbours of deadly ailments by the laying on of hands, and foretold conversions, deaths, and other events with unvarying accuracy. By prolonged private meditation he enjoyed what, from his description, must be a pregustation of the Buddhistic Nirvana, and after this, miracles became quite commonplace with him. He witnessed the " miracle " of the great quail flights into the camp of the fugitive and starving Saints in 1846, and helped to collect the birds and to eat them ; he saw also the " miraculous " flights of seagulls that rescued the Mormons from starvation by destroying the locusts in 1848.

But his personal experiences, narrated with a simplicity of speech and unquestioning confidence that are bewildering, were really marvellous. If cattle were lost, he could always dream where they were. If sickness prevailed, he knew beforehand who would suffer, and which of them would die, and which of them recover. If Indians were about, angels gave him in his sleep the first warnings of his danger. His sympathy with the Indians was, however, very early awakened, and being strengthened in it by the conciliatory Indian policy of Brigham Young, he became before long the only recognized medium of friendly communication with them. Everybody, whether Federal officials, California emigrants, Mormon missionaries, or Indians themselves, enlisted his influence whenever trouble with the tribes was anticipated. His own explanation of this influence is remarkable enough. As a young man, he says, he was sometimes told off to join retributive expeditions, but he could never bring himself to fire at an Indian, and on one occasion, when he *did* try to do so, his rifle kept missing fire, while " the Lamanites," with equally ineffectual efforts to shed his blood, kept on pincushioning the ground all around him with their futile arrows. After this he and the Indians whenever they met, spared each other's lives with punctual reciprocity.

On one occasion he dreamed that he was walking in a friendly manner with some of the members of a certain tribe, when he picked up a piece of a shining substance, which stuck to his fingers. The more he tried to rub it off the brighter it became. One would naturally, under such circumstances, anticipate the revelation of a gold-mine, but Jacob Hamblin, without any questioning, went off at once to the tribe in question. They received him as friends, and he stayed with them. One day, passing a lodge, "the Spirit" whispered to him, "Here is the shining substance you saw in your dream." But all he saw was a squaw and a boy papoose. However, he went up to the squaw, and asked for the boy. She naturally demurred to the request, but to her astonishment the boy, gathering up his bow and arrows, urged compliance with it, and Hamblin eventually led off his dream-revealed "lump." After a while he asked the boy how it was he was so eager to come, though he had never seen a white man before, and the boy answered, "My Spirit told me that you were coming to my father's lodge for me on a certain day, and that I was to go with you, and when the day came I went out to the edge of the wood, and lit a fire to show you the way to me." And Hamblin then remembered that it was the smoke of a fire that had led him to that particular camp, instead of another towards which he had intended riding !

By way of a parenthesis, let me remark here that if there are any "Spiritualists" among my readers, they should study Mormonism. The Saints have long ago formulated into accepted doctrines those mysteries of the occult world which Spiritualists outside the faith are still investigating. Your "problems" are *their* axioms.

This Indian boy became a staunch Mormon, and to the

last was in communion with the other world. Remember I am quoting Hamblin's words, not in any way endorsing them. In 1863 he was at St. George, and one day when his friends were starting on a mission to a neighbouring tribe, he took farewell of them "for ever." "I am going on a mission, too," he said. "What do you mean?" asked Hamblin. "Only that I shall be dead before you come back," was the Indian's reply. "I have seen myself in a dream preaching the gospel to a multitude of my people, and my ancestors were among them. So I know that I must be a spirit too before I can carry the Word to spirits." In six weeks Hamblin returned to St. George; and the Indian was dead.

Brigham Young, as I have said, insisted upon a conciliatory policy towards the Indians. He made in person repeated visits to the missions at work among them, and was never weary of advising and encouraging. Here is a portion of one of his letters: does it read like the words of a thoroughly bad man?—"Seek by words of righteousness to obtain the love and confidence of the tribes. Omit promises where you are not sure you can fulfil them. Seek to unite your hearts in the bonds of love. . . . May the Spirit of the Lord direct you, and that He may qualify you for every duty is the constant prayer of your fellowlabourer in the gospel of salvation, Brigham Young." Here is a part of another letter: "I trust that the genial and salutary influences now so rapidly extending to the various tribes, may continue till it reaches every son and daughter of Abraham in their fallen condition. The hour of their redemption draws nigh, and the time is not far off when they shall become a people whom the Lord will bless. . . . The Indians should be encouraged to keep and take care of stock. I highly approve of your design in doing your farming through the natives; it teaches them to obtain a subsistence by their own industry, and leaves you more liberty to extend your labours among others. . . . You should always be careful to impress upon them that they should not infringe on the rights of others, and our brethren should be very careful not to infringe upon their rights in any particular, thus cultivating honour and good principles in their midst by example as well as by precept. As ever, your brother in the gospel of salvation, Brigham Young."

These and other letters are exactly in the spirit of the correspondence which, in the early days of England in Hindostan, won for the old Court of Directors the eternal admiration of mankind and for England the respect of Asia. Yet in Brigham Young's case is it ever carried to his credit that he spent so much thought and time and labour over the reclamation of the Indians, by a policy of kindness, and their exaltation by an example of honourable dealing?

It was in this spirit that the Mormon missionaries went out to the Indians then living in the part of the Territory over which I travelled, and Jacob Hamblin was one eminently characteristic of the type. Beyond all others, however, he sympathized with the red man's nature. "I argue with him just as he argues," he said. He was on good terms with the medicine-men, and took a delightful interest in their ceremonies. But when they failed to bring rain with bonfires and howling, he used to pray down abundant showers; when they gave up tormenting the sick as past all hope, Hamblin restored the invalid to life by the laying on of hands!

Once more let me say that I am only *quoting*, not indorsing. But I do him a great injustice in not being able to convey in writing the impressive simplicity of his language, his low, measured tones, his contemplative, earnest attitude, his Indian-like gravity of countenance. That he speaks the implicit truth, according to his own belief, I am as certain as that the water of the Great Salt Lake is salt.

His "occult" sympathies seemed at times to be magnetic, for when in doubt as to whom to choose for his companion on a perilous journey, some brother or other, the fittest person for the occasion, would always feel mysteriously influenced to go to him to see if his services were needed. His displeasure killed men, that is to say they went from his presence, sickened and died. So frequent was this inexplicable demise that the Indians worked out a superstition that evil befalls those who rob or kill a Mormon ; and so marked were the special manifestations of the missionaries' spirit power, that, as Hamblin says, "the Indians were without excuse for refusing conversion," and were converted. "They looked to us for counsel, and learned to regard our words as law." Though the missionaries were sometimes alone, and the tribes around them of the most desperate kind, as "plundersome" as wolves and at perpetual blood-feud with each other, the Mormons' lives were quite safe. When they had determined on an atrocity— burning a squaw, for instance—they would do it in the most nervous hurry, lest a Mormon should come along and stop it, and when they had done it and were reproached, they used to cry like children, and say they were only Indians.

Tragedy and comedy went hand in hand ; laughter at the ludicrous is cut short by a shudder of horror. "We cannot be good ; we must be Piutes. Perhaps some of our children will be good. We're going off to kill so-and-so. Whoop !" And away they would go, putting an arrow into the missionary's horse as they passed. By-and-by the man who shot the arrow would be found dead, killed by a Mormon's curse, and the rest would be back at work in the settlement hoeing pumpkins—"for all the world like Christians!" Through all these alternations of temper and fortune, Jacob Hamblin retained his tender sympathy with the red men.

Their superstitious piety which, quaintly enough, he does not seem to think is exactly like his own, attracted him. He found among them tribes asking the blessing of the Great Father on their food before they ate it; invoking the Divine protection on behalf of their visitors; praying for protection when about to cross a river; returning thanks for a safe return from a journey; always sending one of their religious men to accompany any party about to travel, and so on. All this the pious Mormon naturally respected. But over and above these more ordinary expressions of piety, he found tribes that believed in and acted upon dreams; that accepted the guidance of "second sight;" that relied upon prayer for obtaining temporal necessaries; that lived "by faith," and were awaiting the fulfilment of prophecy. In all this the Mormon missionary sees nothing but common sense. For instance, Hamblin said, "I know that some people do not believe in dreams and night-visions. I myself do not believe in them when they arise from a disordered stomach, but in other kinds I have been fore-warned of coming events, and received much instruction!" And, in the spirit of these words, he thinks it the most natural thing in the world that Indians should start off after a dream and find their lost cattle; suddenly alter their course in a waterless journey, and come upon hitherto unknown springs; predict the most impossible meetings with friends, and avoid dangers that were not even anticipated. In the

most serious manner possible, he acquiesces in the Indians'
theory of rain-getting, and acts upon their clairvoyant advice.
" The Lord," he says, " is mindful of the prayers of these
poor barbarians, and answers them with the blessings they
need." Seeing them quite sincere in their faith, he joins
them in their ceremonies of scattering consecrated meal to
ensure protection on a journey, believing himself that
simple reliance on Providence is all that men of honest
lives need.

One tribe has a tradition that three prophets are to come
to lead them back to the lands that their fathers once
possessed, that these are to be preceded by good white
men, but that the Indians are not to go with them until
after the three prophets have reappeared and told them
what to do. The Indians accept the Mormons as " the
good white men " of the tradition, but " the three prophets "
not having reappeared, they refuse to leave their villages (as
the Mormons have wanted them to do), and Hamblin has
not a word to say against such " reasonable " objections.

Is it not wonderful to find men thus reverting to an
intellectual type that the world had supposed to be extinct ?
to find men, shrewd in business, honest in every phase
of temporal life, going back to cheiromancy and hydromancy, and transacting temporal affairs at the guidance of
visions ? An Indian prays for rain on his pumpkins, in
apparently the most unreasonable way, but the Mormon
postpones his departure till the rain that results is over.
On his way he nearly dies of thirst, prays for deliverance,
and in half an hour snow falls over a mile and a half of
ground, melts and forms pools of water ! What are we to
say of men who say such things as these ? Are they all
crazy together ? And what shall we think of the thousands

here who believe that miracles are the most ordinary, reasonable, natural, every-day phenomena of a life of faith, and quote point-blank the promises of the New Testament as a sufficient explanation? The best thing, perhaps, is to say *Hum* meditatively, and think no more about it.

CHAPTER XVII.

THROUGH MARYSVALE TO KINGSTON.

Piute County—Days of small things—A swop in the sage-brush ; two
Bishops for one Apostle—The Kings of Kingston—A failure in
Family Communism.

FROM the brow of the cedared hill south of Munroe a
splendid view is obtained, and Piute County opens with fair
promises ; for a superb-looking valley, all natural meadow,
lies spread out on either side of the Sevier, while from a
gulch in the mountains on the right, a stream of vegetation seems to have poured down across the level, carrying
along with its flood of cotton-wood and willow a few
stately old pine-trees. From among the vegetation
peeps out a cluster of miners' houses—for there are the
Sevier mines up beyond that pine gulch—and a ranch or
two. Much of the enchantment of distance vanishes of
course as we come down to the level of the plains ourselves
and skirt it close under the hills on the left. But it is a fine
location nevertheless, and some day, no doubt, may be a
populous valley. After a mile or two it narrows, and we
cross the river—a wooden bridge, with a store and barns—
("Lisonbee's place") making a pleasant interval of civilization.

From "Lisonbee's" the road passes up on to and over a
stony plateau, and then descends into the valley again.

Cattle and horses are grazing in the meadow, and the dark patches of wire-grass are spangled with yellow lupins, and tinted pink in places with patches of a beautiful orchid-like flower. On the edge of this pleasant-looking tract stand two small cottages, and to one of these we are welcomed by its Mormon occupants. To me the whole country had an aspect of desperate desolation. Yet our host had just come back from "the Post;" his children were away "at school;" the newspaper on his table was the latest we had ourselves seen. It is true that the post was literally a post, with a cigar-box nailed on the top of it, standing all by itself among the brushwood on the roadside. The school was a mile or two off, "just over the hill," and, till the regular teacher came, a volunteer was making shift to impart education to the little scholars who came straggling over the dreary hill-sides by twos and threes. Yet, rudimentary though they be, these are the first symptoms of a civilization triumphing over sage-brush, and give even to such desperately small beginnings a significance that is very interesting. All the thriving settlements I have visited began exactly in the same way—and under worse conditions, too, for the Indian was then a stronger power than the Mormon.

Our host here had shot among the reeds in his meadow a large bird, the size of an average goose, black with white spots, which he had been told was "a loon." It was one of the larger "divers," its neck being very long and snake-like, terminating in a comparatively small head, its wings very short and its legs (the feet webbed) set, as in all diving birds, far back on the body.

Leaving this very young "settlement," we found ourselves again in a wretched, waterless country, where the vegetation did not compensate for its monotony by any attractions of colour, nor the mountains for their baldness by any variety of contour. Here and there stunted cedars had huddled together for company into a gulch, as if afraid to be scattered about singly on such lonesome hill-sides, and away on the right, in a dip under the hills, we caught a glimpse of Marysvale.

Traversing this forbidding tract, we met another waggon on its way to Munroe, and stopping to exchange greetings, it suddenly occurred to one of the strangers that by our exchanging vehicles the horses and their teamsters would both be going home instead of away from it, and thus everybody be advantaged ! The exchange was accordingly effected, our teamster getting two Bishops in exchange for an Apostle and a correspondent, and the waggons being turned round in their tracks, the teams, to their uncon- cealed satisfaction, started off towards their respective homes.

Sage-brush and sand, with occasional patches of tiresome rock fragments and unlimited lizards—nature's hieroglyphics for sultry sterility—were the only features of the journey. Away on our left, however, the track of a water-channel, that when completed will turn many thousands of these arid acres into farm-lands, scarred the red hill-side, and told the same old story of Mormon industry. Where it came from I have forgotten, where it was going to I do not remember, but it was in sight off and on for some thirty miles, and was probably carrying the waters of the Sevier on to the Circle- ville plains.

We are there ourselves in the evening, and passing through some ploughed land and meadow, find ourselves upon the wind-swept, lonesome, location of

The Kings of Kingston.

Among the social experiments of Mormonism, the family

communism of the Kings of Kingston deserves a special notice, for, though in my own opinion it is a failure, both financially and socially, the scheme is probably one of the most curious attempts at solving a great social problem that was ever made.

Kingston is the name of a hamlet of fifteen wooden cottages and a stock-yard which has been planted in the centre of one of the most desolate plains in all the Utah Territory—a very Jehunnam of a plain. Piute County, in which it is situated, is, as a rule, a most forbidding section of country, and the Kingston "Valley" is perhaps the dreariest spot in it. The mountains, stern and sterile, ring it in completely, but on the south-east is a great cañon which might be the very mouth of the cavern in which the gods used to keep their winds, for a persistent, malignant wind is perpetually sweeping through it on to the plain below, and the soil being light and sandy, the people live for part of the year in a ceaseless dust-storm. One year they sowed 300 acres with wheat, and the wind simply blew the crop away. That which it could not actually displace, it kept rubbed down close to the ground by the perpetual passage of waves of sand. They planted an orchard, but some gooseberry bushes are the only remaining vestiges of the plantation, and even these happen to be on the lee side of a solid fence. They also set out trees to shade their houses, but the wind worked the saplings round and round in their holes, so that they could not take root. It can be easily imagined, therefore, that without a tree, without a green thing except the reach of meadow land at the foot of the hills, the Kingston plain, with its forlorn fifteen tenements, looks for most of the year desolation itself. That any one should ever have settled there is a mystery to all ; that he should have *remained* there is a simple absurdity, a very

P

Jumbo of a folly. Yet here, after five years of the most dismal experiences, I found some twenty households in occupation.

At the time when Brigham Young was exerting himself to extend the " United Order " (of which more when I come to Orderville), one of the enthusiasts who embraced its principles was a Mr. King, of Fillmore. He was a prosperous man, with a family well settled about him. Nevertheless, he determined from motives of religious philanthropy to begin life anew, and having sold off all that he possessed he emigrated with his entire family into the miserable Piute country, selected in an hour of infatuation the Kingston— then " Circleville "—location, and announced that he was about to start a co-operative experiment in farming and general industry on the basis of a household, with patriarchal government, a purse in common, and a common table for all to eat at together.

Having been permitted to examine the original articles of enrolment, dated May 1, 1877—a document, by the way, curiously characteristic of the whole undertaking, being a jumble of articles and by-laws written on a few slips of ordinary paper, a miracle of unworldly simplicity and in very indifferent spelling—I found the objects of " the company," as it is called, were "agricultural, manufacturing, commercial, and other industrial pursuits," and the establishment and maintenance of " colleges, seminaries, churches, libraries, and any other charitable or scientific associations." It was to be superintended by a Board, who were to be elected by a majority of the members, and to receive for their services " the same wages as are paid to farm hands or other common labourers."

To become members of this Family Order it was necessary that they should " bequeath, transfer, and convey into

the company all their right, title, and interest to whatever
property, whether personal or real estate, that they were
then possessed of, or might hereafter become possessed of
by legacy, will, or otherwise for the purposes above mentioned, and further that they would labour faithfully and
honourably themselves, and cause their children who were
under age to labour under the direction of the Board of
Directors, the remuneration for which shall be as fixed by the
board both as to price and kind of pay he or she shall
receive." It was "furthermore understood and agreed that
a schedule or inventory of all property bequeathed or trans-
ferred to the company should be kept, together with the
price of each article, that in case any party becomes dissatisfied or is called away, or wishes to draw out, he can
have as near as may be the same kind of property, but in no
case can he have real estate, only at the option of the
Board, nor shall interest or a dividend be paid on such
property."

"We further agree" (so run the articles of this curious
incorporation) "that we will be controlled and guided in all
our labour, in our food, clothing, and habitations for our
families" (by the Board), "being frugal and economical in
our manner of living and dress, and in no case seek to
obtain that which is above another."

"We also covenant and agree that all credits for labour
that stand to our names in excess of debits for food and
clothing, shall become the property of the company."

In these four articles is contained the whole of the
principles of this astonishing experiment. Men were to
sell their all, and put the proceeds into a family fund.
Out of this, as the wages of their labour, they were to
receive food and other necessaries to the value of $1 a
day, and if at the end of the year their drawings exceeded

the amount of work put in the company " forgave " them the excess, while if their earnings exceeded their drawings, they " forgave " the company. Thus the accounts were annually squared by reciprocal accommodation.

If any one seceded from the Order, he was entitled to receive back exactly what he had contributed. Mr. King, the father, started by putting in some $20,000, and his sons and others following suit, the fund rose at once to some $40,000. (I would say here that the entirely original method of " keeping the books " makes balance-striking a difficulty.) With this sum, and so much labour at their disposal, the Family Company should have been a brilliant success. But several circumstances conspired disastrously against it. The first was the unfortunate selection of location, for, in spite of the quantity of promising land available elsewhere, Mr. King pitched his camp in the wretched sand-drifts of the Piute section. The next was the ill-advised generosity of the founders in inviting all the country round to come and join them, with or without means, so long as they would be faithful members of the Order. The result, of course, was an influx of " deadheads "—the company indeed having actually to send out waggons to haul in families who were too poor to be able to move themselves. Of these new-comers only a proportion were worth anything to the young settlement, for many came in simply for the certainty of a roof over their heads and sufficient food. The result was most discouraging, and in a short time the more valuable adherents were disheartened, and began to fall off, and now, five years from the establishment of the company, there are only some twenty families left, and these are all Kings or relatives of the Kings. The father himself is dead, but four sons divide the patriarchal government between them, and, having again reduced the scheme to a strictly family concern, they are thinking of a fresh start.

What may happen in the future is not altogether certain, but it will be strange if in this country where individual industry, starting without a dollar, is certain of a competence, co-operative labour commencing with funds in hand does not achieve success. At present the company possesses, besides its land in the valley, and a mill and a woollen factory, both commencing work, cattle and sheep worth about $10,000, and horses worth some $12,000 more. This is a tolerable capital for an association of hard-working men to begin with, but it is significant of errors in the past that after five years of almost superhuman toil they should find themselves no better off materially than when they started. Nor, socially, has the experiment hitherto been a success, for Kingston is, in my opinion, beyond comparison the lowest in the scale of all the Mormon settlements that I have seen. It is poverty-stricken in appearance; its houses outside and inside testify, in unmended windows and falling plaster, to an absence of that good order which characterizes so many other villages. The furniture of the rooms and the quality of the food on the tables are poorer than elsewhere, and altogether it is only too evident that this family communism has dragged all down alike to the level of the poorest and the laziest of its advocates, rather than raised all up to the level of the best off and the hardest working. The good men have sunk, the others have not risen, and if it were not so pathetic the Kingston phenomenon would be exasperating.

But there is a very sincere pathos about this terrible sacrifice of self for the common good. I do not mean theoretically, but practically. The men of " the company " are the most saddening community I have ever visited. They seem, with their gentle manners, wonderful simplicity of speech, and almost womanly solicitude for the welfare of their guests, to have lost the strong, hearty spirit which characterizes these Western conquerors of the deserts. Yet even the hard-working Mormons speak of them as veritable heroes in work. It is a common thing to hear men say that " the Kingston men are simply killing themselves with toil ;" and when Western men talk of work as being *too* hard, you may rely upon it it is something very exceptional. Almost against hope these peasants have struggled with difficulties that even they themselves confess seem insuperable. They have given Nature all the odds they could, and then gone on fighting her. The result has been what is seen to-day—a crushed community of men and enfeebled women, living worse than any other settlement on the whole Mormon line. Their own stout hearts refuse to believe that they are a failure; but failure is written in large capital letters on the whole hamlet, and in italics upon every face within it. The wind-swept sand-drifts in which the settlement stands, the wretchedness of the tenements and their surroundings, the haphazard composition of their food, their black beans and their buffalo berries, the whistling of the wind as it drives the sand through the boards of the houses, the howling of the coyotes round the stock-yard — everything from first to last was in accord to emphasize the desperate desolation. But those who have known them for all the five years that the experiment has been under trial declare that their present condition, lamentable as it is, is an improvement upon their past. When they ate at a common table, the living, it is said, was even more frugal than it is now, and there was hardly a piece of crockery among them all, the "family" eating and drinking out of tin vessels. The women, either from mismanagement among themselves, or want of order among the men, were unable to bear the burden of ceaseless cooking, and the common table was thereupon abandoned by a unanimous vote.

Yet they are courtesy and hospitality itself, and their sufferings have only clinched their piety. They have not lost one iota of their faith in their principles, though staggering under the conviction of failure. Their children have regular schooling, the women are scrupulously neat in their dress, while profanity and intemperance are unknown.

CHAPTER XVIII.

FROM KINGSTON TO ORDERVILLE.

On the way to Panguitch—Section-houses not Mormon homes—
Through wild country—Panguitch and its fish—Forbidden plea-
sures—At the source of the Rio Virgin—The surpassing beauty of
Long Valley—The Orderville Brethren—A success in Family
Communism.

NEXT day we started over the hills for Panguitch, some forty
miles off. And here, by the roadside, was pointed out to
me one of those "section-houses" which a traveller in
Utah once mistook for Mormon "homes," and described
as "cabins, ten feet by six, built of planks, one window
with no glass in it, one doorway with no door in it." This
is an accurate description enough of a section-house, but it
is a mistake to suppose that any one ever lives in it, as
section-houses are only put up to comply with the Homestead Act, which stipulates for a building with one doorway
and one window being erected upon each lot within a
certain period of its allotment. But they do duty all the
same in a certain class of literature as typical of the squalid
depravity of the Mormons, for, being inhabited by Mormons,
it follows, of course, that several wives, to say nothing of
numerous children, have all to sleep together "on the floor
of the single room the house contains!" Isn't this a
dreadful picture! And are not these large polygamous
families who live in section-houses a disgrace to America?

But, unfortunately for this telling picture, the only " inhabitants " of these section-houses are Gentile tramps.

A rough hill-road, strewn with uncompromising rocks, jolted us for some miles, and then we crossed a stream-bed with some fine old pines standing in it, and beds of blue lupins brightening the margin, and so came down to the river level, and along a lane running between hedges of wild-rose and redberry (the " opie " of the Indians) tangled with clematis and honeysuckle, and haunted by many birds and brilliant butterflies. The river bubbled along among thickets of golden currant and red willow, and mallards with russet heads floated in the quiet backwaters, by the side of their dames all dressed in dainty grey. It was altogether a charming passage in a day of such general dreariness, reminding one of a pleasant quotation from some pretty poem in the middle of a dull chapter by some prosy writer.

But the dulness recommences, and then we find ourselves at a wayside farm, where a couple of fawns with bells round their necks are keeping the calves company, and some boys are fishing on a little log bridge. These fish must have been all born idiots, or been stricken with unanimous lunacy in early youth, for the manner of their capture was this. The angler lay on his stomach on the " bridge " (it was a three foot and a half stream), with one eye down between two of the logs. When he saw any fish he thrust his " rod " —it was more like a penholder—through the space, and held it in front of the fishes' noses. At the end of the rod were some six inches of string, with a hook tied on with a large knot, and baited with a dab of dough. When the fish had got thoroughly interested in the dough, the angler would jerk up his rod, and by some unaccountable oversight on the part of the fishes it was found that about once in fifty jerks a fish came up out of the water ! They seemed to me to be young trout ; but, whatever the species, they must have been the most imbecile of finned things. I suggested catching them with the finger and thumb, but the boys giggled at me, as " the fish wouldn't let ye." But I am of a different opinion, for it seemed to me that fish that would let you catch them with such apparatus, would let you catch them without any at all.

From here to Panguitch the road lies through stony country of the prevalent exasperating type until we reach the precincts of the settlement, heralded long before we reach it by miles of fencing that enclose the grazing-land stretching down to the river. A detestable road, broken up and swamped by irrigation channels, leads into the settle-ment, and the poor impression thus received is not removed as we pass through the treeless " streets " and among the unfenced lots. But it is an interesting spot none the less, for apart from its future, it is a good starting-point for many places of interest. But I should like to have visited Red Lake and Panguitch Lake. " Panguitch," by the way, means " fish " in the red man's language, and it is no wonder, therefore, that at breakfast we enjoyed one of the most splendid dishes of mountain-lake trout that was ever set before man. It is a great fish certainly—and I prefer it broiled. To put any sauce to it is sheer infamy.

The beaver, by the way, is still to be trapped here, and the grizzly bear is not a stranger to Panguitch.

Looking out of the window in the evening, I saw a cart standing by the roadside, and a number of men round it. Their demeanour aroused my curiosity, for an extreme dejection had evidently marked them for its own. Some sate in the road as if waiting in despair for Doomsday ; others prowled round the cart and leant in a melancholy

manner against it.   The cart, it appeared, had come from
St. George, the vine-growing district in the south of the
territory, and contained a cask of wine.   But as there was
no licence in Panguitch for the sale of liquors, it could not
be broached !   I never saw men look so wretchedly thirsty
in my life, and if glaring at the cask and thumping it could
have emptied it, there would not have been a drop left.   It
was a delightful improvement upon the tortures of Tantalus,
but the victims accepted the joke as being against them,
and though they watched the cart going away gloomily
enough, there was no ill-temper.

From Panguitch to Orderville, fifty miles, the scenery
opens with the dreary hills that had become so miserably
familiar, alternating with level pasture-lands, among which
the serpentine Sevier winds a curiously fantastic course.
But gradually there grows upon the mind a sense of coming
change.   Verdure creeps over the plains, and vegetation
steals on to the hill-sides, and then suddenly as if for a
surprise, the complete beauty of Long Valley bursts upon
the traveller.   I cannot in a few words say more of it than
that this valley—through which the Rio Virgin flows, and
in which the Family Communists of Orderville have pitched
their tents—rivals in its beauty the scenery of Cashmere.

Springing from a hill-side, beautiful with flowering shrubs
and instinct with bird life, the Virgin River trickles through
a deep meadow bright with blue iris plants and walled in on
either side by hills that are clothed with exquisite vegetation,
and then, collecting its young waters into a little channel,
breaks away prattling into the valley.   Corn-fields and
orchards, and meadows filled with grazing kine, succeed
each other in pleasant series, and on the right hand and on
the left the mountains lean proudly back with their loads of
magnificent pine.   And other springs come tumbling down

to join the pretty river, which flows on, gradually widening
as it goes, past whirring saw-mills and dairies half buried
among fruit-trees, through park-like glades studded with
pines of splendid girth, and pretty brakes of berry-bearing
trees all flushed with blossoms.   And the valley opens away
on either side into grassy glens from which the tinkle of
cattle-bells falls pleasantly on the ear, or into bold cañons
that are draped close with sombre pines, and end in the
most magnificent cathedral cliffs of ruddy sandstone.

What lovely bits of landscape ! What noble studies of
rock architecture !   It is a very panorama of charms, and,
travelled widely as I have, I must confess to an absolute
novelty of delight in this exquisite valley of

The Orderville Brethren.

Among the projects which occupied Joseph Smith's active
brain was one that should make the whole of the Mormon
community a single family, with a purse in common, and the
head of the Church its head.   In theory they are so already.
But Joseph Smith hoped to see them so in actual practice
also, and for this purpose—the establishment of a universal
family communism—he instituted " The Order of Enoch,"
or " The United Order."

Why Enoch ?   The Mormons themselves appear to have
no definite explanation beyond the fact that Enoch was holy
beyond all his generation.   But for myself, I see in it only
another instance of that curious sympathy with ancient
tradition which Joseph Smith, and after him Brigham
Young, so consistently showed.   They were both of them
as ignorant as men could be in the knowledge that comes
from books, and yet each of them *must* have had some
acquaintance with the mystic institutions of antiquity, or
their frequent coincidence with primitive ideas and schemes

appears to me inexplicable. No man can in these days think and act like an antediluvian by accident. Josephus is, I find, a favourite author among the Mormons, and Josephus may account for a little. Moreover, many of the Mormons, notably both Presidents, are or were Freemasons, and this may account for some more. But for the balance I can find no explanation. Now I remember reading somewhere—perhaps in Sir Thomas Browne—that "the patriarchal Order of Enoch" is an institution of prodigious antiquity ; that Enoch in the Hebrew means "the teacher;" that he was accepted in prehistoric days as the founder of a self-supporting, pious socialism, which was destined (should destruction overtake the world) to rescue one family at any rate from the general ruin, and perpetuate the accumulated knowledge of the past. And it is exactly upon these conditions that we find Joseph Smith, fifty years ago, promulgating in a series of formulated rules, the scheme of a patriarchal "Order of Enoch."

All Mormons are "elect." But even among the elect there is an aristocracy of piety. Thus in Islam we find the Hajji faithful above the faithful. In Hindooism the brotherhood of the Coolins is accepted by the gods above all the other "twice-born." Is it not, indeed, the same in every religion —that there are the chosen within the chosen—"though they were mighty men, yet they were not of the three"—a tenth legion among the soldiers of Heaven—the *arch*angels in the select ministry of the Supreme? In Mormonism, therefore, if a man chooses, he may consecrate himself to his faith more signally than his fellows, by endowing the Church with all his goods, and accepting from the Church afterwards the "stewardship" of a portion of his own property ! It is no mere lip-consecration, no Ritualists' "Order of Jesus," no question of a phylactery. It means the absolute transfer of all property and temporal interests, and of all rights of all kinds therein, to the Church by a formal, legal process, and a duly attested deed.   Here is one :—

" Be it known by these presents, that I, Jesse W. Fox, of Great Salt Lake City, in the county of Great Salt Lake, and territory of Utah, for and in consideration of the sum of one hundred ($100) dollars and the good-will which I have to the Church of Jesus Christ of Latter-Day Saints, give and convey unto Brigham Young, trustee in trust for the said Church, his successor in office and assigns, all my claims to and ownership of the following-described property, to wit :

One house and lot	$1000
One city lot	100
East half of lot 1, block 12 . . .	50
Lot 1, block 14	75
Two cows, $50 ; two calves, $15 . .	65
One mare, $100 ; one colt, $50 . .	150
One watch, $20 ; one clock, $12 . ,	32
Clothing, $300 ; beds and bedding, $125 .	425
One stove, $20 ; household furniture, $210	230

Total	$2127

together with all the rights, privileges, and appurtenances thereunto belonging or appertaining.   I also covenant and agree that I am the lawful claimant and owner of said property, and will warrant and for ever defend the same unto the said trustee in trust, his successor in office and assigns, against the claims of my heirs, assigns, or any person whomsoever."

Then follows the attestation of the witness, and the formal certificate of the Judge of the Probate Court that "the signer of the above transfer, personally known to me, appeared the second day of April, 1857, and acknowledged that he, of his own choice, executed the foregoing transfer"

Such transfers of property are not, I know, infrequent in other religions, notably the Roman Catholic, but the object of the Mormon's piety distinguishes his act from that of others. Had Brigham Young persevered in his predecessor's project, it is almost certain that he would have established a gigantic " company " that would have controlled all the temporal interests of the territory, and eventually comprised the whole Mormon population. It is just possible that he himself foresaw that such success would be ruin ; that the foundations of the Order would sink under such a prodigious superstructure, for he diverted his attention from the main to subsidiary schemes. Instead of one central organization sending out colonies on all sides of it, he advised the establishment of branch communities, which might eventually be gathered together under a single headquarters' control. The two projects were the same as to results ; they differed only as to the means ; and the second was the more judicious.

A few individuals came forward in their enthusiasm to give all they possessed to a common cause, but the Order flagged, though, nominally, many joined it. Thus, travelling through the settlements, I have seen in a considerable number of homes the Rules of the Order framed upon the walls. At any time these would be curious ; *to-day*, when the morality of the principles of Mormonism is challenged, they are of special interest :—

"RULES THAT SHOULD BE OBSERVED BY MEMBERS OF THE UNITED ORDER.

" We will not take the name of the Deity in vain, nor speak lightly of His character or of sacred things.

"We will pray with our families morning and evening, and also attend to secret prayer.

"We will observe and keep the Word of Wisdom according to the spirit and the meaning thereof.

"We will treat our families with due kindness and affection, and set before them an example worthy of imitation. In our families and intercourse with all persons, we will refrain from being contentious or quarrelsome, and we will cease to speak evil of each other, and will cultivate a spirit of charity towards all. We consider it our duty to keep from acting selfishly or from covetous motives, and will seek the interest of each other and the salvation of all mankind.

"We will observe the Sabbath day to keep it holy, in accordance with the Revelations.

"That which is committed to our care we will not appropriate to our own use.

"That which we borrow we will return according to promise, and that which we find we will not appropriate to our own use, but seek to return it to its proper owner.

"We will, as soon as possible, cancel all individual indebtedness contracted prior to our uniting with the order, and, when once fully identified with said order, will contract no debts contrary to the wishes of the Board of Directors.

"We will patronize our brethren who are in the order.

"In our apparel and deportment we will not pattern after nor encourage foolish and extravagant fashions, and cease to import or buy from abroad any article which can be reasonably dispensed with, or which can be produced by combination of home labour. We will foster and encourage the producing and manufacturing of all articles needful for our consumption as fast as our circumstances will permit.

"We will be simple in our dress and manner of living,

using proper economy and prudence in the management of all intrusted to our care.

" We will combine our labour for mutual benefit, sustain with our faith, prayers, and works those whom we have elected to take the management of the different departments of the order, and be subject to them in their official capacity, refraining from a spirit of fault-finding.

" We will honestly and diligently labour and devote ourselves and all we have to the order and to the building up of the Kingdom of God."

Under these general regulations a great number, as I have said, enrolled themselves, and they may be considered therefore to constitute, as it were, a Knight Templar commandery within a Fellowcraft lodge. All are " brethren ;" these are *illustrious* brethren. All are pashas ; these are " of many tails." All are mandarins of heaven ; these wear the supreme button.

But the temporal object of the Order was not served by such transfers of moral obligations ; by the hypothecation of personal piety ; by the investment of spiritual principles in a common fund. You cannot get much working capital out of mortgages on a man's soul. Calchas complained bitterly when the Athenian public paid their vows to the goddess in squashes. The collector, he said, would not take them in payment of the water-rates. So it has fared with the Order of Enoch. It is wealthy in good intentions, and if promises were dollars could draw large checks.

Here and there, however, local fervour took practical shape. The Kings of Kingston planted their family flag on the wind-swept Circleville plain. At Sunset another communistic colony was established, and in Long Valley, in the cañons of the Rio Virgin, was inaugurated the " United Order of Orderville."

Situated in a beautiful valley that needs nothing more
added to it to make its inhabitants entirely self-supporting;
directed and controlled with as much business shrewdness
as fervent piety; supported by its members with a sensible
regard for mutual interests—this Orderville experiment
bids fair to be a signal success. In their Articles of
Association the members call themselves a Corporation
which is "to continue in existence for a period of twenty-
five years," and of which the objects are every sort of
"rightful" enterprise and industry that may render the
Order independent of outside produce and manufactures,
"consistent with the Constitution of the United States and
the laws of this Territory." Its capital is fixed at $100,000,
in 10,000 shares of $10 each, and the entire control of its
affairs is vested in a board of nine directors, who are
elected by a ballot of the whole community. Article 13
states that "the individual or private property of the
stockholders shall not be liable for the debts or obligations
of the company." Article 15 is as follows: "The directors
shall have the right and power to declare dividends on said
stock whenever, in their judgment, there are funds for that
purpose due and payable."

Now, in these two last articles lie the saving principles of
the Orderville scheme. Hitherto, from the beginning of
the world, experiments in communism have always split
upon this rock, namely, that individuality was completely
crushed out. No man was permitted to possess "private"
property—he was *l'enfant de la République*, body and soul
—and no man, therefore, had sufficient personal identity
to make it possible for individual profits to accrue to him.
And so the best of the young men—let the experiment
be at any date in history you like—became dissatisfied
with the level at which they were kept, and they seceded.

They insisted on having names of their own, and refused to be merely, like the members of a jail republic, known by numbers. Individuality and identity are the original data of human consciousness. They are the first solid facts which a baby masters and communicates; they are the last that old age surrenders to infirmity and death. But in Orderville, it will be seen, the notion of "private" property exists. It is admitted that there is such a thing as "individual" ownership. Moreover, it is within the power of the board to pay every man a dividend. This being the case, this particular experiment in communism has the possibility of great success, for its members are not utterly deprived of all individuality. They have some shreds of it left to them.

To become a member of the Order there is no qualification of property necessary. The aged and infirm are accepted in charity. Indeed, at one time they threatened to swamp the family altogether, for the brethren seemed to have set out with a dead-weight upon them heavier than they could bear. But this has righted itself. The working members have got the ship round again, and in one way or another a place and a use has been found for every one. Speaking generally, however, membership meant the holding of stock in the corporation. If a man wished to join the Order, he gave in to the Bishop a statement of his effects. It was left to his conscience that this statement should be complete and exhaustive; that there should be no private reservations. These effects—whatever they might be, from a farm in another part of the Territory to the clothes in his trunk—were appraised by the regular staff, and the equivalent amount in stock, at $10 a share, was issued to them. From that time his ownership in his property ceased. His books would perhaps go into

the school-house library, his extra blankets next door, his
horse into a neighbour's team. According to his capacities,
also, he himself fell at once into his place among the
workers, going to the woollen factory or the carpenter's
shop, the blacksmith's forge or the dairy, the saw-mills or
the garden, the grist-mill or the farm, according as his
particular abilities gave promise of his being most useful.
His work here would result, as far as he was personally
concerned, in no profits. But he was assured of a comfortable house, abundant food, good clothes. The main
responsibilities of life were therefore taken off his shoulders.
The wolf could never come to his door. He and his were
secured against hunger and cold. But beyond this? There
was only the approbation of his companions, the reward of
his conscience. With the proceeds of his labour, or by
the actual work of his own hands, he saw new buildings
going up, new acres coming under cultivation. But none
of them belonged to him. He never became a proprietor,
an owner, a master. While therefore he was spared the
worst responsibilities of life, he was deprived of its noblest
ambitions. He lived without apprehensions, but without
hopes too. If his wife was ill or his children sickly, there
were plenty of kind neighbours to advise and nurse and
look after them. No anxieties on such matters need trouble
him. But if he had any particular taste—music, botany,
anything—he was unable to gratify it, unless these same
kindly neighbours agreed to spend from the common fund
in order to buy him a violin or a flower-press—and they
could hardly be expected to do so. Quite apart from the
fact that a man learning to play a new instrument is an
enemy of his kind, you could not expect a community of
graziers, farmers, and artisans to be unanimously enthusiastic
about the musical whims of one of their number, still less

for his " crank " in collecting " weeds "—as everything that is not eatable (or is not a rose) is called in most places of the West. Tastes, therefore, could not be cultivated for the want of means, and any special faculties which members might individually possess were of necessity kept in abeyance. Amid scenery that might distract an artist, and fossil and insect treasures enough to send men of science crazy, the community can do nothing in the direction of Art or of Natural History, unless they all do it together. For the Order cannot spare a man who may be a good ploughman, to go and sit about in the cañons painting pictures of pine-trees and waterfalls. Nor can it spare the money that may be needed for shingles in buying microscopes for a " bug-hunter." The common prosperity, therefore, can only be gained at a sacrifice of all individual tastes. This alone is a very serious obstacle to success of the highest kind. But in combination with this is of course the more general and formidable fact that even in the staple industries of the community individual excellence brings with it no individual benefits. A moral trades-unionism planes all down to a level. It does not, of course, prevent the enthusiast working his very hardest and best in the interests of his neighbours. But such enthusiasm is hardly human. Men will *insist*, to the end of all time, on enjoying the reward of their own labours, the triumphs of their own brains. Some may go so far as nominally to divide their honours with all their friends. But where shall we look for the man who will go on all his life toiling successfully for the good of idler folks, and checking his own free stride to keep pace with their feebler steps? And this is the rock on which all such communities inevitably strike.

Security from the ordinary apprehensions of life ; a

general protection against misfortune and " bad seasons;" the certainty of having all the necessaries of existence, are sufficient temptations for unambitious men. But the stronger class of mind, though attracted to it by piety, and retained for a while by a sincere desire to promote the common good, must from their very nature revolt against a permanent alienation of their own earnings, and a permanent subordination of their own merits. At Orderville, therefore, we find the young men already complaining of a system which does not let them see the fruits of their work. Their fathers' enthusiasm brought them there as children. Seven years later they are grown up into independent-minded young men. They have not had experience of family anxieties yet. All they know is, that beyond Orderville there are larger spheres of work, and more brilliant opportunities for both hand and head.

Fortunately, however, for Orderville, the articles of incorporation give the directors the very powers that are necessary, and if these are exercised the ship may miss the rock that has wrecked all its predecessors. If they can declare dividends, open private accounts, and realize the idea of personal property, the difference in *possibilities* between the outer world and Orderville will be very greatly reduced, while the advantage of *certainties* in Orderville will be even further increased. Young men would then think twice about going away, and any one if he chose could indulge his wife with a piano or himself with a box of water-colours. Herein then lies the hopefulness of the experiment; and fortunately Mr. Howard Spencer, the President of the community, has all the generosity to recognize the necessity for concession to younger ambition, and all the courage to institute and carry out a modification of communism which shall introduce more individuality.

I anticipate, therefore, that this very remarkable and interesting colony will survive the "twenty-five years" period for which it was established, and will encourage the foundation of many other similar " Family Orders."

Seven years have passed since Mr. Spencer pitched his camp in the beautiful wilderness of the Rio Virgin cañons. He found the hills of fine building-stone, their sides thickly grown with splendid pine timber, and down the valley between them flowing a bright and ample stream. The vegetation by its variety and luxuriance gave promise of a fertile soil ; some of the cañons formed excellent natural meadows, while just over the ridge, a mile or two from the settlement, lay a bed of coal. Finally, the climate was delightfully temperate ! Every condition of success, therefore, was found together, and prosperity has of course responded to the voice of industry. Acre by acre the wild gardens have disappeared, and in their place stand broad fields of corn; the tangled brakes of wild-berry plants have yielded their place to orchards of finer fruits; cattle and sheep now graze in numbers where the antelope used to feed ; and from slope to slope you can hear among the pines, above the idle crooning of answering doves and the tinkling responses of wandering kine, the glad antiphony of the whirring saw-mill and the busy loom.

The settlement itself is grievously disappointing in appearance. For as you approach it, past the charming little hamlet of Glendale, past such a sunny wealth of orchard and meadow and corn-land, past such beautiful glimpses of landscape, you cannot help expecting a scene of rural prettiness in sympathy with such surroundings. But Orderville at first sight looks like a factory. The wooden shed-like buildings built in continuous rows, the adjacent mills, the bare, ugly patch of hillside behind it, give the

actual settlement an uninviting aspect. But once within
the settlement, the scene changes wonderfully for the better.
The houses are found, the most of them, built facing in-
wards upon an open square, with a broad side-walk, edged
with tamarisk and mulberry, box-elder and maple-trees, in
front of them. Outside the dwelling-house square are
scattered about the school-house, meeting-house, blacksmith and carpenters' shops, tannery, woollen-mill, and so
forth, while a broad roadway separates the whole from the
orchards, gardens, and farm-lands generally. Specially
noteworthy here are the mulberry orchard—laid out for the
support of the silk-worms, which the community are now
rearing with much success—and the forcing-ground and
experimental garden, in which wild flowers as well as
" tame " are being cultivated. Among the buildings the
more interesting to me were the school-houses, well fitted
up, and very fairly provided with educational apparatus ; and
the rudimentary museum, where the commencement of a
collection of the natural curiosities of the neighbourhood is
displayed. What this may some day grow into, when
science has had the chance of exploring the surrounding
hills and cañons, it is difficult to say ; for Nature has favoured
Orderville profusely with fossil strata and mineral eccentricities, a rich variety of bird and insect life, and a prodigious
botanical luxuriance. Almost for the first time in my
travels, too, I found here a very intelligent interest taken in
the natural history of the locality ; but the absence of books
and of necessary apparatus, as yet of course prevents the
brethren from carrying on their studies and experiments to
any standard of scientific value.

Though staying in Orderville so short a time, I was
fortunate enough to see the whole community together.
For on the evening of my arrival there was a meeting at

which there was a very full gathering of the adults—and the babies in arms. The scene was as curious as anything I have ever witnessed in any part of the world. The audience was almost equally composed of men and women, the latter wearing, most of them, their cloth sun-bonnets, and bringing with them the babies they were nursing.

Brigham Young used to encourage mothers to bring them, and said that he liked to hear them squalling in the Tabernacle. Whether he really liked it or not, the mothers did as he said, and the babies too, and the perpetual bleating of babies from every corner of the building makes it seem to this day as if religious service was being held in a sheepfold. Throughout the proceedings at Orderville babies were being constantly handed across from mother to neighbour and back from neighbour to mother. Others were being tossed up and down with that jerky, perpendicular motion which seems so soothing to the very young, but which reminded me of the popping up and down of the hammers when the "lid" of a piano is lifted up during a performance. But the baby is an irrepressible person, and at Orderville has it very much its own way. The Apostle's voice in prayer was accepted as a challenge to try their lungs, and the music (very good, by the way) as a mere obligato to their own vocalization. The patient gravity of the mothers throughout the whole performance, and the apparent indifference of the men, struck me as very curious —for I come from a country where one baby will plunge a whole church congregation into profanity, and where it is generally supposed that *two* crying together would empty heaven. Of the men of Orderville I can say sincerely that a healthier, more stalwart community I have never seen, while among the women, I saw many refined faces, and remarked that robust health seemed the rule. Next

morning the children were paraded, and such a brigade
of infantry as it was !   Their legs (I think, though, they are
known as "limbs" in America) were positively columnar,
and their chubby little owners were as difficult to keep
quietly in line as so much quicksilver.   Orderville boasts
that it is self-supporting and independent of outside help,
and certainly in the matter of babies there seems no necessity for supplementing home manufactures by foreign
imports.   The average of births is as yet five in each family
during the six years of the existence of the Order !   Two
were born the day I arrived.

Unfortunately one of the most characteristic features of
this family community was in abeyance during my visit—
the common dining-table.   For a rain-flood swept through
the gorge above the settlement last winter and destroyed
"the bakery."   Since then the families have dined apart or
clubbed together in small parties, but the wish of the
majority is to see the old system revived, for though they
live well now, they used, they say, to live even better when
"the big table" was laid for its 200 guests at once.

Self-supporting and well-directed, therefore, the Orderville
"communists" bid fair to prove to the world that pious
enthusiasm, if largely tempered with business judgment, can
make a success of an experiment which has hitherto baffled
all attempts based upon either one or the other alone.

CHAPTER XIX.

MORMON VIRTUES.

Red ants and anti-Mormons—Ignorance of the Mormons among Gentiles in Salt Lake City—Mormon reverence for the Bible—Their struggle against drinking-saloons in the city—Conspicuous piety in the settlements—Their charity—Their sobriety (to my great inconvenience)—The literature of Mormonism utterly unreliable—Neglect of the press by the Saints—Explanation of the wide-spread misrepresentation of Mormonism.

From Orderville (after a short tour in the south-west of the Territory) I returned to Salt Lake City, and during my second sojourn there, over a month, I saw nothing and learned nothing either from Mormon or Gentile to induce me to erase a single word I had written during my previous visit. Indeed, a better acquaintance only strengthened my first favourable opinions of " the Saints of the Rocky Mountains."

I was walking one day up the City Creek, when I became aware of an aged man seated on a stone by the roadside. His trousers were turned up to his knees, and he was nursing one of his legs as if he felt a great pity for it. As I approached I perceived that he was in trouble—(I perceived this by his oaths)—and getting still nearer I ventured to inquire what annoyed him. " Aged person," said I, " what aileth thee ? "—or words to that effect. But there was no response, at least not worth mentioning. He only bent further over his leg, and I noticed that his coat had split down the back seam. His cursing accounted for that. It was sufficient to make any coat split. And then his hat fell off his head into the dust, in judgment upon him. At this he swore again, horribly. By this time I had guessed that he had been bitten by red ants (and they are the shrewdest reptiles at biting that I know of), so I said, "Bitten by red ants, eh?"   At this he exploded with wrath, and looked up.   And such a face ! He had a countenance on him like the ragged edge of despair. His appearance was a calamity.   "Red *ants*," said he; "red Indians, red devils, red hell!" and then, relapsing into the vernacular, he became unintelligibly profane, but ended up with "*this damned Mormon city*."

Now here was a man, fairly advanced in years, fairly clothed, fairly uneducated. As I had never seen him before, he may have been, for all I know, "the average American" I so often see referred to.   Anyhow, there he was, cursing the Mormons because he had been bitten by red ants ! Of his own stupidity he had gone and stood upon an ants' nest, thrust his hippopotamus foot into their domicile, overwhelming the nurseries and the parlours in a common catastrophe, crushing with the same heel the grandsire ant and the sucking babe at its mother's breast, mashing up the infirm and the feeble with the eggs in the cells and the household provisions laid up in the larder— ruining in fact an industrious community simply by his own weight in butcher's meat. Some of the survivors promptly attacked the intruding boot, and, running up what the old man was pleased to call "his blasted pants," had bitten the legs which they found concealed within them.   And for this, "the average American" cursed *the Mormons and their city !*

The incident interested me, for, apart from my sympathy with the ants, I couldn't help thinking what a powerful adversary to Mormonism this trifling mishap might have created. That man went back to his hotel (for he was evidently a "visitor") a confirmed *anti-*Mormon. His darkest suspicions about polygamy were confirmed. His detestation of the bestial licentiousness of the Saints was increased a hundred-fold. He saw at a glance that all he had ever heard about "the Danites" was quite true, and much more too that he had never heard but could now easily invent for himself. There was no need for any one to tell *him*, after the way he had been treated within a mile of the Tabernacle, of the infamous debaucheries of Brigham Young with his "Cyprian maids" and his "cloistered wives." Wasn't it as plain as the sun at noonday that the Mormons were in league with the red Indians, and went halves in the proceeds of each other's massacres?

The ant-bitten man was a very typical "Mormon-eater," for such is the local name of those who revile Mormonism root and branch because they find intelligent men opposed to polygamy. They are under the impression, seeing and talking to nobody but each other, that the United States in a mass, that the whole world, entertain an unreasoning, fanatical abhorrence of the inhabitants of the Territory, and share with them their mean parochial jealousy of the Mormon tradesmen and Mormon farmers who are more thriving than they are themselves.

Here in Salt Lake City there is the most extraordinary ignorance of Mormonism that can be imagined. I have actually been assured by "Gentiles" that the Saints do not believe in the God of the Bible—that adultery among them is winked at by husbands under a tacit understanding of reciprocity—that the Mormons as a class are profane, and drunken, and so forth. Now, if they knew anything whatever of the Mormons, such statements would be impossible (unless of course made in wilful malice), for my personal acquaintance with "the Saints" has shown me that in all classes alike the reverence for the God of the Bible is formulated not only in their morning and evening prayers, but in their grace before every meal; that so far from there being any exceptional familiarity between families, the very reverse is conspicuous, for so strict is the Mormon etiquette of social courtesies, that households which in England would be on the most intimate terms, maintain here a distant formality which impresses the stranger as being cold; that instead of the Mormons being as a class profane, they are as a class singularly sober in their language, and indeed in this respect resemble the Quakers. Now, *my* opinions are founded upon facts of personal knowledge and experience.

Of course it will be said of me that as I was a "guest" of Mormons I was "bound" to speak well of them; that as I was so much among them I was hoodwinked and "shown the best side of everything," &c., &c. Against this argument, always the resource of the gobemouche, common sense is useless. "Against stupidity the gods themselves are powerless." But this I can say—that I will defy any really impure household, monogamous or not, to hoodwink me in the same way—to keep up from morning to night the same unchanging profession of piety, to make believe from week to week with such consummate hypocrisy that they are god-fearing and pure in their lives, and to wear a mask of sobriety with such uniform success. And I am not speaking of one household only, but of a score to which I was admitted simply as being a stranger from whom they need not fear calumny. I do not believe that acting exists anywhere in such perfection that a whole community can assume, at a few hours' notice and for the benefit of a passing stranger, the characters of honest, kind-hearted, simple men and women, and set themselves patiently to a three months' comedy of pretended purity. Such impostors do not exist.

The Mormons drunken! Now what, for instance, can be the conclusion of any honest thinker from *this* fact—that though I mixed constantly with Mormons, all of them anxious to show me every hospitality and courtesy, I was never at any time asked to take a glass of strong drink? If I wanted a horse to ride or to drive I had a choice at once offered me. If I wanted some one to go with me to some point of interest, his time was mine. Yet it never occurred to them to show a courtesy by suggesting " a drink."

Then, seriously, how can any one have respect for the literature or the men who, without knowing anything of the lives of Mormons, stigmatize them as profane, adulterous, and *drunken ?* As a community I know them, from personal advantages of observation such as no non-Mormon writer has ever previously possessed,[1] to be at any rate exceptionally careful in maintaining the *appearance* of piety and sobriety; and I leave it to my readers to judge whether such solid hypocrisy as this, that tries to abolish all swearing and all strong drink both by precept from the pulpit and example in the household, is not, after all, nearly as admirable as the real thing itself.

This, at all events, is beyond doubt—that the Mormons have always struggled hard to prevent the sale of liquor in Salt Lake City, except under strict regulations and supervision. But the fight has gone against them. The courts uphold the right of publicans to sell when and what they choose; and the Mormons, who could at one time boast—and visi-

[1] Except, of course, General Kane.

tors without number have borne evidence to the fact—that
a drunkard was never to be seen, an oath never to be heard,
in the streets of their city, have now to confess that, thanks
to the example of Gentiles, they have both drunkards and
profane men among them.   But the general attitude of the
Church towards these delinquents, and the sorrow that their
weakness causes in the family circle, are in themselves proofs
of the sincerity in sobriety which distinguishes the Mormons.   Nor is it any secret that if the Mormons had the
power they would to-morrow close all the saloons and bars,
except those under Church regulation, and then, they say,
" we might hope to see the old days back when we never
thought of locking our doors at night, and when our wives
and girls, let them be out ever so late, needed no escort in
the streets."

And having travelled throughout the Mormon settlements,
I am at a loss how to convey to my readers with any
brevity the effect which the tour has had upon me.

I have seen, and spoken to, and lived with, Mormon men
and women of every class, and never in my life in any
Christian country, not even in happy, rural England,
have I come in contact with more consistent piety, sobriety, and neighbourly charity.   I say this deliberately.
Without a particle of odious sanctimony these folk are,
in their words and actions, as *Christian* as I had ever
thought to see men and women.   A perpetual spirit
of charity seems to possess them, and if the prayers of
simple, devout humanity are ever of any avail, it must
surely be this wonderful Mormon earnestness in appeals to
Heaven.   I have often watched Moslems in India praying,
and thought then that I had seen the extremity of devotion,
but now that I have seen these people on their knees in
their kitchens at morning and at night, and heard their old

men—men who remember the dark days of the Faith—
pour out from their hearts their gratitude for past mercy,
their pleas for future protection, I find that I have met
with even a more striking form of prayer than I have
ever met with before. Equally striking is the universal
reverence and affection with which they, quite unconscious
of the fact that I was "taking notes," spoke of the authorities of their Church. Fear there was none, but respect
and love were everywhere. It would be a bold man who,
in one of these Mormon hamlets, ventured to repeat the
slanders current among Gentiles elsewhere. And it would
indeed be a base man who visited these hard-living,
trustful men and women, and then went away to calumniate
them.

But it is a fact, and cannot be challenged, that the only
people in all Utah who libel these Mormons are either
those who are ignorant of them, those who have apostatized
(frequently under compulsion) from the Church, or those, the
official clique and their sycophants, who have been charged
with looking forward to a share of the plunder of the Territorial treasury. On the other hand, I know many Gentiles
who, though like myself they consider polygamy itself
detestable, speak of this people as patterns to themselves
in commercial honesty, religious earnestness, and social
charity.

Travelling through the settlements, I found that every
one voluntarily considered his poorer neighbours as a charge
upon himself. When a man arrives there, a stranger and
penniless, one helps to get together logs for his first hut,
another to break up a plot of ground. A third lends him
his waggon to draw some firewood from the cañon or hill-
side; a fourth gives up some of his time to show him how
to bring the water on to his ground—and so on through

R

all the first requirements of the forlorn new-comer. Behind them all meanwhile is the Church, in the person of the presiding Elder of the settlement, who makes him such advances as are considered necessary. It is a wonderful system, and as pathetic, to my mind, as any struggle for existence that I have ever witnessed. But every man who comes among them is another unit of strength, and let him be only a straight-spoken, fair-dealing fellow, with his heart in his work, and he finds every one's hand ready to assist him.

And the first commencement is terribly small. A one-roomed log hut is planted in a desert of sage-brush " with roots that hold as firm as original sin," and rocks that are as hard to get rid of as bad habits. Borrowing a plough here, and a shovel there, the new-comer bungles through an acre or two of furrows, and digs out a trench. Begging of one neighbour some fruit-tree cuttings, he sticks the discouraging twigs into the ground, and by working out some extra time for another gets some lucerne seed. Then he gets a hen, and then a setting of eggs, by-and-by a heifer, and a little later, by putting in work or by an advance from the Church, or with kindly help from a neighbour, he adds a horse to his stock. Time passes, say a year; his orchard (that is to be) has several dozen leaves on it, and the ground is all green with lucerne, the chickens are thriving, and he adds an acre or two more to the first patch, and his neighbours, seeing him in earnest, are still ready with their advice and aid. Adobe bricks are gradually piled up in a corner of the lot, and very soon an extra room or two is built on to the log hut, and saplings of cotton-wood, or poplar, or locust are planted in a row before the dwelling: and so on year by year, conquering a little more of the sage-brush, bringing on the water a furlong further, adding an outhouse, planting another tree. At the end of ten years—years of unsparing, untiring labour, but years brightened with perpetual kindness from neighbours—this man, the penniless emigrant, invites the wayfarer into his house, has a comfortably furnished bedroom at his service, oats and fodder for his team, ample and wholesome food for all. The wife spreads the table with eggs and ham and chicken, vegetables, pickles, and preserves, milk and cream, pies and puddings,—" Yes, sir, all of our own raising." The dismal twigs have grown up into pleasant shade-trees, and a flower-garden brightens the front of the house. In the barn are comfortable, well-fed stock, horses and cows. This is no fancy picture, but one from life, and typical of 20,000 others. Each homestead in turn has the same experience, and it is no wonder, therefore, when the settlement, properly laid out and organized, grows into municipal existence, that every one speaks kindly of, and acts kindly towards, his neighbour. A visitor, till he understands the reason, is surprised at the intimacy of households. But when he does understand it, ought not his surprise to give place to admiration?

Not less conspicuous is the uniform sincerity in religion. A school and meeting-house is to be found in every settlement, even though there may be only half-a-dozen families, and besides the regular attendance of the people at weekly services, the private prayers of each household are as punctual as their meals. In these prayers, after the ordinary generalities, the head of the house usually prays for all the authorities of the Church, from the President downwards, for the local authorities, for the Church as a body, and the missionaries abroad, for his household and its guest, for the United States, and for Congress, and for all the world that feels kindly towards Mormonism.

But quite apart from the matter of their prayers, their manner is very striking, and the scene in a humble house, when a large family meets for prayer—and half the members, finding no article of furniture unoccupied for the orthodox position of devotion, drop into attitudes of natural reverence, kneeling in the middle of the floor— appeals very strongly to the eye of those accustomed to the stereotyped piety of a more advanced civilization.

One more conspicuous feature of Mormon life is sobriety. I have been the guest of some fifty different households, and only once I was offered even beer. That exception was in a Danish household, where the wife brewed her own " öl "—an opaque beverage of home-fermented wheat and home-grown hops—as a curiosity curious, as an "indulgence " doubtful, as a regular drink impossible. On no other occasion was anything but tea, coffee, milk, or water offered. And even tea and coffee, being discouraged by the Church, are but seldom drunk. As a heathen outsider I deplored my beer, and was grateful for coffee ; but the rest of the household, in almost every instance, drank *water*. Tobacco is virtually unused. It *is* used, but so seldom that it does not affect my statement. The spittoon, therefore, though in every room, is behind the door, or in a corner under a piece of furniture. In case it should be needed, it is there—like the shot-gun upstairs— but its being called into requisition would be a family event.

No, let their enemies say what they will, the Mormon settlements are each of them to-day a refutation of the libel that the Mormons are not sincere in their antipathy to strong drink and tobacco. That individual Mormons drink and smoke proves nothing, except that *they* do it. For the great majority of the Mormons, they are strictly sober. I know it to my great inconvenience.

Is it possible then that the American people, so generous in their impulses, so large-hearted in action, have been misled as to the true character of the Mormon "problem"? At first sight this may seem impossible. A whole people, it will be said, cannot have been misled. But I think a general misapprehension is quite within the possibilities.

Whence have the public derived their opinions about Mormonism? *From anti-Mormons only.* I have ransacked the literature of the subject, and yet I really could not tell any one where to go for an impartial book about Mormonism later in date than Burton's "City of the Saints," published in 1862. Burton, it is well known, wrote as a man of wide travel and liberal education— catholic, therefore, on all matters religious, and generous in his views of ethical and social obliquities, sympathetic, consistent, and judicial. It is no wonder, then, that Mormons remember the distinguished traveller, in spite of his candour, with the utmost kindness. But put Burton on one side, and I think I can defy any one to name another book about the Mormons worthy of honest respect. From that truly *awful* book, "The History of the Saints," published by one Bennett (even an anti-Mormon has styled him "the greatest rascal that ever came to the West") in 1842, down to Stenhouse's in 1873, there is not, to my knowledge, a single Gentile work before the public that is not utterly unreliable from its distortion of facts. Yet it is from these books—for there are no others—that the American public has acquired nearly all its ideas about the people of Utah.

The Mormons themselves are most foolishly negligent of the power of the press, and of the immense value in forming public opinion of a free use of type. They affect to be indifferent to the clamour of the world, but when this clamour leads to legislative action against them, they turn round petulantly with the complaint that there is a universal conspiracy against them. It does not seem to occur to them that their misfortunes are partly due to their own neglect of the very weapons which their adversaries have used so diligently, so unscrupulously, and so successfully.

They do not seem to understand that a public contradiction given to a public calumny goes some way towards correcting the mischief done, or that by anticipating malicious versions of events they could as often as not get an accurate statement before the public, instead of an inaccurate one. But enterprise in advertisement has been altogether on the side of the anti-Mormons. The latter never lose an opportunity of throwing in a bad word, while the Mormons content themselves with " rounding their shoulders," as they are so fond of saying, and putting a denial of the libel into the local *News.* They say they are so accustomed to abuse that they are beginning not to care about it—which is the old, stupid self-justification of the apathetic. The fascination of a self-imposed martyrdom seems too great for them, and, like flies when they are being wrapped up into parcels by the spider for greater convenience of transportation to its larder, they sing chastened canticles about the inevitability of cobwebs and the deplorable rapacity of spiders.

" I can assure you," said one of them, " it would be of no use trying to undeceive the public. You cannot make a whistle out of a pig's tail, you know."

" Nonsense," I replied. " *You can*—for I have *seen* a whistle made out of a pig's tail. And it is in a shop in Chicago to this day ! "

It will be understood, then, that the Mormons have made no adequate efforts either in books or the press to meet their antagonists. They prefer to allow cases against them to go by default, and content themselves with privately filing pleas in defence which would have easily acquitted them had they gone before the public. America, therefore, hearing only one side of the case, and so much of it, is certainly not to be blamed for drawing its conclusions from the only facts before it. It cannot be expected to know that three or four individuals, all of them by their own confession "Mormon-eaters," have from the first been the purveyors of nearly all the distorted facts it receives. Seeing the same thing said in many different directions, the general public naturally conclude that a great number of persons are in agreement as to the facts.

But the exigencies of journalism which admit, for instance, of the same correspondent being a local contributor to two or three score newspapers of widely differing views in politics and religion, are unknown to them. And they are therefore unaware that the indignation so widely printed throughout America has its source in the personal animosity of three or four individuals only who are bitterly sectarian, and that these men are actually personally ignorant of the country they live in, have seldom talked to a Mormon, and have never visited Mormonism outside Salt Lake City. These men write of the "squalid poverty" of Mormons, of their obscene brutality, of their unceasing treason towards the United States, of their blasphemous repudiation of the Bible, without one particle of information on the subject, except such as they gather from the books and writings of men whom they ought to know are utterly unworthy of credit, or from the verbal calumnies of apostates. And what the evidence of apostates is worth history has long ago told us. I am now stating facts; and I, who have lived *among* the Mormons and with them, who have seen them in their homes, rich and poor ; have joined in their worship, public and private ; who have constantly conversed with them, men, women, and children; who have visited their out-lying settlements, large and small— as no Gentile has ever done before me—can assure my readers that every day of my residence increased my regret at the misrepresentation these people have suffered.

CHAPTER XX.

DOWN THE ONTARIO MINE.

"*Been down a mine!* What on earth did you do that for?" said the elder Sheridan to the younger.

"Oh, just to say that I *had* done it," was the reply.

"To *say* that you had done it! Good gracious! Couldn't you have said that *without going down a mine?*"

No, Mr. Sheridan, you could not; at least not in these latter days. Too many people do it now for the impostor to remain undiscovered. Take my own case, for instance. I had often read descriptions of mine descents, and thought I knew how it happened, and how ore was got out. But no one ever told me that you had to go paddling about in water half the time, or that mines were excavated upwards. Now, then, if I had tried to pretend that I had been down a mine I should have been promptly found out, by my ignorance of the two first facts that strike one. Again, it is very simple work imagining the descent of a "shaft" in a "cage." But unfortunately a cage is only a platform to stand on without either sides or top, and not, therefore, such a cage as one would buy to keep a bird in, or as would keep a bird in if one *did* buy it. Nor, without actually experiencing it, could anybody guess that the first sensation of whizzing down a pipe, say 800 feet, is that of seeming to lose all your specific gravity, and that the next (after you had partially collected your faculties) is that you are stationary yourself, but that the dripping timbers that line the shaft are all flying upwards past you like sparks up a chimney.

Mines, of course, differ from one another just as the men who go down them do, but as far as I myself am concerned all mines are puddly places, and the sensations of descent are ridiculous—for I have only been down two in my life, and both "demned, damp, moist, unpleasant" places. But the mine to which I now refer is the "Ontario," in Utah, which may be said, in the preposterous vernacular of the West, to be a "terrible fine" mine, or, in other words, "a boss mine," that is to say, "a daisy."

As for daisies, anything that greatly takes the fancy or evokes especial admiration is called a daisy. Thus I heard a very much respected Mormon Bishop, who is also a director of a railway, described by an enthusiastic admirer as "*a daisy!*"

Finding myself in Park "City" one evening—it is a mining camp dependent chiefly upon the Ontario—I took a walk up the street with a friend. Every other house appeared to be a saloon, with a doctor's residence sandwiched in between—a significantly convenient arrangement perhaps in the days when there was no "Protective Committee" in Park City, but—so I am told—without much practical benefit to the public in these quiet days, when law-abiding citizens do their own hanging, without troubling the county sheriff, who lives somewhere on the other side of a distance. The result of this is that bad characters do not stay long enough in Park City now to get up free fights, and make work for the doctors. The Protective

Committee invites them to "git" as soon as they arrive, and, to do them credit, they do "git."

However, as I was saying, I took a walk with a friend along the street, and presently became aware above me, high up on the hillside, of a great collection of buildings, with countless windows (I mean that I did not try to count them) lit up, and looking exactly like some theatrical night-scene. These were the mills of the Ontario, which work night and day, and seven days to the week, a perpetual flame like that of the Zoroastrians, and as carefully kept alive by stalwart stokers as ever was Vestal altar-fire by the girl-priestesses of Rome. It was a picturesque sight, with the huge hills looming up black behind, and the few surviving pine-trees showing out dimly against the darkening sky.

Next morning I went up to the mine—and down it

Having costumed myself in garments that made getting dirty a perfect luxury, I was taken to the shaft. Now, I had expected to see an unfathomably black hole in the ground with a rope dangling down it, but instead of that I found myself in a spacious boarded shed, with a huge wheel standing at one end and a couple of iron uprights with a cross-bar standing up from the floor at the other. Round the wheel was coiled an enormous length of a six-inch steel-wire band, and the disengaged end of the band, after passing over a beam, was fastened to the cross-bar above mentioned. On the bridge of the wheel stood an engineer, the arbiter of fates, who is perpetually unwinding victims down from stage to stage of the Inferno, and winding up the redeemed from limbo to limbo. Having propitiated him by an affectation of intelligence as to the machinery which he controlled, we took our places under the cross-bar, between the stanchions, and suddenly the floor—as innocent-looking and upright-minded a bit of boarded floor as you could wish to stand on—gave way beneath us, and down we shot *apud inferos*, like the devils in "Der Freischütz." We had our lamps in our hands, and they gave just light enough for me to see the dripping wooden walls of the shaft flashing past, and then I felt myself becoming lighter and lighter—a mere butterfly— imponderable. But it doesn't take many seconds to fall down 800 feet, and long before I had expected it I found we were "at the bottom."

Our explorations then began; and very queer it all was, with the perpetual gushing of springs from the rock, and the bubble and splash of the waters as they ran along on either side the narrow tunnels; the meetings at corners with little cars being pushed along by men who looked, as they bent low to their work, like those load-rolling beetles that Egypt abounds in; the machinery for pump- ing, so massive that it seemed much more likely that it was found where it stood, the vestiges of a long-past sub- terranean civilization, than that it had been brought down there by the men of these degenerate days; the sudden endings of the tunnels which the miners were driving along the vein, with a man at each ending, his back bent to fit into the curve which he had made in the rock, and reminding one of the frogs that science tells us are found at times fitted into holes in the middle of stones; the climbing up hen-roost ladders from tunnel to tunnel, from one darkness into another; the waiting at different spots till "that charge had been blasted," and the dull, deadened roar of the explosion had died away; the watching the solitary miners at their work picking and thumping at the discoloured strips of dark rock that looked to the uninitiated only like water-stained, mildewy accidents in the general structure, but which, in reality, was silver, and yielding, it might be, $1600 to the ton !

" This is all very rich ore," said my guide, kicking a heap that I was standing on. I got off it at once, reverentially.

But reverence for the Mother of the Dollar gradually dies out, for everything about you, above you, beneath you, is silver or silverish—dreadful rubbish to look at, it is true, but with the spirit of the great metal in it all none the less ; that fairy Argentine who builds palaces for men, and gives them, if they choose, all the pleasures of the world, and the leisure wherein to enjoy them. And there they stood, these latter-day Cyclops, working away like the gnomes of the Hartz Mountains, or the entombed artificers of the Bear-Kings of Dardistan, with their lanterns glowing at the end of their tunnels like the Kanthi gem which Shesh, the fabled snake-god, has provided for his gloomy empire of mines under the Nagas' hills. Useless crystals glittered on every side, as if they were jewels, and the water dripping down the sides glistened as if it was silver, but the pretty hypocrisy was of no avail. For though the ore itself was dingy and ugly and uninviting, the ruthless pick pursued it deeper and deeper into its retreat, and only struck the harder the darker and uglier it got. It reminded me, watching the miner at his work, of the fairy story where the prince in disguise has to kill the lady of his love in order to release her from the enchantments which have transformed her, and how the wicked witch makes her take shape after shape to escape the resolute blows of the desperate lover. But at last his work is accomplished, and the ugly thing stands before him in all the radiant beauty of her true nature.

And it is a long process, and a costly one, before the 'umps of heavy dirt which the miner pecks out of the

inside of a hill are transformed into those hundredweight
blocks of silver bullion which the train from Park City
carries every morning of the year into Salt Lake City.
From first to last it is pretty much as follows.   Remember
I am not writing for those who live inside mines ; very
much on the contrary.   I am writing for those who have
never been down a mine in their lives, but who may care
to read an unscientific description of " mining," and the
Ontario mine in particular.

In 1872 a couple of men made a hole in the ground,
and finding silver ore in it offered the hole for sale at
$30,000.   A clever man, R. C. Chambers by name, hap-
pened to come along, and liking the look of the hole,
joined a friend in the purchase of it.   The original diggers
thus pocketed $30,000 for a few days' work, and no
doubt thought they had done a good thing.   But alas !
that hole in the ground which they were so glad to get
rid of ten years ago now yields *every day* a larger sum in
dollars than they sold it for !   The new owners of the hole,
which was christened " The Ontario Mine," were soon at
work, but instead of following them through the different
stages of development, it is enough to describe what that
hole looks like and produces to-day.

A shaft, then, has been sunk plumb down into the mountain for 900 feet, and from this shaft, at every 100 feet as
you go down, you find a horizontal tunnel running off to
right and left.   If you stop in your descent at any one of
these " stages " and walk through the tunnel—water rushing
all the way over your feet, and the vaulted rock dripping overhead—you will find that a line of rails has been laid down
along it, and that the sides and roofs are strongly supported
by timbers of great thickness.   These timbers are necessary
to prevent, in the first place, the rock above from crushing

down through the roof of the tunnel, and, in the next, from squeezing in its sides, for the rock every now and then swells and the sides of the tunnels bulge in. The rails are, of course, for the cars which the miners fill with ore, and push from the end of the tunnel to the "stage." A man there signals by a bell which communicates with the engineer at the big wheel in the shed I have already spoken of, and there being a regular code of signals, the engineer knows at once at which stage the car is waiting, and how far therefore he is to let the cage down. Up goes the car with its load of ore into the daylight,—and then its troubles begin.

But meanwhile let us stay a few minutes more in the mine. Walking along any one of the main horizontal tunnels, we come at intervals to a ladder, and going up one of them we find that a stope, or smaller gallery, is being run parallel with the tunnel in which we are walking, and of course (as it follows the same direction of the ore), immediately over that tunnel, so that the roof of the tunnel is the floor of the stope. The stopes are just wide enough for a man to work in easily, and are as high as he can reach easily with his pickaxe, about seven feet. If you walk along one of these stopes you come to another ladder, and find it leads to another stope above, and going up this you find just the same again, until you become aware that the whole mountain above you is pierced throughout the length of the ore vein by a series of seven-foot galleries lying exactly parallel one above the other, and separated only by a sufficient thickness of pine timber to make a solid floor for each. But at every hundred feet, as I have said, there comes a main tunnel, down to which all the produce of the minor galleries above it is shot down by "shoots," loaded into cars and pushed along to the "stage."

'But silver ore is not the only thing that the Company gets out of its mine, for unfortunately the mountain in which the Ontario is located is full of springs, and the miner's pick is perpetually, therefore, letting the water break into the tunnels, and in such volume, too, that I am informed it costs as much to rid the works of the water as to get out the silver! Streams gurgle along all the tunnels, and here and there ponderous bulkheads have been put up to keep the water and the loosened rock from falling in. Pumps of tremendous power are at work at several levels throwing the water up towards the surface—one of these at the 800-foot level throwing 1500 gallons a minute up to the 500-foot level.

Following a car-load of ore, we find it, having reached the surface, being loaded into waggons, in which it is carried down the hill to the mills, weighed, and then shot down into a gigantic bin—in which, by the way, the Company always keeps a reserve of ore sufficient to keep the mills in full work for two years. From this hour, life becomes a burden to the ore, for it is hustled about from machine to machine without the least regard to its feelings. No sooner is it out of the waggon than a brutal crusher begins smashing it up into small fragments, the result of this meanness being that the ore is able to tumble through a screen into cars that are waiting for it down below. These rush upstairs with it again and pour it into " hoppers," which, being in the conspiracy too, begin at once to spill it into gigantic drying cylinders that are perpetually revolving over a terrific furnace fire, and the ore, now dust, comes streaming out as dry as dry can be, is caught in cars and wheeled off to batteries where forty stampers, stamping like one, pound and smash it as if they took a positive delight in it. There is an intelligent, deliberate determination about this fearful stamping which makes one feel almost afraid of the machinery. Some pieces, however, actually manage to escape sufficient mashing up and slip away with the rest down into a "screw conveyor," but the poor wretches are soon found out, for the fiendish screw conveyor empties itself on to a screen, through which all the pulverized ore goes shivering down, but the guilty lumps still remaining are carried back by another ruthlesss machine to those detestable stamps again. They cannot dodge them. For these machines are all in the plot together. Or rather, they are the honest workmen of good masters, and they are determined that the work shall be thoroughly done, and that not a single lump of ore shall be allowed to skulk. So without any one to look after them these cylinders and stampers, hoppers and dryers, elevators and screens go on with their work all day, all night, relentless in their duty and pitiless to the ore. Let a lump dodge them as it may, it gets no good by it, for the one hands it over to the other, just as constables hand over a thief they have caught, and it goes its rounds, again and again, till the end eventually overtakes it, and it falls through the screen in a fine dust.

For its sins it is now called " pulp," and starts off on a second tour of suffering—for these Inquisitors of iron and steel, these blind, brutal Cyclops-machines, have only just begun, as it were, their fun with their victim. Its tortures are now to be of a more searching and refined description. As it falls through the screen, another screw-conveyor catches sight of it and hurries it along a revolving tube into which salt is being perpetually fed from a bin overhead—this salt, allow me to say for the benefit of those as ignorant as myself, is " necessary as a chloridizer "—and thus mixed up with the stranger, falls into the power of a hydraulic elevator, which carries it up forty feet to the top of a roast-

s

ing furnace and deliberately spills the mixture into it! Looking into the solid flame, I appreciated for the first time in my life the courage of Shadrach, Meshach, and Abednego.

The mixture which fell in at the top bluish-grey comes out at the bottom yellowish-brown—I only wonder at its coming out all—and is raked into heaps that have a wicked, lurid colour and give out such fierce short flames of brilliant tints, and such fierce, short blasts of a poisonous gas, that I could not help thinking of the place where bad men go to, and wondering if a Dante could not get a hint or two for improving his Inferno by a visit to the Ontario roasting-furnace. The men who stir these heaps use rakes with prodigious handles, and wear wet sponges over their mouths and noses, and as I watched them I remembered the poet's devils who keep on prodding up the damned and raking them about over the flames.

But the ore submits without any howling or gnashing of teeth, and is dragged off dumb, and soused into great churns, kept at a boiling heat, in which quicksilver is already lying waiting, and the ore and the quicksilver are then churned up together by revolving wheels inside the pans, till the contents look like huge caldrons of bubbling chocolate. After some hours they are drained off into settlers and cold water is let in upon the mess, and lo ! silver as bright as the quicksilver with which it is mixed comes dripping out through the spout at the bottom into canvas bags.

Much of the quicksilver drips through the canvas back into the pans, and the residue, silver mixed with quicksilver, makes a cold, heavy, white paste called " amalgam," which is carried off in jars to the retorts. Into these it is thrown, and while lying there the quicksilver goes on dripping away from the silver, and after a time the fires are lighted and the retort is sealed up. The intense heat that is obtained volatilizes the quicksilver; but this mercurial vapour is caught as it is escaping at the top of the retort, again condensed into its solid form, and again used to mix with fresh silver ore. Its old companion, the silver, goes on melting inside the retort all the time, till at last when the fires are allowed to cool down, it is found in irregular lumps of a pink-looking substance. These lumps are then taken to the crucibles, and passing from them, molten and refined, fall into moulds, each holding about a hundred-weight of bullion.

And all this bother and fuss, reader, to obtain these eight or ten blocks of metal !

True, but then that metal is *silver*, and with one single day's produce from the Ontario Mine in the bank to his credit a man might live at his leisure in London, like a nobleman in Paris, or like a prince among the princes of Eulenspiegel-Wolfenbüttel-Gutfürnichts.

CHAPTER XXI.

FROM UTAH INTO NEVADA.

Rich and ugly Nevada—Leaving Utah—The gift of the Alfalfa—
Through a lovely country to Ogden—The great food-devouring
trick—From Mormon to Gentile : a sudden contrast—The son
of a cinder—Is the red man of no use at all ?—The papoose's
papoose—Children all of one family.

IT is a far cry from the City of the Saints to the city of the
Celestials, for Nevada stretches all its hideous length between them, and thus keeps apart the two American problems of the day—pigtails and polygamy. But mere length
in miles is not all that goes to make a journey seem long,
for dreariness of landscape stretches every yard to six feet,
and turns honest miles into rascally versts, or elongates them
into the still more infamous "kos" of the East, the so-called
mile, which seems to lengthen out at the other end as you
travel along it, and about nightfall to lose the other end altogether. And Nevada is certainly dreary enough for anything. It is abominably rich, I know. There is probably
more filthy lucre in it per acre (in a crude state, of course)
than in any other state in the Union, and more dollars
piled up in those ghastly mountains than in any other range
in America. But, as a fellow-passenger remarked, "There's
a pile of land in Nevada that don't amount to much," and it
is just this part of Nevada that the traveller by railway sees.

"That hill over there is full of silver," said a stranger to
me, by way of propitiating my opinion.

" Is it ?" I said, " *the brute.*" I really couldn't help it. I had no ill-feeling towards the hill, and if it had asked a favour of me, I believe I should have granted it as readily as any one. But its repulsive appearance was against it, and the idea of its being full of silver stirred my indignation. I grudged so ugly a cloud its silver lining, and like the sailor in the Summer Palace at Pekin felt moved to insult it. The sailor I refer to was in one of the courts of the palace looking about for plunder. It did not occur to his weather-beaten, nautical intelligence that everything about him was moulded in solid silver. He thought it was lead. A huge dragon stood in the corner of the room, and the atrocity of its expression exasperated Jack so acutely that he smote it with his cutlass, and lo ! out of the monster's wound poured an ichor of silver coinage.

" Who'd have thought it ! " said Jack, " *the ugly devil !* "

Nevada, moreover, lies under the disadvantage of having on one side of it the finest portion of California, on the other the finest portion of Utah, and sandwiched between two such Beauties, such a Beast naturally looks its worst. For the northern angle of Utah is by far the most fertile part of the territory, possessing, in patches, some incomparable meadows, and corn-lands of wondrous fertility. As compared with the prodigious agricultural and pastoral wealth of such states as Missouri, Illinois, or Ohio, the Cache Valleys and Bear Valleys of Utah seem of course insignificant enough ; but at present I am comparing them only with the rest of poor Utah, and with ugly, wealthy Nevada.

Starting from Salt Lake City northwards, the road lies through suburbs of orchards and gardens, many of them smothered in red and yellow roses, out on to the levels of the Great Valley. Here, beyond the magic circle of the Water-wizard, there are patches of fen-lands still delightful to wild-fowl, and patches of alkali blistering in the sun, but all about them stretch wide meadows of good grazing-ground, where the cattle, good Devon breed many of them, and here and there a Jersey, loiter about, and bright fields of lucerne, or alfalfa, just purpling into blossom and haunted by whole nations of bees and tribes of yellow butterflies. What a gift this lucerne has been to Utah! Indeed, as the Mormons say, the territory could hardly have held its own had it not been for this wonderful plant. Once get it well started (and it will grow apparently anywhere) the "alfalfa" strikes its roots ten, fifteen, twenty feet into the ground, and defies the elements. More than this, it becomes aggressive, and, like the white races, begins to encroach upon, dominate' over, and finally extinguish the barbarian weeds, its wild neighbours.

Scientific experiments with other plants have taught us that vegetables wage war with each other, under principles and with tactics, curiously similar to those of human communities.

When a strong plant advancing its frontiers comes upon a nation of feeble folk, it simply falls upon it pell-mell, relying upon mere brute strength to crush opposition. But when two plants, equally hardy, come in contact, and the necessity for more expansion compels them to fight, they bring into action all the science and skill of old gladiators and German war-professors. They push out skirmishers, and draw them in, throw out flanking parties, plant outposts, race for commanding points, manœuvre each other out of corners, cut off each others' communications with the water, sap and mine —in fact go through all the artifices of civilized war. If they find themselves well-matched, they eventually make an alliance, and mingle peacefully with each other, dividing the richer spots equally, and going halves in the water. But as a rule one gives way to the other, accepts its dominion, and gradually accepts a subordinate place or even extirpation.

Now this lucerne is one of the fightingest plants that grows. It is the Norwegian rat among the vegetables, the Napoleon of the weeds. Nothing stops it. If it comes upon a would-be rival, it either punches its head and walks over it, or it sits down to besiege it, drives its own roots under the enemy, and compels it to capitulate by starvation. Fences and such devices cannot of course keep it within bounds, so the lucerne overflows its limits at every point, comes down the railway bank, sprouts up in tufts on the track, and getting across into the Scythian barbarism of the opposite hill-side, advances as with a Macedonian phalanx to conquest and universal monarchy. Three times a year can the farmer crop it, and there is no fodder in the world that beats it. No wonder then that Utah encourages this admirable adventurer. In time it will become the Lucerne State.

And so, passing through fields of lucerne, we reach the Hot Springs. From a cleft in a rock comes gushing out an ample stream of nearly boiling water as clear as diamonds, and so heavily charged with mineral that the sulphuretted air, combined with the heat, is sometimes intolerable, while the ground over which the water pours becomes in a few weeks thickly carpeted with a lovely weed-like growth of purest malachite green. Passing across the road, from its first pool under the rock, the stream spreads itself out into the Hot Springs Lake, where the water soon assimilates in temperature to the atmosphere, but possesses, for some reason known to the birds, a peculiar attraction for wild-fowl, which congregate in great numbers about it. Where it issues from the rock no vegetable of course can grow in it, and there is a rim all round its edge about a foot in width where the grass and weeds lie brown and dead, suffocated by the fumes. The fungoid-like growth at the bottom of the pool exactly resembles a vegetable, but is as purely mineral, though sub-aqueous, as the stalactites on a cave-roof.

And so, on again through a wilderness of lucerne, with a broad riband of carnation-coloured phlox retreating before its advancing borders—past a perpetual succession of cottages coming at intervals to a head in delightful farming hamlets of the true Mormon type—past innumerable orchards, and here and there intervals of wild vegetation, willows, and cotton-wood, with beds of blue iris, and brakes of wild pink roses (such a confusion of beauty !) among which the birds and butterflies seem to hold perpetual holiday.

Then Salt Lake comes in sight, lying along under the mountains on the left, and on the right the Wasatch range closes in, with the upper slopes all misty with grey clouds of sage-brush, and the lower vivid with lusty lucerne. Each settlement is in turn a delightful repetition of its predecessor, meadow and orchard and corn-land alternating, with the same pleasant features of wild life, flocks of crimson-winged or yellow-throated birds wheeling round the willow copses, or skimming across the meadows, bitterns tumbling out from among the reeds, doves darting from tree to tree, butterflies of exquisite species fluttering among the beds of flowers, and overhead in the sky, floating on observant wings, the hawk—one of those significant touches of Nature that redeems a country-side from Arcadian mawkishness, and throws into an over-sweet landscape just that dash of sin and suffering that lemons it pleasantly to the taste.

Round the corner yonder lies Ogden, one of the most promising towns of all the West, and as we approach it the great expanses of meadow stretching down to the lake and the wide alfalfa levels give place to a barren sage *veldt*, where the sunflower still retains ancestral dominion, and the jackass rabbits flap their ears at each other undisturbed by agriculture or by grazing stock. Nestling back into a nook of the hills which rise up steeply behind it, and show plainly on the front their old water-line of "Lake Bonneville" (of which the Great Salt Lake is the shrunken miserable relict), lies a pretty settlement, cosily muffled up in clover and fruit trees, and then beyond it, across another interval of primeval sage, comes into view the white cupola of the Ogden court-house.

Ogden is the meeting-point of the northern and southern Utah lines of rail, and, more important still, of the Union Pacific and the Central Pacific also. As a "junction town," therefore, it enjoys a position which has already made it prosperous, and which promises it great wealth in the near future. Nature too has been very kind, for the climate is one of the healthiest (if statistics may be believed) in the world; and wood and water, and a fertile soil, are all in abundance. Fortunately also, the Mormons selected the site and laid it out so that the ground-plan is spacious, the roadways are ample, the shade-trees profuse, and the drainage good. Its central school is, perhaps, the leading one in the territory, while in manufactures and industry it will probably some day outstrip Salt Lake City. For the visitor who does not care about statistics, Ogden has another attraction as the centre of a very beautiful cañon country, and excursions can be made in a single day that will give him as exhaustive an idea of the beauties of western hill scenery, as he will ever obtain by far more extended trips. The Ogden and Weber cañons alone exhaust such landscapes, but if the tourist has the time and the will, he may wander away up into the Wasatch range, past Ogden valley and many lovely bits of scenery, towards Bear Valley. But for myself, having seen nearly all the cañons of Utah and many of Colorado, I confess that the Weber and Ogden would have sufficed for all mere sight-seeing purposes.

It was in the Ogden refreshment-room, waiting for the train for San Francisco, that I saw a performance that filled me with astonishment and dismay. It was a man eating his dinner. And let me here remark, with al possible courtesy, that the American on his travels is the most reprehensible eater I have ever seen. In the first place, the knives are purposely made blunt—the back and the front of the blade being often of the same "sharpness" —to enable him to eat gravy with it. The result is that the fork (which *ought* to be used simply to hold meat steady on the plate while being cut with the knife) has to be used with great force to wrench off fragments of food. The object of the two instruments is thus materially abused, for he holds the meat down with the knife and tears it into bits with his fork! Now, reader, don't say *no*. For I have been carefully studying travelling Americans at their food (all over the West at any rate), and what I say is strictly correct. This abuse of knife and fork then necessitates an extraordinary amount of elbow-room, for in forcing apart a tough slice of beef the elbows have to stick out as square as possible, and the conse- quence is, as the proprietor of a hotel told me, only four Americans can eat in a space in which six Englishmen will dine comfortably. The latter, when feeding, keep their elbows to their sides; the former square them out on the line of the shoulders, and at right angles to their sides. Having thus got the travelling American into position, watch him consuming his food! He has ordered a dozen "por- tions" of as many eatables, and the whole of his meal, after

the detestable fashion of the " eating-houses " at which travellers are fed, is put before him at once. To eat the dozen or
so different things which he has ordered, he has only one knife
and fork and one tea-spoon. Bending over the table, he
sticks his fork into a pickled gherkin, and while munching this
casts one rapid hawk-like glance over the spread viands,
and then proceeds to eat. Mehercule ! what a sight it is !
He dabs his knife into the gravy of the steak, picks up with
his fork a piece of bacon, and while the one is going up to his
mouth, the other is reaching out for something else. He never
apparently chews his food, but dabs and pecks at the dishes
one after the other with a rapidity which (merely as a juggling
trick) might be performed in London to crowded houses
every day, and with an impartiality that, considered as
" *dining*," is as savage as any meal of Red Indians or of
Basutos. Dab, dab, peck, peck, grunt, growl, snort ! The
spoon strikes in every now and then, and a quick sucking-up
noise announces the disappearance of a mouthful of huckle-
berries on the top of a bit of bacon, or a spoonful of cus-
tard-pie on the heels of a radish. It is perfectly prodigious.
It defies coherent description. But how on earth does he
swallow ? Every now and then he shuts his eyes, and
strains his throat ; this, I suppose, is when he swallows,
for I have seen children getting rid of cake with the same
sort of spasm. Yet the rapidity with which he shovels in
his food is a wonder to me, seeing that he has not got any
"pouch" like the monkey or the pelican. Does he keep
his miscellaneous food in a " crop ' like a pigeon, or a
preliminary stomach like the cow, and " chew the cud "
afterwards at his leisure ? I confess J am beaten by it.
The mixture of his food, if it pleases him, does not annoy
me, for if a man likes to eat mouthfuls of huckle-berries,
bacon, apple-pie, pickled mackerel, peas, mutton, gherkins,
oysters, radishes, tomatoes, custard, and poached eggs (this

is a *bonâ-fide* meal copied from my note-book on the spot) in indiscriminate confusion, it has nothing to do with me. But what I want to know is, why the travelling American does not stop to chew his food ; or why, as is invariably the case, he will despatch in five minutes a meal for which he has half an hour set specially apart? He falls upon his food as if he were demented with hunger, as if he were a wild thing of prey tearing victims that he hated into pieces ; and when the hideous deed is done, he rushes out from the scene of massacre with a handful of toothpicks, and leans idly against the door-post, as if time were without limit or end! The whole thing is a mystery to me. When I first came into the country I used to waste many precious moments in gazing at "the fine confused feeding" of my neigh-bours at the table, and waiting to see them choke. But I have given that up now. I plod systematically and delibe-rately through my one dish, content to find myself always the last at the table, with a tumult of empty platters scattered all about me. Nothing can choke the travelling American. In the meantime, I wish that young man of Ogden would exhibit his great eating trick in London. It beats Maskelyne and Cook into fits.

From Ogden northwards the road lies past perpetual cottage-farms, separated only by orchards or fields, and clustering at intervals into pleasant villages, where the people are all busy gathering in their lucerne crops. The same profusion of wild-flowers, and exquisite rose-brakes, the same abundance of bird and insect life is conspicuous.

But gradually our road bears away westward from the hills, leaving cultivation and cottages to follow the line of irriga-tion along their lower slopes, and while to our right the narrow-gauge line runs northward up into the Cache Valley, the granary of Utah, we trend away to the left. The northern end of the Salt Lake comes in sight, and the track running for a while close to its side gives me a last look at this sheet of wonderful water.

I was sorry to see the last of it, for I was sorry to leave Utah and the kind-hearted, simple, hard-working Mormon people. But the Lake gradually comes to a point, dwindles out into a marsh, and is gone, and as we speed away across levels of dreary alkaline ground, we can only recall its site by the wild duck streaming across to settle for the night in the reeds that grow by its edges.

Away from Mormon industry, the sage-brush flourishes like green bay-trees. To the east, the line of white-walled cottages speaks of a civilization which we are leaving behind us. To the west, the dreary mountains of Nevada already herald a region of barren desolation. And so the sun begins to set, and in the dim moth-time, as the mists begin to blur the outlines of Antelope Island in the Salt Lake, the small round-faced owls come out upon the railway fencing and chuckle to each other, and crossing the Bear River, all ruddy with the sunset, we see the night-hawks skimming the water in chase of the creatures of the twilight.

And so to Corinne, ghastly Corinne, a Gentile failure on the very skirts of Mormon success. It had once a great carrying-trade, for being at the terminus of the Utah Railway, Montana depended upon it for its supplies, and bitterly had Montana cause to regret it, for the Corinne freight-carriers (I wish I could remember their expressive slang name) seemed to think that railway enterprise must always terminate at Corinne, and so they carried just what they chose, at the price they chose, and when they chose. But the railway ran past them one fine day, and so now there is Corinne, stranded high and dry, as discreditable a settlement as ever men put together. Without any plan, treeless and roadless, the scattered hamlet of crazy-looking shanties stands half the year in drifting dust and half the year in sticky mud, and the Mormons point the finger of scorn at the place the Gentiles used to boast of. And Corinne seems to strike the keynote of the succeeding country, for cultivation ceases and habitations are not on the desolate plain we enter. And so to Promontory and then darkness.

We awake to find ourselves still in calamitous Nevada. What heaps of British gold have been sunk in those ugly hills in the hope of getting up American silver !

But here is Halleck, a government post, and soldiers from the barracks are lounging about in uniforms that make them look like butcher-boys, and with a drowsy gait that makes one suspect them to be burthened with the saddening load of yesterday's whisky. Then, after an interval of desert, we cross the Humboldt river, thick with the mud of melting snows, and, snaking across a plain warted over with ant-hills, arrive at Elko.

It is possible that Allah in his mercy may forgive Elko the offal which it put before us for breakfast. For myself, mere humanity forbids me to forgive it. But Elko was otherwise of interest. A waiter, very black, and, in proportion to his nigritude, insolent, had triumphed over my unconcealed disgust with my food. Yet I turned to him civilly and said, " Isn't there a warm spring here which is worth going to see ? "

" *No*," said the negro, " *our spring been burned up !*"

" Burned up ! " I exclaimed in astonishment; " the *spring* been burned up ! "

" Yes," said the abominable one, " *burned up*. Everybody know *dat*."

"Was your mother there?" I asked courteously, pretending not to be exasperated by the blackamoor.

"My mother? No. My mother's—"

"Ah!" I replied, "I thought she might have been burned up at the same time, for you look like the son of a cinder."

My sally—mean effort that it was—was a complete triumph, and I left Ham squashed. It proved, of course, that it was the wooden shanty at the spring that had been burned down, but in any case it was too far off for us to go to see. So we consoled ourselves with the Indians, who always gather on the platform at Elko, in the assurance of begging or showing their papooses to some purpose. Nor were they wrong. I paid a quarter to see "the papoose," and got more than my money's worth in hearing this poor brown woman talking to her child the same sweet nursery nonsense that my own wife talks to mine. And the papoose understood it all, and chuckled and smiled and looked happy, for all the world as if it were something better than a mere Indian baby. Poor little Lamanite! In a year or two it will be strutting about the camp with its mimic bow and arrows, striking its mother, and sneering at her as "a squaw," and ten years later (if the end of the race has not then arrived) may be riding with his tribe on some foul errand of murder, while his mother carries the lodge-poles and the cooking-pots on foot behind the young brave's horse. Imagine a life in which begging is the chief dissipation, and horse-stealing the only industry!

But I can feel a sympathy for the red man. It may be true that neither gunpowder nor the Gospel can reform him, that his code of morality is radically incurable, that he is, in fact, "the red-bellied varmint" that the Western man believes him to be. Yet all the same, remembering the miracles that British government has worked with the Gonds and other seemingly hopeless tribes of India, I entertain a lurking suspicion that under other and more kindly circumstances the Red Indian might have been to-day a better thing than he is.

At any rate, a people cannot be altogether worthless that in the deepest depths of their degradation still maintain a lofty wild-beast scorn of white men, and think them something lower than themselves. And is not pride the noblest and the easiest of all fulcrums for a government to work on?

Is it quite certain, for instance, that, given arms, and drilled as soldiers, detachments of the tribes, as auxiliaries of the regulars, might not do good service at the different military posts, in routine duty, of course, and that the prestige of such employment would not appeal to the military spirit of the tribes at large? What is there at Fort Halleck that Indians could not do as well as white men? It is a notorious fact, and as old as American history, that the red man holds sacred everything that his tribe is guarding. Why should not this chivalry, common to every savage race on earth, and largely utilized by other governments in Asia and in Africa, be turned to account in America too, and Indians be entrusted with the peace of Indian frontiers?

I know well enough that many will think my suggestion sentimental and absurd, but fortunately it is just the class who think in that way that have no real importance in this or in any other country. They are the men who think the "critturs" ought to be "used up," and who, when they are in the West, "would as soon shoot an Injun as a coyote." These men form a class of which America, when she is three generations older, will have little need for, and who, in a more settled community, will find that they must either conform to civilization or else "git." There are a great number of these coarse, thick-skinned, ignorant men floating about on the surface of Western America : for Western America still stands in need of men who will do the reckless preliminary work of settlement, and shoot each other off over a whisky bottle when that work is done. Now, these men, and those of a feebler kind who take their opinions from them, believe and preach that annihilation of the Indian is the only possible cure for the Indian evil. I have heard them say it in public a score of times that "the Indian should be wiped clean out." But a larger and more generous class is growing up very fast in the West, who are beginning to see that the red men are really a charge upon them : and that as a great nation they must take upon themselves the responsibilities of empire, and protect the weaker communities whom a rapidly advancing civilization is isolating in their midst.

But it is a pity that those in authority cannot see their way to giving practical effect to such sentiments, and devise some method for utilizing the Indian. For myself, seeing what has been done in Asia and in Africa with equally difficult tribes, I should be inclined to predict success for an experiment in military service, if the routine duties of barracks and outpost duty, in unnecessary places, can be called "military service."

For one thing, drilled and well-armed Indians would very soon put a stop to cow-boy disturbances in Arizona, or anywhere else. Or, again, if Indians had been on his track, James, the terror of Missouri, would certainly not have flourished so long as he did.

But by this time we have got far past Elko, and the

T

train is carrying us through an undulating desert of rabbit-bush and greasewood, with dull, barren hills on either hand, and then we reach Carlin, another dreadful-looking hamlet of the Corinne type, and, alas ! Gentile also, without a tree or a road, and nearly every shanty in it a saloon.

More Indians are on the platform. They are allowed, it appears, under the Company's contract with the government, to ride free of charge upon the trains, and so the poor creatures spend their summer days, when they are not away hunting or stealing, in travelling backwards and forwards from one station to the next, and home again. This does not strike the civilized imagination as a very exhilarating pastime, nor one to be contemplated with much enthusiasm of enjoyment. Yet the Indians, in their own grave way, enjoy it prodigiously.

Curiously enough, they cannot be persuaded to ride anywhere, except on the platforms between the baggage-cars. But here they cluster as thick as swarming bees, the "bucks" in all the fantastic combination of vermilion, tag-rag and nudity, the squaws dragging about ponderous bison robes and sheep-skins, and laden with papooses, the children, grotesque little imitations of their parents, with their playthings in their hands.

For the "papoose" is a human child after all, and the little Shoshonee girls nurse their dolls just as little girls in New York do, only, of course, the Red Indian's child carries on her back an imitation papoose in an imitation pannier, instead of wheeling an imitation American baby in an imitation American "baby-carriage." I watched one of these brown fragments of the great sex that gives the world its wives and its mothers, its sweethearts and its sisters, and it was quite a revelation to me to hear the wee thing crooning to her wooden baby, and hushing it to sleep, and making believe to be anxious as to its health and comforts. Yes, and my mind went back on a sudden to the nursery, on the other side of the Atlantic, thousands of miles away, where another little girl sits crooning over her doll of rags and wax, and on her face I saw just the same expression of troubled concern as clouded the little Shoshonee's brow, and the same affectation of motherlycare.

So it takes something more than mere geographical distance to alter human nature.

CHAPTER XXII.

FROM NEVADA INTO CALIFORNIA.

Of Bugbears—Suggestions as to sleeping-cars—A Bannack chief, his
hat and his retinue—The oasis of Humboldt—Past Carson Sink—
A reminiscence of wolves—"Hard places"—First glimpses of
California—A corn miracle—Bunch-grass and Bison—From
Sacramento to Benicia.

Is a bugbear most bug or bear? I never met one yet
fairly face to face, for the bugbear is an evasive insect. Nor,
if I *did* meet one, can I say whether I should prefer to find
it mainly bug or mainly bear. The latter is of various sorts.
Thus, one, the little black bear of the Indian hills, is about
as formidable as a portmanteau of the same size. Another,
the grizzly of the Rockies, is a very unamiable person. His
temper is as short as his tail; and he has very little more
sense of right and wrong than a Land-leaguer. But he
is not so mean as the bug. You never hear of grizzly
bears getting into the woodwork of bedsteads and creeping out in the middle of the night to sneak up the
inside of your night-shirt. He does not go and cuddle
himself up flat in a crease of the pillow-case, and then slip
out edgeways as soon as it is dark, and bite you in the nape
of the neck. It is not on record that a bear ever got inside
a nightcap and waited till the gas was turned out, to come
forth and feed like grief on the damask cheek of beauty.
No, these are not the habits of bears, they are more

manly than bugs. If you want to catch a bear between your finger and thumb, and hold it over a lighted match on the point of a pin, it will stand still to let you try. Or if you want to have a good fair slap at a bear with a slipper, it won't go flattening itself out in the crevices of furniture, in order to dodge the blow, but will stand up square in the road, in broad daylight, and let you do it. So, on the whole, I cannot quite make up my mind whether bugs or bears are the worst things to have about a house. You see you could shoot at the bear out of the window ; but it would be absurd to fire off rifles at bugs between the blankets. Besides, bears don't keep you awake all night by leaving you in doubt as to whether they are creeping about the bed or not, or spoil your night's rest by making you sit up and grope about under the bed-clothes and try to see things in the dark. Altogether, then, there is a good deal to be said on the side of the bear.

I am led to these remarks by remembering that at Carlin, in Nevada, I found two bugs in my " berth " in the sleeping-car. The porter thought I must have " brought them with me." Perhaps I did, but, as I told him, I didn't remember doing so, and with his permission would not take them any further. Or perhaps the Shoshonees brought them. All Indians, whether red or brown, are indifferent to these insects, and carry them about with them in familiar abundance.

And this reminds me to say a little about sleeping-cars in general. During my travels in America I have used three kinds, the Pullman Palace, the Silver Palace, and the Baltimore and Ohio, and except in " high tone," and finish of ornament, where the Pullman certainly excels the rest, there is very little to choose between them. All are extremely comfortable *as sleeping-cars*. In the Silver Palace, however, there is a custom prevalent of not pulling down the upper berth when it is unoccupied, and this improvement on the Pullman plan is certainly very great. The two shelves, one at each end of the berth, are ample for one's clothes, while the sense of relief and better ventilation from not having the bottom of another bedstead suspended eighteen inches or so above your face is decidedly conducive to better rest. The general adoption of this practice, wherever possible, would, I am sure, be popular among passengers. As *day-cars*, the "sleepers" have one or two defects in common, which might very easily be remedied. For one thing, every seat should have a removable head-rest belonging to it. As it is, the weary during the day become very weary indeed, and the attempts of passengers to rest their heads by curling themselves up on the seats, or lying crosswise in the "section," are as pathetic as they are often absurd, and give a Palace car the appearance, on a hot afternoon, of a ward in some Hospital for Spinal Complaints. Another point that should be altered is the hour for closing the smoking-room. When not required for berths *for passengers* (for the company's *employés* ought not to be considered when the convenience of the company's customers is in question) there is no reason whatever for closing the smoking-room at ten. As a rule it is not closed ; but sometimes it is ; and it should not be placed in the power of a surly conductor—and there are too many ill-mannered conductors on the railways —to annoy passengers by applying such a senseless regulation. A third point is the apple-and-newspaper-boy nuisance. This wretched creature, if of an enterprising kind, pesters you to purchase things which you have no intention of purchasing, and if you express any annoyance at his importunity, he is insolent. But apart from his insolence, he is an unmitigated nuisance. What should be done is this : a printed slip, such as the boy himself carries and showing what he sells, should be put on to the seats by the porter, and when any passenger wants an orange or a book, he could send for the vendor. But the vendor should be absolutely forbidden to parade his wares in the sleeping-cars, unless sent for. Anywhere else, except on a train, he would be handed over to the police for his importunities ; but on the train he considers himself justified in badgering the public, and impertinently resents being ordered away. These are three small matters, no doubt, but changes in the direction I have suggested would nevertheless materially increase the comfort of passengers.

And now let me see. When I fell into these digressions I had just said good-bye to the Mormons and Mormonland, and had got as far into Nevada as Carlin. From there a dismal interval of wilderness brings the traveller to Palisade, a group of wooden saloons haunted by numbers of yellow Chinese. In the few minutes that the train stopped here, I saw a curious sight.

A number of our Shoshonee passengers—the " deadheads " on the platform between the baggage-cars—had got off, and one of them was the squaw that had the papoose. As she sat down and unslung her infant from her back, a group gathered round her—one Englishman, one negro, three mulattoes, and a Chinaman. And they were all laughing at the Indian. Not one of them all, not even the negro, but thought himself entitled to make fun of her and her baby ! The white man looks down on the mulatto, and the mulatto on the negro, and the negro and the Chinaman reciprocate a mutual disdain ; yet here they were, all four together, on a common platform, loftily ridiculing the Shoshonee ! It was a delightful spectacle for the cynic. But I am no cynic, and yet I laughed heartily at them all— at them all except the Shoshonee.

I cannot, for the life of me, help venerating these repre-

sentatives of aprodigious antiquity, these relics of a civilization that dates back before our Flood.

Then we reach the Humboldt River, a broad and full-
watered stream, lazily winding along among ample meadows
But not a trace of cultivation anywhere. And then on to the
desert again with the surface of the alkali land curling up
into flakes, and the lank grey greasewood sparsely scattered
about it. The desolation is as utter as in Beluchistan or the
Land of Goshen, and instead of Murrees there are plenty of
Shoshonees to make the desolation perilous to travellers by
waggon. At Battle Creek station they are mustered in quite
a crowd, listless men with faces like masks and women
burnished and painted and wooden as the figure-heads of
English barges. I do not think that in all my travels, in Asia
or in Africa, or in the islands of eastern or southern seas, I
have ever met a race with such a baffling physiognomy.
You can no more tell from his face what an Indian is thinking of than you can from a monkey's. Their eyes brighten
and then glaze over again without a word being spoken or a
muscle of the face moved, and they avert their glance as
soon as you look at them. If you look into an Indian's
eyes, they seem to deaden, and all expression dies out of
them ; but the moment you begin to turn your head away,
you are conscious of the rapid furtive glance that they dart
at you. They are hieroglyphics altogether, and there is
something " uncanny " about them.

At Battle Creek we note that (with irrigation) trees will
grow, but in a few minutes we are out again on the wretched
desert, the eternal greasewood being the only apology
for vegetation, and little prairie owls the only representatives
of wild life. And so to Winnemucca, where, being watered,
a few trees are growing ; but the desolation is nevertheless
so complete that I could not help thinking of the difference

a little Mormon industry would make! A company of Bannack Indians were waiting here for the train, and such a wonderful collection as they were! One of them was the chief who not long ago gave the Federal troops a good deal of trouble, and his retinue was the most delightful medley of curiosities—a long thin man with the figure of a lamp-post, a short fat one with the expression of a pancake, a half-breed with a beard, and a boy with a squint. The chief, with a face about an acre in width, wore a stove-pipe hat with the crown knocked out and the opening stuffed full of feathers, but the rest of his wonderful costume, all flapping about him in ends and fringes of all colours and very dirty, is indescribable. His suite were in a more sober garb, but all were grotesque, their headgear being especially novel, and showing the utmost scorn of the hatter's original intentions. Some wore their hats upside down and strapped round the chin with a ribbon; others inside out, with a fringe of their own added on behind—but it was enough to make any hatter mad to look at them.

They travelled with us across the next interval of howling wilderness, and got out to promenade at Humboldt, where we got out to dine—and, as it proved, to dine well.

Humboldt is an exquisite oasis in the hideous Nevada waste. A fountain plays before the hotel door, and on either side are planted groves of trees, poplar and locust and willow, with the turf growing green beneath them, and roses scattered about.

No wonder that all the birds and butterflies of the neighbourhood collect at such a beautiful spot, or that travellers go away grateful, not only for the material benefits of a good meal, but the pleasures of green trees and running water and the song of birds. An orchard, with lucerne strong and thick beneath them, promises a continuance of cultivation, but on a sudden it stops, and we find ourselves out again on the alkali plain, as barren and blistered as the banks of the Suez Canal.   A tedious hour or two brings us to the river again; but man here is not agricultural, so the desert continues in spite of abundant water.   And so to Lovelocks, where girls board the train as if they were brigands, urging us to buy "sweet fresh milk—five cents a glass."   Indians, as usual, are lounging about on the platform, and some more of them get on to the train, and away we go again into the same Sahara as before.   Humboldt Lake, the "sink" where the river disappears from the surface of the earth, and a distant glimpse of Carson's "Sink," hardly relieve the desperate monotony, for they are hideous levels of water without a vestige of vegetation, and close upon them comes as honest a tract of desert as even Africa can show, and with no more "features" on it than a plate of cold porridge has.   A wolf goes limping off in a three-legged kind of way, as much as to say that, having to live in such a place, it didn't much care whether we caught it or not; and what a contrast to the pair of wolves I remember meeting one morning in Afghanistan !

I was riding a camel and looking away to my right across the plain.   I saw coming towards me, over the brushwood, in a series of magnificent leaps, a couple of immense wolves. I knew that wolves grew sometimes to a great size, but I had no idea that, even with their winter fur on, they could be so large as these were.

And there was a majesty about their advance that fascinated me, for every bound, though it carried them twelve or fifteen feet, was so free and light that they seemed to move by machinery rather than by prodigious strength of muscle.   But it suddenly occurred to me that they were crossing my path, and I saw, moreover, that our relative speeds, if maintained, might probably bring us into actual collision at the point of intersection. But it was not for me to yield the road, and the wolves thought it was not for them. And so we approached, the wolves keeping exact time and leaping together, as if trained to do it, and then, without swerving a hair's-breadth from their original course they bounded across the path only a few feet behind my camel. It was superb courage on their part, and as an episode of wild-beast life, one of the most picturesque and dramatic I ever witnessed.

The next station we halted at was Wadsworth, a "hard place," so men say, where revolvers are in frequent use and Lynch is judge. Here the broad-faced Bannack chief got down, and, followed by his tag-rag retinue, disappeared into the cluster of wigwams which we saw pitched behind the station. I noticed a man standing here with a splendid cactus in his hand, covered with large magenta blossoms, and this reminded me to note the conspicuous change in the botany that about here takes place. The flowers that had borne us company all through Utah and now and then brightened the roadside in Nevada had disappeared, and were replaced by others of species nearly all new to me. I saw here for the first time a golden-flowered cactus and a tall lavender-coloured spiræa of singular beauty. A little beyond Wadsworth the change becomes even more marked, for striking the Truckee river, we exchange desolation for pretty landscape, and the desert for green bottom lands. The alteration was a welcome one, and some of the glimpses, even if we had not passed through such a melancholy region, would have claimed our admiration on their own merits. The full-fed river poured along a rapid stream, through low-lying meadow-lands fringed with tall cotton-wood, the valley sometimes narrowing so much

that the river took up all the room, and then widening out
so as to admit of large expanses of grass and occasional
fields of corn. And so to Greeno, where we supped
heartily off " Truckee trout," one of the best fish that ever
wagged a fin. As we got back into the cars it.was getting
dark, for with the usual luck of travel the Central Pacific
has to run its trains so as to give passengers ugly Nevada
by day and beautiful California by night.

Awaking next morning was a wonderful surprise. We
had gone to sleep in Nevada in early summer, and we awoke
in California late in autumn ! In Utah, two days ago, the
crops had only just begun to ·flush the ground with green.
Here, to-day, the corn-fields were the sun-dried stubble of
crops that had been cut weeks ago !

And the first glimpses of it were fortunate ones, for when
I awoke it was in a fine park-like, undulating country,
studded with clumps of oak-trees, but one continuous corn-
field. Great mounds of straw and stacks of corn dotted
the landscape as far as the eye could see, and already the
fields were alive with carts and men all busy with the splendid
harvest. After a while came vast expanses of meadow,
prettily timbered, in which great flocks of sheep and herds
of cattle were grazing, " ranches " such as I had never seen
before. And then we passed some houses, broad-eaved and
verandahed, with capacious barns standing in echelon behind, and all the signs of an ample prosperity, deep shaded
in walnut-trees laden with nuts, overrun by vines already
heavy with clusters, and brightened by clumps of oleanders
ruddy with blossom. And then came the corn-fields again,
an unbroken expanse of stubble, yellow as the sea-sand, and
seemingly as interminable. What a country ! It is a
kingdom in itself.

And its rivers ! The American River soon came in sight,

rolling its stately flood along between brakes of willow and elder, and aspen, and then the Sacramento, a noble stream. And the two conspire and join together to take liberties with the solid earth, swamp it into bulrush beds by the league together, and create such jungles as almost rival the great Himalaya Terai. And so to Sacramento.

Sacramento was *en fête*, for it was the race week. So bunting was flapping from every conspicuous point, and everything and everybody wore a whole holiday, morning-cocktail, go-as-you-please sort of look. This fact may account for the very ill-mannered conductor who boarded us here.

I am sitting in the smoking-car. Enter conductor with his mouth too full of tobacco to be able to speak. He points at me with his thumb. I take no notice of his thumb. He spits in the spittoon at my feet and jerks his thumb towards me again. I disregard his thumb. "*Ticket!*" he growls. I give him my ticket. He punches it and thrusts it back to me so carelessly and suddenly that it falls on the floor. He takes no notice, but passes on into the car. I take out my pocket-book and make a note :—

"Such a man as this goes some way towards discrediting the administration of a whole line. It seems a pity therefore to retain his services."

However, of Sacramento, I was very sorry not to be able to stay there, for next to the Los Angeles country I had been told that it was one of the finest "locations" in all California, and I can readily believe it, for the botany of the place is sub-tropical, and snow and sunstroke are equally unknown. Fruits of all kinds grow there in delightful abundance, and I cherish it therefore as a personal grudge against Sacramento that there was not even a blackberry procurable at breakfast.

Passing from Sacramento, and remarking as we go, the patronage which that vegetable impostor, the eucalyptus globulus (or " blue-gum " of Australia) has secured, both as an ornamental—save the mark !—and a shade-tree, two purposes for which by itself the eucalyptus is specially unfitted, we find ourselves once more in a world given up to harvesting. A monotonous panorama of stubble and standing crops, with clumps of pretty oak timber studding the undulating land, leads us to the diversified approaches to San Francisco.

It is old travellers' ground, but replete with the interest which attaches to variety of scenery, continual indications of vast wealth, and a rapidly growing prosperity. But one word, before we reach the town, for that wonderful natural crop—the " wild oats," which clothe every vacant acre of the country on this Pacific watershed with harvests as close and as regular as if the land had been tilled, and the ground sown, by human agency. This surprising plant is said to have been brought to California by the Spaniards, and to have run wild from the original fields. But whatever its origin, it is now growing in such vast prairies that whole tribes of Indians used to look to it as the staple of their food. But better crops are fast displacing it, and as for the Indian, California no longer belongs to him or his bison-herds. Further east, that is to say, from the Platte Valley to the Sierra Nevada, the " bunch grass " was the great natural provision for the wild herds of the wild man, and it still ranks as one of the most valuable features of otherwise barren regions in Colorado, Utah, and Nevada. To the student of Nature, however, it is far more interesting as one of the most beautiful examples of her kindly foresight, for the bunch grass grows where nothing else can find nourishment, and just when all other grasses are useless as fodder, it throws out young juicy shoots, thrives under the snow, and then in May, when other grasses are abundant, it dies ! Somebody has said that without the mule and the pig America would never have been colonized. That may be as it may be. But the real pioneer of the West was the bison, for the first emigrants followed exactly in the footsteps of the retiring herds, and these in their turn grazed their way towards the Pacific in the line of the bunch grass.

Mount Diavolo is the first "feature" that arouses the traveller's inquisitiveness, and then the Martines Straits with their yellow waters spread out at the feet of rolling, yellow hills, and then great mud flats on which big vessels lie waiting for the tide to come and float them on, and then a bay which, with its girdle of hills and its broad margin, reminds me of Durban in Natal. So to Benicia, the place of "the Boy," with the blacksmith's forge where Heenan used to work still standing near the water's edge, and where the hammer that the giant used to use is still preserved " in memoriam," and then on to the ferry-boat (train and all !) and across a bay of brown water and brown mud and brown hills—dismally remindful of Weston-super-Mare —and on to dry land again, past Berkley, with its college among the trees, Oakland, and other suburban resorts of the San Franciscan, to the fine new three-storeyed Station at the pier. Once more on to the ferry-boat, but this time leaving our train behind us and across another bay, and so into San Francisco. Outside the station stands a crowd of chariot-like omnibuses, as gorgeously coloured, some of them, as the equipages of a circus, and empanelled with gaudy pictures. In one of them we find our proper seats, and are soon bumping over the cobble-stones into "the most wonderful city, sir, of America."

CHAPTER XXIII.

San Franciscans, their fruits and their falsehoods—Their neglect of opportunities—A plague of flies—The pig-tail problem—Chinamen less black than they are painted—The seal rocks—The loss of the *Eurydice*—A jeweller's fairyland—The mystery of gems.

SOMEBODY has poked fun at San Francisco, by calling it "the Venice of the West," and then qualifying the compliment by explaining that the only resemblance between the two cities is in the volume and variety of the disagreeable smells that prevail in them. But the San Franciscans take no notice of this explanation. They accept the comparison in its broadest sense, and positively expect you to see a resemblance between their very wonderful, but very new town, and *Venice!* Indeed, there is no limit to the San Franciscan's expectations from a stranger.

Now, I was sitting in the hotel one day and overheard a couple of San Franciscans bragging in an off-hand way to a poor wretch who had been brought up, I should guess, in New Mexico, and calmly assuring him that there was no place "in the world" of greater beauty than San Francisco, or of more delicious fruit. I pretended to fall into the same easy credulity myself, and drew them on to making such monstrous assertions as that San Francisco was a revelation of beauty to all travellers, and the perfection of its fruit a never-ceasing delight to them! I then ventured deferentially to inquire what standard of comparison they had for their self-laudation, what other countries they had visited, and what fruits they considered California produced in such perfection. Now, it turned out that these three impostors had never been out of America: in fact, that, except for short visits on business to the Eastern States, they had never been out of California and Nevada! I then assured them that, for myself, I had seen, in America alone, many places far more beautiful, while "in the world" I knew of a hundred with which San Francisco should not venture to compare itself. As for its fruits, there was not in its market, nor in its best shops, a single thing that deserved to be called first-class. From the watery cherries to the woolly apricots, every fruit was as flavourless as it dared to be, while, as a whole, they were so second-rate that they could not have found a sale in the best shops of either Paris or London. The finest fruit, to my mind, was a small but well-flavoured mango, imported from Mexico. Its flavour was almost equal to that of the *langra* of the Benares district, or the green mango of Burmah; and if the Maldah was grafted on to this Mexican stock, the result would probably be a fruit that would be as highly prized in New York and in England, as it is all over Asia. But very few people in San Francisco ever buy mangoes. "No, sir," I said at last to the barbarian who had been imposed upon; "don't you believe any one who tells you that San Francisco is the most lovely spot on earth, or that its fruits are extraordinary in flavour. San Francisco is a wonderful city; it is *the* Wonder of the West. But you must not believe all that San Franciscans tell you about it."

It is a great pity that San Franciscans should have this

weakness. They have plenty to be proud of, for their city is a marvel. But it has as yet all the disadvantages of newness. Its population, moreover, is as disagreeably un-settled as in the towns of the Levant. All the mud and dirt are still in suspension. I know very well, of course, that improvement is making immense and rapid strides, but to the visitor the act of *transition* is, of course, invisible, and he only sees the place at a period of apparent repose between the last point of advance and the next. He can *imagine* anything he pleases—and it is difficult to imagine the full splendour of the future of the Californian capital. But this is not what he actually sees. For myself, then, I found San Francisco as so many other travellers have described it, disorderly, breathless with haste, unkempt. Here and there, where trees have been planted, and there is the grace of flowers and creeping plants, the houses look as if rational people might really *live* in them. But for the vast majority of the buildings, they seem merely places to lodge in, dak-bungalows or rest-houses, perches for passing swallows, any-thing you like—except houses to pass one's life in. They are not merely wooden, but they are sham too, with their im-posing " fronts " nailed on to the roofs to make them look finer, just as vulgar women paste curly " bangs " on to the fronts of their heads. There is also an inexcusable dearth of ornament. I say inexcusable, because San Francisco might be a perfect paradise of flowers and trees. Even the " weeds " growing on the sand dunes outside the city are flowers that are prized in European gardens. But as it is, François Jeannot,—" French gardener, with general enter-prise of gardens," as his signboard states,—has evidently very little to do. There is little " enterprise of gardens." Yet what exquisite flowers there are ! The crimson salvia grows in strong hedges, and 'plots are fenced in with geraniums. The fuchsias are sturdy shrubs in which birds might build their nests, and the roses and jessamines and purple clematis of strange, large-blossomed kinds, form natural arbours of enchanting beauty. Lobelias spread out into large cushions of a royal blue, and the canna, wherever sown, sends up shafts of vivid scarlet, orange, and yellow.

If I only knew the names of other plants I could fill a page with descriptions of the wonderful luxuriance of San Franciscan flowers. But all I could say would only emphasize the more clearly the apparent neglect by the San Franciscans of the floral opportunities they possess.

It is curious how enthusiastic California has been in its reception of the eucalyptus globulus, the blue-gum tree of Australia. And I am afraid there has been some job put upon the San Franciscans in this matter. Has anybody, with a little speculation in blue-gums on hand, been telling them that the eucalyptus was a wonderful drainer of marshes and conqueror of fevers ? If so, it is a pity they had not heard that *that* hoax was quite played out in Europe, and the eucalyptus shown to be an impostor. Or were they told of its stately proportions, its rapid growth, its beautiful foliage, and its splendid shade ? If so, that hoax will soon expose itself. Given a site where no wind blows, the eucalyptus will grow straight, but offered the smallest provocation it flops off to one side or the other, while its foliage is liable probably beyond that of all other trees to discoloration and raggedness. In Natal it has proved itself very useful as fencing, for neither wood nor stone being procurable, slips and shreds of eucalyptus have soon grown up into permanent hedges. But no one thinks of valuing it anywhere, except in Australia, either for its timber, its appearance, or its medicinal virtues.

In many ways the Queen of the Pacific was a surprise ;

I had expected to find it "semi-tropical." It is nothing of the kind. Women were wearing furs every afternoon (in June) because of the chill wind that springs up about three o'clock, and men walked about with great-coats over their arms ready for use. The architecture of the city is not so "semi-tropical" as that of suburban New York, while vegetation, instead of being rampant, is conspicuously absent. Three· women out of every four wore very thick veils, but why they were *so* thick I could not discover. In hot countries they do not wear them, nor in "semi-tropical." Perhaps they were vestiges of some recent visitation of dust, which appears to be sometimes as prodigious here as it is in Pietermaritzburg. But they might, very properly, have been an armour against the flies which swarmed in some parts of the town in hideous multitudes. I went into a large restaurant, the "Palace" something it was called, with the intention of eating, but I left without doing so, appalled by the plague of flies. I found Beelzebub very powerful in Washington, and at some of "the eating places" in the South his hosts were intolerable ; but San Francisco has streets as completely given over to the fly-fiend as an Alexandrian bazaar.

Before I went to San Francisco, I had an idea that a "Chinese question" was agitating the State of California, that every white man was excited about the expulsion of the heathen, that it was the topic of the day, and that passion ran high between the rival populations. I very soon found that I had been mistaken, and that there is really no "Chinese question" at all in California. At least, the one question *now* is, how to evade the late bill stopping Chinese immigration ; and it was gleefully pointed out to me that though the importation of Celestials by sea was prohibited, there was no provision to prevent them being brought into the State by land; and that the numbers of the arrivals would not probably diminish in the least!

I had intended to "study" the Chinese question. But there is not much study to be done over a ghost. Besides, every Californian manufacturer is agreed on the main points, that Chinese labour is absolutely necessary, that there is not enough of it yet in the State, that more still must be obtained. And where a "problem" is granted on all hands, it is hardly worth while affecting to search for profound social, political, or economical complication in it. There is not much more mystery about it than about the nose on a man's face.

Of course those who organized the clamour have what they call "arguments," but they are hardly such as can command respect. In the first place they allege two apprehensions as to the future: 1. That the Chinese, if unrestricted, will swamp the Americans in the State; and 2. That they will demoralize those Americans. Now the first is, I take it, absurd, and if it is not, then California ought to be ashamed of itself. And as for the second, who can have any sympathy with a State that is unable to enforce its police regulations, or with a community in which parents say they cannot protect the purity of their households? If the Chinaman, as a citizen, disregards sanitary bye-laws, why is he not punished, as he would be everywhere else: and if as a domestic servant he misbehaves, why is he not dispensed with, as he would be everywhere else?

Besides these two apprehensions as to the future, they have three objections as to the present. The first is, that the Chinese send their earnings out of the country; the second, that they spend nothing in San Francisco; the third, that they underwork white men. Now the first is foolish, the second and the third, I believe, untrue. As to the Chinese carrying money out of the country—why should they not do so? Will any one say seriously that America, a bullion-producing country, is injured by the Chinese taking their money earnings out of the States, in exchange for that which America cannot produce, namely, labour? Is political economy to go mad simply to suit the sentiment of extra-white labour in California?

As to the Chinese spending nothing in this country, this is hardly borne out by facts, and, in the mouths of San Franciscans, specially unfortunate. For they have not only raised their prices upon the Chinese, but have actually forbidden them to spend their money in those directions in which they wished to do so. As it is, however, they spend, in exorbitant rents, taxes, customs-dues, and in direct expenditure, a perfectly sufficient share of their earnings, and if permitted to do so, would spend a great deal more. A ludicrous superstition, that the Chinese are *economical*, underlies many of the misstatements put forward as "arguments" against them. Yet they are not economical. On the contrary, the Chinese and the Japanese are exceptional among Eastern races for their natural extravagance.

It is further alleged that they underwork white men. This statement will hardly bear testing; for the wages of a Chinese workman, in the cigar trade, for instance, are not lower than those of a white man, say, in Philadelphia. They do not, therefore, "underwork" the white man; but they do undoubtedly underwork *the white Californian.* For the white Californian will not work at Eastern rates. On the contrary, he wishes to know whether you take him for "a —— fool," to think that he, in California, is going to accept the same wages that he could have stopped in New York for! Yet why should he not do so? It will hardly be urged that the Californian Irishman is a superior individual to the Eastern American, or that the average San Franciscan workman is any better than the men of his own class on the Atlantic coast? Yet the Californian claims higher wages, and abuses the Chinese for working at rates which white men are elsewhere glad to accept. He says, too, that living is dearer. Facts disprove this. As a matter of fact, living is cheaper in San Francisco than in either Chicago or New York.

How did I spend my time in San Francisco? Well, friends were very kind to me, and I saw everything that a visitor "ought to see." But after my usual fashion I wandered about the streets a good deal alone, and rode up and down in the street-cars, and I had half a mind at first to be disappointed with the city of which I had heard so much. But later in the evening, when the gas was alight and the pavement had its regular *habitués*, and the pawnbrokers' and bankrupts'-stock stores were all lit up, I saw what a wild, strange city it was. Indeed, I know of no place in the world more full of interesting incidents and stirring types than this noisy, money-spending San Francisco.

One night, of course, I spent several hours in the Chinese quarter, and I cannot tell why, but I took a great fancy to the Celestial, as he is to be seen in San Francisco. Politically, nationally, and commercially, I hate Pekin and all its works. But individually I find the Chinaman, all the world over, a quiet-mannered, cleanly-living, hard-working servant. And in all parts of the world, except California, my estimate of Johnnie is the universal one. In California, however, so the extra-white people say, he is a dangerous, dirty, demoralizing heathen. And there is no doubt of it that, in the Chinese quarter of the city, he is crowded into a space that would be perilous to the health of men accustomed to space and ventilation, but I was told by a Chinaman that he and his people had been *prevented* by the city authorities from expanding into more commodious lodgings. As for cleanliness, I have travelled too much to forget that this virtue is largely a question of geography, and that, especially in matters of food, the habits of Europeans áre considered by half the world so foul as to bring them within the contempt of a hemisphere. As regards personal cleanliness, the Chinese are rather scrupulous.

But I wonder San Francisco does not build a Chinatown, somewhere in the breezy suburbs, and lay a tramway to it for the use of the Chinamen, and then insist upon its sanitary regulations being properly observed. San Francisco would be rather surprised at the result. For the settlements of the Chinese aré very neat and cleanly in appearance, and the people are very fond of curious gardening and house-ornamentation. The Chinese themselves would be only too glad to get out of the centre of San Francisco and the quarters into which they are at present compelled to crowd, while their new habitations would very soon be one of the most attractive sights of all the city. As it is, it is picturesque, but it is of necessity dirty—after the fashion of Asiatic dirtiness. Smells that seem intolerable assail the visitor perpetually, but after all they were better than the smell from an eating-house in Kearney Street which we passed soon after, and where creatures of Jewish and Christian persuasions were having fish fried. I am not wishing to apologize for the Chinese. I hate China with a generous Christian vindictiveness, and think it a great pity that dismemberment has not been forced upon that empire long ago as a punishment for her massacres of Catholics, and her treason generally against the commerce and polity of Europe. But I cannot forget that California owes much to the Chinese.

Next to the Chinese, I found the sea-lions the most interesting feature of San Francisco. To reach them, however (if
you do not wish to indulge the aboriginal hackman with an
opportunity for extortion), you have to undergo a long drive
in a series of omnibuses and cars, but the journey through
the sand-waste outskirts of the city is thoroughly instructive,
for the intervals of desert remind you of the original condition of the country on which much of San Francisco has
been built, while the intervals of charming villa residences
in oases of gardens, show what capital can do, even with
only sea-sand to work upon. We call Ismailia a wonder—
but what is Ismailia in comparison with San Francisco !
After a while solid sand dunes supervene, beautiful, however, in places with masses of yellow lupins, purple rocket,
and fine yellow-flowered thistles, and then the broad sea
comes into sight, and so to the Cliff House.

Just below the House, one of the most popular resorts
of San Francisco, the "Seal Rocks" stand up out of
the water, and it is certainly one of the most interesting
glimpses of wild life that the whole world affords to see the
herds of "sea-lions" clambering and sprawling about their
towers of refuge. For Government has forbidden their
being killed, so the huge creatures drag about their bulky
slug-shaped bodies in confident security. It would not be
very difficult I should think for an amateur to make a sea-
lion. There is very little shape about them. But, nevertheless, it is such a treat as few can have enjoyed twice
in their lives to see these mighty ones of the deep basking
on the sunny rocks, and ponderously sporting in the
water.

And looking out to sea, beyond the sea-lions, I saw a
spar standing up out of the water. It was the poor *Escambia* that had sunk there the day before, and there, on the

beach to the left of the Cliff House, was the spot where the three survivors of the crew managed to make 'good their hold in spite of the pitiless surf, and to clamber up out of reach of the waves. And all through the night, with the lights of the Cliff House burning so near them, the men lay there exhausted with their struggle. It was a strange wreck altogether. When she left port, every one who saw her careening over said " she *must* go down;" every one who passed her said " she *must* go down;" the pilot left her, saying " she *must* go down;" the crew came round the captain, saying " she *must* go down." But the skipper held on his way awhile, and at last he too turned to his mate ; " she *must* go down," he said. Then he tried to head her to port again, but a wave caught her broadside as she was clumsily answering the helm ; and while the coastguard, who had been watching her through his glass, turned for a moment to telephone to the city that " she *must* go down,"—*she did.* When he put up the glasses to his eyes again, there was no *Escambia* in sight ! She *had* gone down.

And the sight of that lonely spar, signalling so pathetically in the desolate waste of waves the spot of the ship's disaster, brought back to my mind a Sunday in Ventnor, where the people of the town, looking out across to sea, stood to watch the beautiful *Eurydice* go by in her full pomp of canvas. A bright sun glorified her, and her crew, met for Divine Service, were returning thanks to Heaven for the prosperous voyage they had made. And suddenly over Dunnose there rushed up a dark bank of cloud. A squall, driving a tempest of snow before it, struck the speeding vessel, and in the fierce whirl of the snowdrift the folk on shore lost sight of the *Eurydice* for some minutes. But as swiftly as it had come, the squall had passed. The sun shone brightly again, but on a troubled sea. And where was the gallant ship, homeward bound, and all her gallant company? She had gone down, all sail set, all hands aboard. And the boats dashed out from the shore to the rescue! But alas! only two survivors out of the three hundred and fifty souls that manned the barque ever set foot on shore again! And the news flashed over England that the *Eurydice* was "lost." For days and weeks afterwards there stood up out of the water, half-way between Shanklin and Luccombe Chine, one lonely spar, like a gravestone, and those who rowed over the wreck could see, down below them under the clear green waves, the shimmer of the white sails of the sunken war-boat. She was lying on her side, the fore and mizzen top-gallant masts gone, her top-gallant sails hanging, but with her main-mast in its place, and all the other sails set. The squall had struck her full, and she rolled over at once, the sea rising at one rush above the waists of the crew, and her yards lying on the water. Then, righting for an instant, she made an effort to recover herself. But the weight of water that had already poured in between decks drove her under. The sea then leaped with another rush upon her, and in an awful swirl of waves the beautiful ship, with all her crew, went down. The Channel tide closed over the huge coffin, and except for the two men saved, and the corpses which floated ashore, there was nothing to tell of the sudden tragedy.

And then back into the city and amongst its shipping. I have all the Britisher's attraction towards the haunts of the men that "go down to the sea in ships." Indeed, walking about among great wharves and docks, with the shipping of all nations loading and discharging cargo, and men of all nations hard at work about you, is in itself a liberal education.

But it can nowhere be enjoyed in such perfection as in London. There, emphatically, is the world's market; and

written large upon the pavement of her gigantic docks is the
whole Romance of Trade.   A single shed holds the products
of all the Continents ; and what a book it would be that told
us of the strange industries of foreign lands !   Who cut that
ebony and that iron-wood in the Malayan forests ? and how
came these palm-nuts here from the banks of the Niger ?
Mustard from India, and coffee-berries from Ceylon lie
together to be crushed under one boot, and here at one
step you can tread on the chili-pods of Jamaica and the
pea-nuts of America.   That rat that ran by was a thing
from Morocco ; this squashed scorpion, perhaps, began life
in Cyprus or in Bermuda.   Queer little stowaways of insect
life are here in abundance, the parasites of Egyptian lentils
or of Indian corn.   The mosquito natives of Bengal swamps
are brought here, it may be, in teakwood from some drift on
the Burman coast.   All the world's produce is in convention
together.   Here stands a great pyramid of horned skulls, the
owners of which once rampaged on Brazilian pampas, or
the prairies of the Platte River, and hard by them lie piled
a multitude of hides that might have fitted the owners of
those skulls, had it not been that they once clothed the
bodies of cattle that grazed out their lives in Australia.
Juxtaposition of packages here means nothing   It does not
argue any previous affinities.   This ship happens to be discharging Norwegian pine, in which the capercailzies have
roosted, and for want of space the logs are being piled on
to sacks of ginger from the West Indies.   Next them there
happens to-day to be cutch from India ; to-morrow there
may be gamboge from Siam, or palm oil from the Gold
Coast.   These men here are trundling in great casks of
Spanish wine that have been to the Orient for their health ;
but an hour ago they were wheeling away chests of Assam
tea, and in another hour may be busy with logwood from

the Honduras forests. One of them is all white on the shoulders with sacks of American wheat flour, but his hands are stained all the same with Bengal turmeric, and he is munching as he goes a cardamum from the Coromandel coast. What a book it would make—this World's Work !

And then back through this city of prodigious bustle, through fine streets with masses of solid buildings that stand upon a site which, a few years ago, was barren sea-sand, and some of it, too, actually sea-beach swept by the waves !

The frequency of diamonds in the windows is a point certain to catch the stranger's eye, but his interest somewhat diminishes when he finds that they are only "California diamonds." They are exquisite stones, however, and, to my thinking, more beautiful than coloured gems, ruby, sapphire, or amethyst, that are more costly in price. But the real diamond can, nevertheless, be seen in perfection in San Francisco. Go to Andrews' "Diamond Palace," and take a glimpse of a jeweller's fairyland. The beautiful gems fairly fill the place with light, while the owner's artistic originality has devised many novel methods of showing off his favourite gem to best advantage. The roof and walls, for instance, are frescoed with female figures adorned on neck and arm, finger, ear, and waist, with triumphs of the lapidary's art.

There is something very fascinating to the fancy in gems, for the one secret that Nature still jealously guards from man is the composition of those exquisite crystals which we call "precious stones." We can imitate, and do imitate, some of them with astonishing exactness, but after all is done there still remains something lacking in the artificial stone. Wise men may elaborate a prosaic chemistry, producing crystals which they declare to be the fac-similes of Nature's delightful gems ; but the world will not accept the ruddy residue of a crucible full of oxides as rubies, or the shining fragments of calcined bisulphides as emeralds. No crucible yet constructed can hold a native sapphire, and all the alchemy of man directed to this point has failed to extort from carbon the secret of its diamond—the little crystal that earth with all her chemistry has made so few of, since first heat and water, Nature's gem-smiths, joined their forces to produce the glittering stones. They placed under requisition every kingdom of created things, and in a laboratory in mid-earth set in joint motion all the powers that move the volcano and the earthquake, that re-fashion the world's form and substance, that govern all the stately procession of natural phenomena. Yet with all this Titanic labour, this monstrous co-operation of forces, Nature formed only here and there a diamond, and here and there a ruby. Masses of quartz, crystals of every exquisite tint, ame-thystine and blue, as beautiful, perhaps, in delicacy of hue as the gems themselves, were sown among the rocks and scattered along the sands, but only to tell us how near Nature came to making her jewels common, and how—just when the one last touch was needed—she withheld her hand, so that man should confess that the supreme triumphs of her art were indeed "precious"!

CHAPTER XXIV.

I HAD looked forward to my journey from San Francisco
to St. Louis with great anticipations, and, though I had no
leisure to "stop off" on the tour, I was not disappointed.
Six continuous days and nights of railway travelling carried
me through such prodigious widths of land, that the mere
fact of traversing so much space had fascinations. And the
variations of scene are very striking—the corn and grape
lands of Southern California, that gradually waste away into
a hideous cactus desert, and then sink into a furnace-valley,
several hundred feet below the level of the sea; the wild
pastures of Texas, that seem endless, until they end in
swamped woodlands; the terrific wildernesses of Arkansas,
that gradually soften down into the beautiful fertility of
Missouri. It was a delightful journey, and taught me in
one week's panorama more than a British Museum full of
books could have done.

Visitors to America do not often make the journey.
They are beguiled off by way of Santa Fé and Kansas City.
I confess that I should myself have been very glad to have
visited Santa Fé, and some day or other I intend to pitch

my tent for a while in San Antonio. But if I had to give advice to a traveller, I would say:—

" Take the Southern Pacific to El Paso, and the Texan Pacific on to St. Louis, and you will get such an idea of the spaciousness of America as no other trip can give you." You will see prodigious tracts of country that are still in aboriginal savagery and you will travel through whole nations of hybrid people—Mexicans and mulattoes, graduated commixtures of Red Indian, Spaniard, and Negro—that some day or another must assume a very considerable political importance in the Union.

Nothing would do Americans more good than a tour through Upper India. Nothing could do European visitors to America more good than the journey from San Francisco to St. Louis by the Southern-and-Texas route. The Gangetic Valley, the Western Ghats, the Himalayas, are all experiences that would ameliorate, improve, and impress the American. The Arizona cactus-plains, the Texan flower-prairies, the Arkansas swamps, give the traveller from Europe a more truthful estimate of America, as a whole, by their vastness, their untamed barbarism, their contrast with the civilized and domesticated States, than years of travel on the beaten tracks from city to city.

And here just a word or two to those American gentlemen to whom it falls to amuse or edify the sight-seeing foreigner. Do not be disappointed if he shows little enthusiasm for your factories, and mills, and populous streets. Remember that these are just what he is trying to escape from. The chances are, that he would much rather see a prairie-dog city, than the Omaha smelting-works ; an Indian lodge than Pittsburg ; one wild bison than all the cattle of Chicago ; a rattlesnake at home than all the legislature of New York in Albany assembled. He prefers cañons to streets, mountain streams to canals; and when he crosses the river, it is the river more than the bridge that interests him. Of course it is well for him to stay in your gigantic hotels, go down into your gigantic silver-mines, travel on your gigantic river-steamers, and be introduced to your gigantic millionaires. These are all American, and it is good for him, and seemly, that he should add them to his personal experiences. So too, he should eat terrapin and planked shad, clam-chowder, canvas-back ducks, and soft-shelled crabs. For these are also American. But the odds are he may go mad and bite thee fatally, if thou wakest him up at un-Christian hours to go and see a woollen factory, simply because thou art proud of it—or settest him down to breakfast before perpetual beefsteak, merely because he is familiar with that food. The intelligent traveller, being at Rome, wishes to be as much a Roman as possible. He would be as aboriginal as the aborigines. And it is a mistake to go on thrusting things upon him solely on the ground that he is already weary of them. As I write, I remember many hours of bitter anguish which I have endured—*I* who am familiar with Swansea, who have stayed in Liverpool, who live in London—in loitering round smelting works and factories, and places of business, trying to seem interested, and pretending to store my memory with statistics. Sometimes it would be almost on my tongue to say, "And now, sir, having shown off your possessions in order to gratify your own pride in them, suppose you show me something for *my* gratification." I never did, of course, but I groaned in the spirit, at my precious hours being wasted, and at the hospitality which so easily forgot itself in ostentatious display. I have perhaps said more than I meant to have done. But all I mean is this, that when a sojourner is at your mercy, throw him unreservedly upon his own resources for such time as you are busy, and deny yourself unreservedly for *his* amusement when

x

you are at leisure. But do not spoil all his day, and half your own, by trying to work your usual business habits into his holiday, and take advantage of his foreign helplessness to show him what an important person (when at home) you are yourself. Do not, for instance, take him after breakfast to your office, and there settling to your work with your clerks, ask him to "amuse himself" with the morning papers—for three hours; and then, after a hurried luncheon at your usual restaurant, take him back to the office for a few minutes—another hour; and then, having carefully impressed upon him that you are taking a half-holiday solely upon his account, and in spite of all the overwhelming business that pours in upon you, do not take him for a drive in the Mall—in order to show off your new horses to your own acquaintances; and after calling at a few shops (during which time your friend stays in the trap and holds the reins), do not, oh do not, take him back to your house to a solitary dinner "quite in the English style." No, sir; this is not the way to entertain the wayfarer in such a land of wonders as this; and you ought not therefore to feel surprise when your guest, wearied of your mistaken hospitality, and wearied of your perpetual suggestions of your own self-sacrifice on his behalf, suddenly determines not to be a burden upon you any longer, and escapes the same evening to the most distant hotel in the town. Nor when you read this ought you to feel angry. You did him a great wrong in wasting a whole day out of his miserable three, and exasperated him by telling his friends afterwards what a "good time" he had with you. These few words are his retaliation—not written either in the vindictive spirit of reprisal, but as advice to you for the future and in the interests of strangers who may follow him within your gates.

From San Francisco to Lathrop, back on the route we

came by, to Oakland, and over the brown waters of the arrogant Sacramento—swelling out as if it would imitate the ocean, and treating the Pacific as if it were merely "a neighbour,"—and out into thousands and thousands of acres of corn, stubble, and mown hay-fields, the desolation worked by the reaper-armies of peace-time with their fragrant plunder lying in heaps all ready for the carts ; and the camp-followers—the squirrels, and the rats, and the finches—all busy gleaning in the emptied fields, with owls sitting watchful on the fences, and vigilant buzzards sailing overhead. What an odd life this is, of the squirrels and the buzzards, the mice, and the owls ! They used to watch each other in these fields, just in the very same way, ages before the white men came. The colonization of the Continent means to the squirrels and mice merely a change in their food, to the hawks and the owls merely a slight change in the flavour of the squirrels and mice ! So, too, when the Mississippi suddenly swelled up in flood the other day, and overflowed three States, it lengthened conveniently the usual water-ways of the frogs, and gave the turtles a more comfortable amplitude of marsh. Hundreds of negroes narrowly escaped drowning, it is true ; but what an awful destruction there was of smaller animal life ! Scores of hamlets were doubtless destroyed, but what myriads of insect homes were ruined ! It does one good, I think, sometimes to remember the real aborigines of our earth, the worlds that had their laws before ours, those conservative antiquities with a civilization that was perfect before man was created, and which neither the catastrophes of nature nor the triumphs of science have power to abrogate.

Oak trees dot the rolling hills, and now and again we come to houses with gardens and groves of eucalyptus, but for hours we travel through one continuous corn-field, a veritable Prairie of Wheat, astounding in extent and in significance. And then we come upon the backwaters of the San Joacquin, and the flooded levels of meadow, with their beautiful oak groves, and herds of cattle and horses grazing on the lush grass that grows between the beds of green tuilla reeds. It is a lovely reach of country this, and some of the water views are perfectly enchanting. But why should the company carefully board up its bridges so that travellers shall not enjoy the scenes up and down the rivers which they cross? It seems to me a pity to do so, seeing that it is really quite unnecessary. As it was, we saw just enough of beauty to make us regret the boards. Then, after the flooded lands, we enter the vast corn-fields again, and so arrive at Lathrop.

Here we dined, and well, the service also being excellent, for half a dollar. Could not the Union Pacific take a lesson from the Southern Pacific, and instead of giving travellers offal at a dollar a head at Green River and other eating-houses, give them good food of the Lathrop kind for fifty cents? As I have said before, the wretched eating-houses on the Union Pacific are maintained, confessedly, for the benefit of the eating-houses, and the encouragement of local colonization; but it is surely unfair on the "transient" to make him contribute, by hunger, indigestion, and ill-temper, to the perpetration of an imposition. On the Southern and the Texas Pacific there are first-rate eating-places, some at fifty cents, some at seventy-five, and, as we approach an older civilization, others at a dollar. But no one can grudge a dollar for a good meal in a comfortable room with civil attendance; while on the Union Pacific there is much to make the passenger dissatisfied, besides the nature of the food, for it is often served by ill-mannered waiters in cheerless rooms. A very little industry, or still less enterprise, might make other eating-places like Humboldt.

It was at Lathrop that some Californians of a very rough type wished to invade our sleeping-car. They wanted to know the "racket," didn't "care if they had to pay fifty dollars," had "taken a fancy" to it, &c., &c.; but the conductor, with considerable tact, managed to persuade them to abandon their design of travelling like gentlemen, and so they got into another car, where they played cards for drinks, fired revolvers out of the window at squirrels between the deals, and got up a quarrel over it at the end of every hand.

California Felix! Aye, happy indeed in its natural resources. For we are again whirling along through prairies of corn-land, a monotony of fertility that becomes almost as serious as the grassy levels of the Platte, the sage-brush of Utah, or the gravelled sands of Nevada. And so to Modesta, a queer, wide-streeted, gum-treed place, not the least like "America," but a something between Madeira and Port Elizabeth. It has not 2000 people in it altogether, yet walking across the dusty square is a lady in the modes of Paris, and a man in a stove-pipe hat! Another stretch of farm-lands brings us to Merced, and the county of that name, a miracle of fertility even among such perpetual marvels of richness. If I were to say what the average of grain per acre is, English farmers might go mad, but if the printer will put it into some very small type I will whisper it to you that the men of Merced *grumble at seventy bushels per acre.* I should like to own Merced, I confess. I am a person of moderate desires. A little contents me. And it is only a mere scrap, after all, of this bewildering California. On the counter at the hotel at Merced are fir-cones from the

Big Trees and fossil fragments and wondrous minerals from Yosemite, and odds and ends of Spanish ornaments. The whole place has a Spanish air about it. This used to be the staging-point for travellers to the Valley of Wonders, but times have changed, and with them the stage-route, so Merced is left on one side by the tourist stream. Leaving it ourselves, we traverse patches of wild sunflower, and then find ourselves out on wide levels of uncultivated land, waiting for the San Joacquin (pronounced, by the way, Sanwa-Keen) canal, to bring irrigation to them. How the Mormons would envy the Californians if they were their neighbours, and the contrast is indeed pathetic, between the alkaline wastes of Utah and the fat glebes of Merced !

At present, however, a nation of little owls possesses the uncultivated acres, and ground squirrels hold the land from them on fief, paying, no doubt, in their vassalage a feudal tribute of their plump, well-nourished bodies. To right and left lies spread out an immense prairie-dog settlement, deserted now, however ; and beyond it, on either side, a belt of pretty timbered land stretches to the coast range, which we see far away on the right, and to the foot-hills—the " Sewaliks " of the Sierra Nevada, —which rise up, capped and streaked with snow, on the left.

Wise men read history for us backwards from the records left by ruins. Why not do the same here with this vast City of the Prairie-Dogs that continues to right and left of us, miles after miles ? Once upon a time, then, there was a powerful nation of prairie-dogs in this place, and they became, in process of years, debauched by luxury, and weakened by pride. So they placed the government in the hands of the owls, whom they invited to come and live with them, and gave over the protection of the country to the rattlesnakes, whom they maintained as janissaries. But the owls and the rattlesnakes, finding all the power in their own hands, and seeing that the prairie-dogs had grown idle and fat and careless, conspired together to overthrow their masters. Now there lived near them, but in subjection to the prairie-dogs, a race of ground-squirrels, a hard-working, thick-skinned, bushy-tailed folk; and the owls and the rattlesnakes made overtures to the ground-squirrels, and one morning, when the prairie-dogs were out feeding and gambolling in the meadows, the conspirators rushed to arms, and while the rattlesnakes and the ground-squirrels, their accomplices, seized possession of the vacated city, the owls attacked the prairie-dogs with their beaks and wings. And the end of it was disaster, utter and terrible; and the prairie-dogs fled across the plains into the woodland for shelter, but did not stay there, but passed on, in one desolating exodus, to the foot-hills beyond the woodland. And then the owls and the rattlesnakes and the ground-squirrels divided the deserted city among them. And to this day the ground-squirrels pay a tribute of their young to the owls and the rattlesnakes, as the price of possession and of their protection. But they are always afraid that the prairie-dogs may come back again some day (as the Mormons are going back to Jackson County, Missouri), to claim their old homesteads; and so, whenever the ground-squirrels go out to feed and gambol in the meadows, the rattlesnakes remain at the bottom of the holes, and the owls sit on sentry duty at the top. Isn't that as good as any other conjectural history?

And then Madera, with its great canal all rafted over with floating timber, and more indications, in the eating-house, of the neighbourhood of the Big Trees and Yosemite.

For this is the point of departure now in vogue, the distance being only seventy miles, and the roads good. But of the trip to Clark's, and thence on to " Yohamite " and to Fresno Grove—hereafter. Meanwhile, grateful for the good meal at Madera, we are again smoking the meditative pipe, and looking out upon Owl-land, with the birds all duly perched at their posts, and their bushy-tailed companions enjoying life immensely in family parties among the short grass. Herds of cattle are seen here and there, and wonderful their condition, too ; and thus, through flat pastures all pimpled over with old, fallen-in, " dog-houses," we reach Fresno. This monotony of fertility is beginning to exasperate me. It is a trait of my personal character, this objection to monotonous prosperity. I like to see streaks of lean. Thus I begin to think of Vanderbilts as of men who have done me an injury ; and unless Jay Gould recovers his ground with me, by conferring a share upon me, I shall feel called upon to take personal exception to his great wealth. And now comes Fresno, a welcome stretch of land that requires irrigation to be fruitful, a land that only gives her favours to earnest wooers, and does not, like the rest of California, smile on every vagabond admirer. Where the ground is not cultivated, it forms fine parade-ground for the owls, and rare pleasaunces for the squirrels. But what a nymph this same water is ! Look at this patch of greensward all set in a bezel of bright foliage and bright with wild flowers ! In mythology there is a goddess under whose feet the earth breaks into blossoms and leaves. I forget her name. But it should have been Hydore. And now, as the evening gathers round, we see the outlines of the Sierras, away on the left, blurring into twilight tints of blue and grey—and then to bed.

California is blest in the olive. It grows to perfection,

and the result is that the California is no stranger to the priceless luxury of good oil, and can enjoy, at little cost, the delights of a good salad. How often, in rural England, with acres of salad material growing fresh and crisp all round me, have I groaned at the impossibility of a salad, by reason of the atrocious character of the local grocer's oil! But in California all the oil is good, and the vegetable ingredients of the fascinating bowl are superb. But in America there is a fatal determination towards mayonnaise, and every common waiter considers himself capable of mixing one. So that even in California your hopes are sometimes blighted, and your good humour turned to gall, by fools rushing in where even angels should have to pass an examination before admission. A simpler salad, however, is better than any mayonnaise, and once the proportions are mastered, a child may be entrusted with the mixture.

The lettuce, by long familiarity, has come to be considered the true basis of all salad, and in its generous expanse of faintly flavoured leaf, so cool and juicy and crisp when brought in fresh from the garden, it has certainly some claims to the proud position. But a multitude of salads can be made without any lettuce at all, and it is doubtful whether either Greece or Rome used it as an ingredient of the bowl in which the austere endive and pungent onion always found a place. Now-a-days however, lettuce is a deserving favourite, It has no sympathies or antipathies, and no flavour strong enough to arouse enthusiasm or aversion. It is not aggressive or self-assertive, but, like those amiable people with whom no one ever quarrels, is always ready to be of service, no matter what company may be thrust upon it, or what treatment it has to undergo. Opinions of its own it has none, so it easily adopts those of others, and takes upon itself— and so distributes over the whole-- any properties of taste or smell that may be communicated to it by its neighbours. An onion might be rubbed with lettuce for an indefinite period and betray no alteration in its original nature, but the lettuce if only touched with onion becomes at once a modified onion itself, and no ablution will remove from it the suspicion of the contact. The gentle leaf is therefore often ill-used, but, after all, even this, the meekest of vegetables, will turn upon the oppressor, and if not eaten young and fresh, or if slaughtered with a steel blade, will convert the salad that should have been short and sharp in the mouth into a basin of limp rags, that cling together in sodden lumps, and when swallowed conduce to melancholy and repentance. The antithesis of the lettuce is the onion. Both are equally essential to the perfect salad, but for most opposite reasons. The lettuce must be there to give substance to the whole, to retain the oil and salt and vinegar, to borrow fragrance and to look green and crisp. It underlies everything else, and acts as conductor to all, like consciousness in the human mind. It is the bulk of the salad so far as appearances go, and yet it alone could be turned out without affecting the flavour of the dish. It is only the canvas upon which the artist paints.

How different is the onion! It adds nothing to the amount, and contributes nothing to the sight, yet it permeates the whole ; not, however, as an actual presence, but rather as a reflection, a shadow, or a suspicion. Like the sunset-red, it tinges everything it falls upon, and everywhere reveals new beauties. It is the master-mind in the mixed assembly, allowing each voice to be heard, but guiding the many utterances to one symmetrical result. It keeps a strong restraint upon itself, helping out, with a judicious hint only, those who need it, and never interfering with neighbours that can assert their own individuality. I speak, of course, of the onion as it appears in the civilized salad, and not the outrageous vegetable that the Prophet condemned and Italy cannot do without. Some pretend to have a prejudice against the onion, but as an American humourist—Dudley Warner — says, " There is rather a cowardice in regard to it. I doubt not all men and women love the onion, but few confess it."

In simplicity lies perfection. The endive and beetroot, fresh bean, and potato, radish and mustard and cress, asparagus and celery, cabbage-hearts and parsley, tomato and cucumber, green peppers and capers, and all the other ingredients that in this salad or in that find a place are, no doubt, well enough in their way ; but the greatest men of modern times have agreed in saying that, given three vege-tables and a master-mind, a perfect salad may be the result. But for the making there requires to be present a miser to dole out the vinegar, a spendthrift to sluice on the oil, a sage to apportion the salt, and a maniac to stir. The household that can produce these four, and has at command a firm, stout-hearted lettuce, three delicate spring onions, and a handful of cress, need ask help from none and envy none ; for in the consumption of the salad thus ambrosially resulting, all earth's cares may be for the while forgotten, and the consumer snap his fingers at the stocks, whether they go up or down. There is no need to go beyond these frugal ingredients. In Europe it is true men range hazardously far afield for their green meat. They tell us, for instance, of the fearful joy to be snatched from nettle-tops, but it is not many who care thus to rob the hairy caterpillar of his natural food ; nor in eating the hawthorn buds, where the sparrows have been before us, is there such prospect of satisfaction as to make us hurry to the hedges. The dandelion, too, we are told, is a wholesome herb, and so is wild sorrel; but who among us can find the time to go wandering about the country grazing with the cattle, and playing Nebuchadnezzar among the green stuff? In the Orient the native is never at a loss for salad, for he grabs the weeds at a venture, and devours them complacently, relying upon "fate" to work them all up to a good end; and the Chinaman, so long as he can only boil it first, turns everything that grows into a vegetable for the table.

But it would not be safe to send a public of higher organization into the highways and ditches; for a rabid longing for vegetable food, unballasted by botanical knowledge, might conduce to the consumption of many unwholesome plants, with their concomitant insect evils. Dreadful stories are told of the results arising from the careless eating of unwashed watercress; and in country places the horrors that are said to attend the swallowing of certain herbs without a previous removal of the things that inhabit them are sufficient to deter the most ravenously inclined from taking a miscellaneous meal off the roadside, and from promiscuous grazing in hedge-rows.

CHAPTER XXV.

THE ᵢcactus is the Carlyle of vegetation. Here, in Southern California, it assumes many of its most uncouth and affected attitudes, puts on all its prickles and its angles, and its blossoms of rare splendour. Those who are better informed than myself assure me that the cactus is a vegetable. I take their word for it. Indeed, the cactus itself may have said so to them. There is nothing a cactus might not do. But it surely stands among plants somewhere where bats do among animals, and the apteryx among birds. Look for instance at this tract of cactus which we cross before Caliente. There are chair-legs and footstools, pokers, brooms, and telegraph-poles; but can you honestly call them *plants ?*

But stay a moment. Can you not call them plants ? Look ! See those superb blossoms of crimson upon that footstool of thorns, those golden stars upon the telegraph-pole yonder, those beautiful flowers of rosy pink upon that besom-head. Yes, they *are* plants, and worthy of all admiration, for they have the genius of a true originality, and the sudden splendour of the flowers they put forth are made all the more admirable by the surprise of them and the eccentricity.

And with them grows the yucca, that wonderful plant that sends up from its rosette of bayonets—they call it the "Spanish bayonet" in the West—a green shaft, six feet high, and all hung with white waxen bells. I got out of the train at one of its stoppages, and cut a couple of heads of this wonderland plant, and found the blossoms on each numbered between 400 and 406. And there was a certain moral discipline in it too. For we found these exquisite flower-hung shafts were smothered in "blight," those detestable, green, sticky aphides, that sometimes make rose-buds so dreadful, and are the enemy of all hothouses. Looking out at the yuccas as we passed, those splendid coronals of waxen blossoms—pure enough for cathedral chancels—it seemed as if they were things of a perfect and unsullied beauty. My arrival with them was hailed with cries of admiration, and for the first moment enthusiasm was supreme. But the next, alas for impure beauty! the swarms of clinging parasites were detected. Hands that had been stretched out to hold such things of grace, shrank from even touching them, known to be polluted, and so, at last, with honours that were more than half condescension, the yucca-spikes were put out on the platform, to be admired from a distance. Passing through the cactus land we saw numbers of tiny rabbits—the "cotton tails," as distinguished from the "mule-ears" or jack-rabbits—dodging about the stems and grass; but in about an hour the grotesque vegetable began to sober down into a botanical conglomerate that defies analysis, and gives the little rabbits a denser covert. The general result of this change in the botany was as Asiatic, as Indian as it could be, but *why*, it were difficult to say, unless it was the prevalence of the babool-like "muskeet," and the beautiful but murderous dhatura—the "thorn-apple" of Europe. Yet there was sage-brush enough to make

Asia impossible, while the variations of the botany were too sudden for any generalizations of character. And so on, past an oil-mill on the left—petroleum bubbling out of the hillock—and a great farm, "Newhall's," on the right; past Andrews and up the hill to the San Fernando tunnel, 7000 feet in length, and then down the hill again into San Fernando. Has any one ever "stopped off" at San Fernando and spent any time with the monks at their picturesque old mission, smothered in orangeries, and dozed away the summer hours amongst them, watching the peaches ripen and the bees gathering honey, and opening bottles of mellow California wine to help along the intervals between drowsy mass and merry meal-times? I think when my sins weigh too heavily on me to let me live among men, I will retire to San Fernando, to the bee-keeping, orange-growing fathers, ask them to receive my bones, and start a beehive and an orange-tree of my own. It does not seem to me, looking forward to it, a very arduous life, and I might then, at last, overtake that seldom-captured will-o'-the-wisp, fleet-footed Leisure.

The bees, by the way, are kept on a "ranch," whole herds and herds of bees, all hived together in long rows of hives, hundreds to the acre. They fly afield to feed themselves, and come home with their honey to make the monks rich. I am not sure that these fathers have done all they might for the country they settled in, and yet who is not grateful to the brethren for the picturesqueness of comparative antiquity? Their very idleness is a charm, and their quiet, comfortable life, half in cloisters, half in orange groves, is a delight and a refreshment in modern America.

But the loveliness of their country, and the wonder of its possibilities! Can any one be surprised that we are approaching the city of *Los Angeles?* A bright river comes tumbling along under cliffs all hung with flowering creepers, and between banks that are beautiful with ferns and flowers, and the land widens out into cornfield and meadow; and away to right and left, lying under the hills and overflowing into all the valleys, are the vineyards, and orchards, and orangeries that make the City of Angels worthy of a king's envy and a people's pride. As yet, of course, it is the day of small things, as compared with what will be when water is everywhere; but even now Los Angeles is a place for the artist to stay in and the tourist to visit. There is a great deal to remind you of the East, in this valley of dark-skinned men, and in the "bazaars," with their long ropes of chilis dangling on the door-posts, the fruit piled up in baskets on the mules, the brown bare-legged children under hats with wide ragged brims, there are all the familiar features of Southern Europe, hot, strong-smelling, and picturesque. But Los Angeles shares with the rest of California the disadvantage under which all climates of great forcing power and rudimentary science must lie, for its fruits, though exquisite to look upon, often prodigious in size, and always incredible in quantity, fail, as a rule, dismally in flavour. The figs are very large, both green and black, but they seem to have ripened in a perpetual rainstorm ; the oranges look perfection, and are as bad as any I have had in America ; the peaches are splendid in their appearance, for their coarse barbaric skins are painted with deep yellow and red, but they ought not to be called "peaches" at all. They would taste just as well by any other name, and the traveller who knows the peaches of Europe, or the peaches of Persia, would not then be disappointed.

So away from Los Angeles, with its groups of idle, brown-faced men, in their flap-brimmed Mexican hats, leaning against the posts smoking thin cigars, and its groups of listless, dark-eyed women, with bright kerchiefs round their heads or necks, sitting on the doorsteps; away through valleys of corn, broken up by orangeries and vineyards, where the river flows through a tangle of willow and elder and muskeet; past the San Gabriel Mission, overtaken, poor idle old fragment of the past, by the railroad civilization of the present, and already isolated in its sleepiness and antiquity from the busier, younger world about it; on through a scene of perpetual fertility, orange groves and lemon, fields of vegetables and corn, with pomegranates all aglow with scarlet flowers, and eucalyptus-trees in their ragged foliage of blue and brown.

The squash grows here to a monstrous size. " I have seen them, sir," said a passenger, "weighing as much as yourself." The impertinence of it! Think of a squash venturing to turn the scale against me. Perhaps it will pretend that it has as good a seat on a horse? Or will it play me a single-wicket match at cricket? I should not have minded so much if it had been a water-melon, or even a " simlin," or some other refined variety of the family. But that a *squash*, the 'poor relation' of the pumpkin, should——. But enough. Let us be generous, even to squashes.

Some one ought to write the psychology of the squash. There is a very large human family of the same name and character. If you ask what the bulky, tasteless thing is good for, people always say, " Oh, for a pie !" Now that is the only form in which I have tasted it. And I can say, from personal experience, therefore, that it is not good for *that*. It never hurts anybody, or speaks ill of any one – an inoffensive, tedious, stupid person, too commonplace to be either liked or disliked. Economical parents say squashes are " very good for children," espe-

Y

cially in pies. They may be. But they are not conducive to the formation of character.

Some one, too, ought to visit these old Franciscan missions in Southern California—some one who could write about them, and sketch them. They are very delightful ; the more delightful, perhaps, because they are in the United States, in the same continent as "live" towns, as Chicago, and Omaha, and Leadville, and Tombstone. Scattered about among the rolling grassland are hollows filled with orchards, in which old settlements and new are fairly embowered, while the missions themselves are singularly picturesque ; and San Gabriel's Church, they say, has a pretty peal of bells, which the monks carried overland from Mexico in the old Spaniard days, and which still chime for vespers as sweetly as ever. What a wonder it must have been to the wandering Indians to hear that most beautiful of all melodies, the chime of bells, ascending with the evening mists from under the feet of the hills ! No wonder they had campanile legends, these poor poets of the river and prairie, and still speak of Valleys of Enchantment whence music may be heard at nightfall !

Past Savanna and Monte, with its swine droves, and its settlement of men who live on "hog and hominy," past Puente, and Spadra, and Pomona, into Colton, where we dine, and well, for half a dollar, enjoying for dessert a chat with a very pretty girl. She tells us of the beauties of San Bernardino, and I could easily credit even more than she says. For San Bernardino was settled by Mormons some fifty years ago, and has all the charms of Salt Lake City, with those of natural fertility and a profusion of natural vegetaton added. But I can say nothing of San Bernardino, for the train does not enter it. And then, reinforced by another engine—a dumpy engine-of-all-work sort of "help"—clambers up the San Gorgonio pass. All along the road I notice a yellow thread-like epiphyte, or air-plant, tangling itself round the muskeet-trees, and killing them. They call it the "mistletoe" here; but it is the same curious plant that strangles the orange trees in Indian gardens, and the jujubes in the jungles, that cobwebs the aloe hedges, and hangs its pretty little white bells of flower all over the undergrowth. On the bare, sandy ground a wild gourd, with yellow flowers and sharp-pointed spear-head leaves, throws out long strands, that creep flat upon the ground with a curious snake-like appearance. Clumps of wild oleander find a frugal subsistence, and here and there an elder or a walnut manages to thrive. But the profuse fertility of California is fast disappearing. And so to Gorgonio, at the top of the pass; and then we begin to go down, down, down, till we are not surprised to hear that we are far below the level of the sea. The cactus has once more reasserted itself, and to right and left are "forests" of this grotesque candelabra-like vegetable, with stiff arms, covered apparently with some woolly sort of fluff. The soil beneath them is a desperate-looking desert-sand, and here and there are bare levels of white glistening sterility. But water works such wonders that there is no saying what may happen. At present, however, it is pure, unadulterated desert—wilderness enough to delight a camel, were it not for the quantity of stones which strew the waste, and which would make it an abomination to that fastidious beast. Camels were once imported into the country, but the experiment failed —and no wonder. Imagine the modern American trying to drive a camel! The Mexican might do it, but I doubt if any other race in all America could be found with sufficient contempt for time, sufficient patience in idleness, sufficient *camelishness* in fact, to "personally conduct" a camel train. There is a tradition, by the way, that somewhere in Arizona, wild camels, the descendants of the discarded brutes, are to be met with to this day, enjoying a life without occupations.

At present the most formidable animal in possession of these cactus plains is the rabbit. But such a licence of ears as the creature has taken! It must be developing them as weapons of offence : the future "horned rabbit." They call these long-eared animals "mules," and deny that you can make a rabbit-pie of them. This seems to me hardly fair on the rabbit. But in England the small rodent suffers under even more pointed injustice.

A certain railway porter, it is said, was once sorely puzzled by a tortoise which the owner wished to send by train. The official was nonplussed by the inquiry as to which head of the tariff the creature should be considered to fall under ; but, at last, deciding that it was neither "a dog" nor "a parrot" (the broad zoological classification in use on British railways) pronounced the tortoise to be "an insect," and therefore not liable to charge. This profound decision was prefaced by a brief enumeration of the animals which the railway company call "dogs." "Cats is dogs, and rabbits is dogs, and so is guinea-pigs," said the porter, "but squirrels in cages is parrots!"

But please note particularly the porter's confusion of identity with regard to the rabbit. This excellent rodent is emphatically called "a dog." But the rabbit knows much better than to mistake itself for a dog. It might as well think itself a poacher.

Meanwhile, other attempts have been made to confuse it as to its own individuality; and if the rabbit eventually gives itself up as a hopeless conundrum, it is not more than might be expected. Its fur is now called "seal-skin" in the cheap goods market; the fluke has attacked it as if it were a sheep; while in recent English elections, when the Ground Game Bill was to the front, it was a very important factor. All the same, everybody goes on shooting it just as if it were a mere rabbit. This, I would contend, is hardly fair ; for if its skin is really sealskin, the rabbit must, of necessity, be a seal, and, as such, ought to be harpooned from a boat, and not shot at with double-barrelled guns. It is absurd to talk of going out "sealing" in gaiters, with a terrier, for the pursuit of the seal is a marine operation, and concerned with ships and icebergs and whaling line. A sportsman, therefore, who goes out in quest of this valuable pelt should, in common regard for the proprieties, affect Arctic apparel; and, instead of ranging with his gun, should station himself with a harpoon over the "seal's" blow-hole, and, when it comes up to breathe, take his chance of striking it, not forgetting to have some water handy to pour over the line while it is being rapidly paid out, as otherwise it is very liable to catch fire from friction. By this means the rabbit would arrive at some intelligible conception of itself, and be spared much of the discomfort which must now arise from doubts as to its personality. Nothing, indeed, is so precious to sentient things as a conviction of their own "identity" and their "individuality," and I need only refer those who have any doubt about it to the whole range of moral philosophy to assure themselves of this fact. If we were not certain who we were two days running, much of the pleasure of life would be lost to us.

We entered the arid tract somewhere near the station of the Seven Palms. They can be seen growing far away on the left under the "foot-hills." About half way through we find ourselves at the station of Two Palms, but they are

in tubs.   Of course there may be others, and no doubt are.
But all you can see from the cars is a limited wilderness.
Yet on those mountains there, on the right—one is 12,000
feet—there is splendid pine timber ; and on the other side of
them, incredible as it seems, are glorious pastures, where the
cattle are wading knee-deep in grass ! For us, however,
the hideous wilderness continues.   The hours pass in
a monotony of glaring sand, ugly rock fragments, and
occasional bristly cactus.   And then begins a low chapparal
of "camel-thorn" or "muskeet," and as evening closes in
we find ourselves at the Colorado River and at Yuma, where
the sun shines from a cloudless sky three hundred and ten
days in the year.

And the weather ?   I have not mentioned it as we travelled along, for I wished to emphasize it by bringing it in
at the end of the chaper.   Well, *the weather.*   There was
none to speak of, unless you can call a fierce dry over-heat,
averaging 96° in the shade, weather.   And this is all that
we have had for the last twelve hours or so ; heat enough to
blister even a lizard, or frizzle a salamander.   A hot wind,
like the "loo" of the Indian plains, blew across the desperate sands, getting scorched itself as it went, and spitefully
passing on its heat to us.   It was as hot as Cawnpore in
June ; nearly as hot as Aden.   And then the change at
Yuma ! We had suddenly stepped from Egypt in August
into Lower Bengal in September—from a villainous dry
heat into a far more villainous damp one.   The thermometer,
though the sun had set, was at 92°, and, added to all, was
such a plague of mosquitoes as would have subdued even
Pharaoh into docility.   The instant—literally, the *instant*—
that we stepped from our cars our necks, hands, and faces
were attacked, and on the platform everybody, even the
half-breed Indians loafing outside the dining-room, were

hard at work with both hands defending themselves from the small miscreants. The effect would have been ludicrous enough to any armour-plated onlooker, but it was no laughing matter. We were too busy slapping ourselves in two places at once to think of even smiling at others similarly engaged ; and the last I remember of detestable Yuma was the man who sells photographs on the platform, whirling his hands with experienced skill round his head and packing up his wares by snatches in between his whirls.

CHAPTER XXVI.

THROUGH THE COWBOYS' COUNTRY.

The Santa Cruz Valley—The Cactus—An ancient and honourable
Pueblo—A terrible Beverage—Are Cicadas deaf?—A floral
Catastrophe—The Secretary and the Peccaries.

YUMA marks the frontier between California and Arizona.
But it might just as well mark the frontier between India and
Beluchistan, for it reproduces with exact fidelity a portion
of the town of Rohri, in Sind. A broad, full-streamed river
(the Colorado) seems to divide the town into two; on the
top of its steep bank stands a military post, a group of bun-
galows, single-storied, white-walled, green-shuttered, verandahed. On the opposite side cluster low, flat-roofed houses,
walled in with mud, while here and there a white-washed
bungalow, with broad projecting eaves, stands in its own
compound. Brown-skinned men with only a waistcloth
round the loins loaf around, and in the sandy spaces that
separate the buildings lean pariah dogs lie about, languid
with the heat. The dreadful temperature assists to complete the delusion, and finally the mosquitoes of the
Colorado river have all the ferocity of those that hatch on
the banks of the Indus.

Against our will, too, these pernicious insects board our
train and refuse to be blown out again by all the draughts
which we tax our ingenuity to create. So we sit up sulkily

in a cloud of tobacco smoke far into the night and Arizona—watching the wonderful cactus-plants passing our windows in gaunt procession, and here and there seeing a fire flash past us, lit probably by Papajo Indians for the preparation of their abominable "poolke" liquor. But the mosquitoes are satisfied at last, and go to sleep, and so we go too.

We awake in the Santa Cruz Valley, with the preposterous cactus poles and posts standing up as stiff and straight as sentries "at attention," and looking as if they were doing it for a joke. There is no unvegetable form that they will not take, for they mimic the shape of gate posts, semaphores, bee-hives, and even *mops*—anything, in fact, apparently that falls in with their humour, and makes them look as unlike plants as possible. I am not sure that they ought not to be punished, some of them. Such botanical lawlessness is deplorable. But, after all, is not this America, where every cactus "may do as he darned pleases"? These cacti, by the way—the gigantic columnar species, which throws up one solid shaft of flesh, fluted on each side, and studded closely with rosettes of spines—are the same that crowd in multitudinous impis on the side of the hills which slope from the massacre-field of Isandula in Zululand, down to the Buffalo River. How well I remember them!

If it were not for the cactus it would be a miserably uninteresting country, for the vegetation is only the lowest and poorest looking scrub, and water as yet there is none. But now we are approaching what the inhabitants call "the ancient and honourable pueblo of Tucson," pronouncing it *Too son*, and ancient and honourable we found it. For does it not dispute with Santa Fé the title of the most ancient town in the United States? and was not the breakfast which it gave us worthy of all honour?

It takes, reader, as you will have guessed, a very
long journey indeed to knock into a traveller's head a
complete conception of the size of North America. Mere
space could never do it, for human nature is such that when
trying to grasp in the mind any great lapse of time or territory, the two ends are brought together as it were, and all
the great middle is forgotten. Nor does mere variety of
scene emphasize distance on the memory, for the more
striking details here and there crowd out the large monotonous intervals. Thus a mile of an Echo cañon obliterates
half a state's length of Platte Valley pastures, and a single
patch of Arkansas turtle-swamp whole prairies of Texan
meadow. But in America, even though many successive
days of unbroken travel may have run into one, or its
many variations—from populous states to desert ones,
from timber states to pasture ones, from corn states to
mineral ones, from mountain to valley, river to lake, can-
yoned hills to herd-supporting prairies, from pine forest to
oak forest, from sodden marsh to arid cactus-land—may have
got blurred together, there grows at the end of it all upon the
mind a befitting sense of vastness which neither linear mea-
surement in miles nor variety in the panorama fully explain.
It is due, I think, to the size of the *instalments* in which
America puts forward her alternations of scene. She does
not keep shifting her suits, so as to spoil the effect of her
really strong hand, but goes on leading each till she has
established it, and made each equally impressive. You have
a whole day at a time of one thing, and then you go to sleep,
and when you wake it is just the same, and you cannot help
saying to yourself "Twenty-four successive hours of meadow-
land is a considerable pasturage," and you do not forget
it ever afterwards. The next item is twenty-four hours of
mountains, "all of them rich in metals;" and by the time

this has got indelibly fixed on the memory, Nature changes
the slide, and then there is rolling corn-land on the screen
for a day and night. And so, in a series of majestic alternations, the continent passes in review, and eventually
all blends into one vast comprehensible whole.

Apart from physical, there are curious ethnological divisions which mark off the continent into gigantic sub-nationali-
ties. For though the whole is of course "American," there
is always an underlying race, a subsidiary one so to speak,
which allots the vast area into separate compartments.
Thus on the eastern coast we have the mulatto, who gives
place beyond Nebraska to the Indian, and he, beyond Nevada, to the Chinaman. After California comes the
Mexican, and after him the negro, and so back to the East
and the mulatto again.

Here in Arizona, at Tucson, the "Mexican" is in the
ascendant, for such is the name which this wonderful mixture of nationalities prefers to be called by. He is really a
kind of hash, made up of all sorts of brown-skinnned
odds and ends, an *olla podrida*. But he calls himself
"Mexican," and Tucson is his ancient and honourable
pueblo. It is a wretched-looking place from the train, with
its slouching hybrid men, and multitudinous pariah dogs.
Indians go about with the possessive air of those who know
themselves to be at home; and it is not easy to decide
whether they, with their naked bodies and ropes of hair
dangling to the waist, or the half-breed Mexican with their
villainous slouch and ragged shabbiness, are the lower race
of the two. And the dogs! they are legion; having no
homes, they are at home everywhere. I am told there is a
public garden, and some "elegant" buildings, but as usual
they are on "the other side of the town." All that we can
see on *this* side, are collections of squalid Arabic-looking

huts and houses, made of mud, low-roofed and stockaded
with ragged-looking fences. The heat is of course prodigious for eight months of the year, and the dust and the
flies and the mosquitoes are each and all as Asiatic as the
heat—or any other feature of this ancient and honourable
pueblo. It has its interest, however, as an American
" antiquity ; " while the river, the Santa Cruz, which flows
past the town, is one of those Arethusa streams, which
comes to the surface a few miles above the town and
disappears again a few miles below it.

For the student of hybrid life, Tucson must have exceptional attractions ; but for the ordinary traveller, it has
positively none. Kawai Indians have not many points
very different from Papajo Indians, and mud hovels are
after all only mud hovels. But it is an ancient and honourable pueblo.

The only people who look cool are the Mexican
soldiers in blue and white, and that other Mexican, a
civilian, in a broad-brimmed, flimsy hat, spangled with a
tinsel braid and fringe. Have these men ever got anything to do ? and when they have, do they ever do it ? It
seems impossible they could undertake any work more
arduous than lolling against a post, and smoking a yellow-
papered cigarette. Yet only a few days ago these Mexicans,
perhaps those very soldiers there, destroyed a tribe of
Apaches, and then arrested a force of Arizona Rangers who
had pursued the Indians on to Mexican ground ! These
Apaches had kept the State in a perpetual terror for a long
time, but finding the Federal soldiers closing in upon them,
they crossed the frontier line close to Tucson, and there fell
in with the Mexicans, who must at any rate be given the
credit for promptitude and efficiency in all their Indian
conflicts. The Apaches were destroyed, and the force of

Rangers who had followed them were caught by the Mexican general, and under an old agreement between the two Republics, they were made prisoners of war, disarmed, and told to find their way back two hundred and fifty miles into the States as best and as quickly as they could. Some thirty years ago a Mexican general, who captured some American filibusters in a similar way at the village of Cavorca, paraded his captives and shot them all down. So the Arizona men were glad enough to get away.

The cactus country continues, and the plants play the mountebank more audaciously than ever. There is no absurdity they will not commit, even to pretending that they are broken fishing rods, or bundles of riding whips. But the majority stand about in blunt, kerb-stone fashion, as if they thought they were marking out streets and squares for the cotton-tail rabbits that live amongst them. Under the hill on the left is the old mission church of " San'avēre " (San Xavier); and over those mountains, the " Whetstones," lies the mining settlement of Tombstone, where the cowboys rejoice to run their race, and the value of life seldom rises to par in the market. Then we enter upon a plain of the mezcal all in full bloom, and a "lodge" of brown men, partly Indian, partly Mexican, waiting it may be for the plant to mature and the time to come round for distilling its fiery liquor. I tasted mezcal at El Paso for the first time in my life, and I think I may venture to say the last, so whether it was good of its kind or not, I cannot tell. I am no judge of mezcal. But I know that it was thick, of a dull sherry colour, with a nasty vegetable smell, and infinitely more fiery than anything I ever tasted before, not excepting the whisky which the natives in parts of Central India brew from rye, the brandy which the Boers of the Transvaal distil from rotten potatoes, or the "tarantula juice " which you are often offered by the hearty miners of Colorado. It is almost literally "fire-water;" but the red pepper, I suppose, has as much to do with the effect upon the tongue and palate as the juice of the mezcal.

On a sudden, in the midst of this desolate iand, we come upon a ranche with cattle wading about among the rich blue grass; but in a minute it is gone, and lo! a Chinese village, smothered in a tangle of shrubs all overgrown with creeping gourds, with the coolies lying in the shade smoking long pipes of reed.

Have you ever smoked Chinese "tobacco"? If not, be careful how you do. A single pipe of it (and Chinese pipes hold very little) will upset even an old smoker. For myself, I can hardly believe it *is* tobacco, for in the hand it feels of a silky texture, utterly unlike any tobacco I ever saw, while the smell of it, and the taste on the tongue, are as different to the *buena yerba* as possible. It is imported by the Chinese in America for their own consumption, and in spite of duties is exceedingly cheap. A single sniff of it, by the way, completely explains that heavy, stupefying odour which hangs about Chinese quarters and Chinese persons.

But this glimpse of China has disappeared as rapidly as the ranche had done, and in a few minutes later a collection of low mud-walled huts, overshadowed by rank vegetation, an ox or two trying to chew the cud in the shade, an uptilted cart, some brown-skinned children playing with magnolia blossoms, and lo! a glimpse of Bengal.

And then as suddenly we are out again on to the cactus plains with cotton-tail rabbits everywhere, and cicadas innumerable shrilling from the muskeet trees. Above all the noise of the train we could hear the incessant chorus filling the hot out-of-doors, and, stepping on to the rear platform, I found that several had flown or been blown on to the car.

Poor helpless creatures, with their foolish big-eyed heads and little brown bodies wrapped up in a pair of large transparent wings. But fancy living in such a hideous din as these cicadas live in! Do naturalists know whether they are deaf? One would suppose of course that the voice was given them originally for calling to each other in the desolate wastes in which they are sometimes found scattered about. But in the lapse of countless generations that have spent their lives crowded together in one bush, sitting often actually elbow to elbow and screaming to each other at the tops of their voices, it is hardly less rational to suppose that kindly Nature has encouraged them to develop a comfortable deafness. At any rate it is impossible to suppose that even a cicada can enjoy the ear-splitting clamour in which its neighbours indulge, and which now keeps up with us all the way as we traverse the San Pedro Valley, and mounting from plateau to plateau—some of them fine grass land, others arid cactus beds—reach another " Great Divide," and then descend across an immense, desolate prairie, brightened here and there with beautiful patches of flowers, into the San Simon Valley. And all the time we eat our dinner (at the Bowie station) the cicadas go on shrilling, on the hot and dusty ground, till the air is fairly thrilling, with the waves of barren sound. That sounds like rhyme,—and I do not wonder at it,—for even the cicadas themselves manage to drift into a kind of metre in their arid aimless clamour, and the high noon, as we sit on our cars again, looking out on the pink-flowered cactus and the mezcal with its shafts of white blossoms, seems to throb with a regular pulsation of strident sound.

What a desolate land it seems, this New Mexico into which we have crossed! But not for long. We soon find ourselves out upon a vast plain of grassland, upon which the sullen, egotistical cactus will not grow. " You common vegetables may grow there if you like," it says. " Any fool of a plant can grow where there is good soil; but it shows genius to grow on no soil at all." So it will not stir a step on to the grass-land, but stands there out on the barren sun-smitten sand, throwing up its columns of juicy green flesh and bursting out all over into flowers of vivid splendour, just to show perhaps that " Todgers's can do it when it likes." There is about the cactus' conduct something of the superciliousness of the camel, which wades through hay with its nose up in the air as if it scorned the gross provender of vulgar herds, and then nibbles its huge stomach full of the tiny tufts of leaves which is found growing among the topmost thorns of the scanty mimosa.

Here, on this plain, is plenty of the " camel thorn," the muskeet, and a whole wilderness of Spanish bayonet waiting till some one thinks it worth while to turn it into paper, and there is not probably a finer fibre in the world. Nor, because the cactus contemns the easy levels, do other flowers refuse to grow. They are here in exquisite profusion, a foretaste of the Texan " flower-prairies," and when the train stopped for water I got out and from a yard of ground gathered a dozen varieties. Nearly all of them were old familiar friends of English gardens, and some were beautifully scented, notably one with a delicate thyme perfume, and another that had all the fragrance of lemon verbena.

Both to north and south are mountains very rich in mineral wealth, and at Lordsburg, where we halted, I could not resist the temptation of buying some " specimens." I had often resisted the same temptation before, but here somehow the beauty of the fragments was irresistible. Outside the station, by the way, under a heap of rubbish, were lying a score or so of bars of copper bullion, worth, perhaps, twenty pounds apiece. Such bulky plunder probably suits nobody in a climate of everlasting heat, but it is all pure copper nevertheless—pennies *en bloc.*

The plain continues in a monotony of low muskeet scrub, broken· here and there by flowering mezcal. It is utterly waterless, and, except for one fortnight's rain which it receives, gets no water all the year round. Yet beautiful flowers are in blossom even now, and what it must be just after the rain has fallen it is difficult to imagine. To this great flower-grown chapparal succeeds a natural curiosity of a very striking kind—a vast cemetery of dead yuccas. It looks as if some terrific epidemic had swept in a wave of scorching death over the immense savannah of stately plants. Not one has escaped. And there they stand, thousand by thousand, mile after mile, each yucca in its place, but brown and dead. And so through the graveyards of the dead things into Deming—Deming of evil repute, and ill-favoured enough to justify such a reputation. Even the cowboy fresh from Tombstone used to call Deming " a hard place," and there is a dreadful legend that once upon a time, that is to say, about ten years ago, every man in the den had been a murderer ! No one would go there except those who were conscious that their lives were already forfeited to the law, and who preferred the excitement of death in a saloon fight to the dull formalities of hanging. However, *tempora mutantur,* and all that I remember Deming for myself is its appearance of dejection and a very tolerable supper.

And then away again, across the same flower-grown meadow, with its sprinkling of muskeet bushes, and its platoons of yucca, but now all radiant in their bridal bravery of waxen white. The death-line of the beautiful plant seems to have

z

been mysteriously drawn at Deming. I got out at a stoppage and cut two more of the yuccas. The temptation to possess such splendour of blossom was too great to resist. But alas ! as before, the dainty thing in its virginal white was hideous with clinging parasites, and so I fastened them into the brake-wheel on the platform, and sitting in my car smoking, could look out at the great mass of silver bells that thus completely filled the doorway, and in the falling twilight they grew quite ghostly, the spectres of dead flowers, and touching them we find the flowers all clammy and cold. " How it chills one !" said a girl, holding a thick, white, damp petal between her fingers. " It feels like a dead thing."

And sitting out in the moonlight—an exquisite change after the hateful heat of the day that was past—we saw the muskeet growth gradually dwindle away, and then great lengths of wind-swept sand-dunes supervened. And every now and then a monstrous owl—the "great grey owl of California," I think it must have been—tumbled up off the ground and into the sky above us. Otherwise the desolation was utter. But I sat on smoking into the night, and was abundantly repaid after awhile, for the country, as if weary of its monotony, suddenly swells up into billows and sinks into huge troughs, a land-Atlantic that beats upon the rocks of the Colorado range to right and left ; and as we cut our way through the crests of its waves, the land broke away from before us into bay-like recesses, crowned with galleries of pinnacled rock and curved round into great amphitheatres of cliff. But away on the left it seemed heaving with a more prodigious swell, and every now and then down in the hollows I thought I could catch glimpses of moon-lit water glittering. And the train sped on, winding in and out of the upper ridges of the valley brim, and then, descending, plunged into a dense growth of willows, and lo !

the Rio Grande, and "the shining levels of the mere." It was *it* then, this splendid stream, that had been disturbing the land so, thrusting the valley this way and that, shaping the hills to its pleasure, and that now rolled its flood along the stately water-way which it had made, with groves of trees for reed beds and a mountain range for banks !

We cross it soon, seeing the Santa Fé line pass underneath us with the river flowing underneath it again—and then with the Rio Grande gradually curving away from us, we reach El Paso. And it is well perhaps for El Paso, that we see it under the gracious witchery of moonlight, for it is a place to flee from. Without one of the merits of Asia, it has all Asia's plagues of heat and insects and dust. And no one plants trees or sows crops ; and so, sun-smitten, and waterless, it lies there blistering, with all its population of half-breeds and pariah dogs, a place, as I said, to flee from. And yet on the other side of the river, a rifle-shot off, is the Mexican town of El Paso—for the river here separates the States from their neighbour Republic—and *there*, there are shade trees and pleasant houses, well-ordered streets, and all the adjuncts of a superior civilization.

A brawl alongside the station platform, with a horrible admixture of polyglot oaths and the flash of knives, is the only incident of El Paso life we travellers had experience of. But it may be characteristic.

One of the party who had been incidentally concerned in the disagreement travelled with us. He knew both New and Old Mexico well, and among other things which he told me I remember that he said that he had seen peccaries in New Mexico, on the borders of Arizona. I had thought till then that this very disagreeable member of the pig family confined itself to more southern regions.

Treed by pigs is not exactly the position in which we should expect to find a Colonial Secretary—at least, not often. But when one of the Secretaries in Honduras was recently exploring the interior of the country, he was overtaken by a drove of peccaries, and had only time to take a snap shot at the first of them and scramble up a tree, dropping his rifle in the performance, before the whole pack were round his perch, gnashing their teeth at him, grunting, and sharpening their tusks against his tree. Now the peccary is not only ferocious but patient, and rather than let a meal escape it, it will wait about for days, so that the Secretary had only two courses—either to remain where he was till he dropped down among the swine from sheer exhaustion and hunger, or else to commit suicide at once by coming down to be killed there and then. While he was in this dilemma, however, what should come along—and looking out for supper too—but a jaguar. Never was beast of prey so opportune! For the jaguar has a particular fondness for wild pork, and the peccaries know it, for no sooner did they see the great ruddy head thrust out through the bushes than they bolted helter-skelter, forgetting, in their anxiety to save their own bacon, the meal they were themselves leaving up the tree. The jaguar was off after the swine with admirable promptitude, and the Secretary, finding the coast clear, came down—reflecting, as he walked towards the camp, upon the admirable arrangements of Nature, who, having made peccaries to eat Colonial Secretaries, provided also jaguars to eat the peccaries.

And so to sleep, and sleeping, over the boundary into Texas.

CHAPTER XXVII.

American neglect of natural history—Prairie-dogs again ; their courtesy and colouring—Their indifference to science—A hard crowd—Chuckers out—Makeshift Colorado.

"Have we struck another city?" I asked on awaking, and finding the train at a standstill.

"No, sir," said the conductor, "only a water-tank."

"You see," I explained, "there are so many 'cities' on the Railway Companies' maps that one hardly dares to turn one's head from the window, lest one should let slip a few—so I thought it best to ask."

No, it didn't look like a country of many cities. It was Texas. And the grazing land stretched on either side of us to the horizon, without even a cow to break the dead level of the surface. It was patched, however, with wildflowers. Yellow verbena and purple grew in acres together. And then the breakfasting station suddenly overtook us. It was called Coya, and we ate refuse. When we complained, the man and his wife—knock-kneed folk—deplored almost with tears their distance from any food supply, and vowed they had done their best. And while they vowed, we starved on damaged tomatoes ; and on paying the man I gave him advice to go and buy some potter's field with the proceeds, and to act accordingly.

What I hate about being starved is, that you can't smoke afterwards. The best part of a good meal is the pipe afterwards, and the more ample the meal the better the subsequent weed. But on a pint of bad tomatoes no man can smoke with comfort to his stomach. But I ate bananas till I thought I had qualified for tobacco, and with my pipe came more kindly thoughts. Outside the cars the country was doing all it could to soothe me, for the meadows were fairly ablaze with flowers. They were in distracting profusion and of beautiful kinds. I knew most of them as garden and hothouse flowers in England, but not their names; the verbenas, however, were unmistakable, and so was the "painted daisy." It suffices, however, that the country seemed a wild garden as far as the eye could reach, yellow and orange being as usual the prevailing colours.

This determination of wild flowers to these colours is a point worth the notice of science. And why are the very great majority of Spring flowers *yellow ?*

One of my companions called this distraction of colour a "weed-prairie," which reminds me to say that it is perfectly amazing how indifferent the present generation of Western Americans are to the natural history of their country. They cannot easily mistake a crow or a rose. But all other birds, except "snipe" and "prairie chickens," seem to be divided into "robins," and "sparrows;" and all flowers, except the sunflower and the violet, into lilies and primroses. They have not had time yet, they say, to notice the weeds and bugs that are about. But, in the meantime, a most appalling confusion of nomenclature is taking root. As with eatables and other things, the emigrants to the States have taken with them from Europe the names of the most familiar flowers and birds, and anything that takes their fancy is at once christened with their names.

As the sun rose the population of these painted meadows came abroad, multitudes of rabbits, a few "chapparal hens," and myriads—literally myriads—of brilliant butterflies.

And so on for a hundred miles. And then Texas gets a little tired of so much level land and begins to undulate. Dry river-beds are passed, and then a muskeet "chapparal" commences, and with it a prodigious city of prairie-dogs. But the inhabitants are partially civilized. The train does not alarm them in the least. It does not even arouse their curiosity. They sit a few feet off the rails, with their backs to the passing trains. Perhaps they may look over their shoulders at it. But they do not interrupt their gambols nor their work for such a trifle as a train. They eat and squabble and flirt—do anything, in fact, but run away. Now and then, as if out of good taste and not to appear too affected, they make a show of moving a little out of the way. But the motive is so transparent that the trivial change of position counts for nothing. The jack-rabbit imitates the prairie-dog, just as the Indian imitates the white man, and pretends that it too does not care about the train. But there is an expression on its ears that betrays its nervousness; and why, too, does it always manage to get under the shady side of the nearest bush?

One thing more about the prairie-dog, and I have done with him. The soil east of Colorado city changes for a while in colour, being reddish. Before this it had been sandy. And the prairie-dog alters its colour to suit its soil. You might say of course that the dust round its burrows tinged its fur, just as dust will tinge anything it settles on. But it is a fact that the fur itself is redder where the soil is redder, and that in the two tracts the little animal assimilates itself to the ground it sits upon. And the advantage is obvious. Dozens of prairie-dogs sitting motionless on the soil harmonized so exactly with their surroundings that for a time I did not observe them. Detecting one I soon learned to detect all. Now one of the grey prairie dogs on the red soil would have been very conspicuous, just as conspicuous in fact as a red one would have been trying to pass unobserved on the lighter soil.

The undulations now increase into valleys, and splendid they are, with their rich crops of wild hay and abundant life. The train stops at a "station" (I am not sure that it has earned a name yet), and some cowboys, and dreadful of their kind, get on to the train. But it is only for an hour or so. But during that-hour the prairie-dogs had much excitement given them by the perpetual discharging of revolvers into the middle of their family parties. It is impossible to say whether any of them were hit, for the prairie-dog tumbles into his hole with equal rapidity, whether he is alive or dead. But I hope they escaped. For I have a great tenderness for all the small ministers of Nature, in fur and in feathers.

> " Their task in silence perfecting,
>   Still working, blaming still our vain turmoil,
>   Labours that shall not fail, when man is gone."

And yet I would be reluctant to say that their indifference to express trains should be encouraged. I don't like to see prairie-dogs thus regardless of the latest triumphs of science. And so if the cowboys' revolvers frightened them a little, let it pass.

The train stopped again at another " station," and our cow-

boy passengers got out, being greeted by two evil-look-
ing vagabonds lying in the shade of a shrub. The meeting
of these worthies looked unmistakably like that of thieves
re-assembling after some criminal expedition. All alike
seemed eager to converse, but they evidently had to wait
till the train was gone. One man had a bundle which he
held very tight (so it seemed to us) between his legs. A
few muttered sentences were exchanged, the speakers turning their heads away from the train while they talked, and
the rest assuming a most ludicrous affectation of indifference
to what was being said. We started off, and looking out at
them from the rear platform of the car, I saw they were
already in full talk. Their animated gestures were almost
as significant as words. Had I referred to the conductor
I might have saved myself all conjecture. For mentioning
my suspicions to him, he said, " Oh, yes ! Those Rangers
who got off at Coya are after that crowd : and they're a hard
crowd too."

They were, without doubt, a terribly " hard crowd " to
look at, these cowboy-men. In England they would probably have followed " chucking out " as a profession. I remember in a police court, during election time, seeing some
hulking victims of the police charged with " rioting." But
they pleaded, in justification of turbulence, that they were
" *chuckers out of meetings !* " They had been captured when
expelling the supporters of a rival candidate from a public
hall with the fag ends of furniture, and made no attempt at
concealment of their misdemeanour. They were paid, they
said, to chuck out, and chucked out accordingly, to the best
of their intelligence and ability, and when overpowered by the
police attempted no subterfuge. Their stock-in-trade were
broad shoulders and prodigious muscle. For any odd job
of fancy work they would perhaps provide themselves with a

few old eggs or put a dead cat or two into their pockets.
But, as a rule, when they went out to business they took only
their fists and their hob-nailed boots with them, relying
upon the meeting room to provide them with table legs and
chairs.   As soon as the signal for the disturbance was given,
the chuckers-out " went for " the furniture, and, armed with
a convenient fragment, looked about for people whom they
ought to chuck.   There were plenty to choose from, for a
meeting consists, as a rule, of several or more persons, and
the chuckers-out having marked down a knot of the enemy,
would proceed to eject them, individually if refractory, in a
body if docile, and would thus, if unopposed by police,
gradually empty the room.   There is something very
humorous in this method of invalidating an obnoxious
orator's arguments, for nothing weakens the force of a
speech so much as the total absence of the audience.
Nevertheless, the chucker-out sees no humour in his job.
It is all serious business to him, and so he goes through his
chucking with uncompromising severity.   Now and then,
perhaps, he expels the wrong man, or visits the political
offences of an enemy upon the innocent head of one of
his own party ; but in political discussions with the legs
of tables and brickbats, such mistakes can hardly help
occurring.

And the beautiful undulating meadows continue, sprinkled
over with shrub-like trees, and populous with rabbits and
prairie-dogs and chapparal hens.   Here and there we come
upon small companies of cattle and horses, most contented
with their pastures ; but what an utter desolation this vast
tract seems to be !   The " stations " are, as yet, mere single
houses, and we hardly see a human being in an hour.
And then comes Colorado, a queer makeshift-looking town,

with apparently only one permanent place of habitation in it—the jail.

Beyond the town we passed some Mexicans supposed to be working, but apparently passing time by pelting stones at the snakes in the water, and soon after stopped to take up some Texan Rangers for the protection of our train during the night. These Rangers reminded me very much of a Boer patrol, and there is no doubt that both cowboys and Indians find them far too efficient for comfort. They are, as a rule, good shots, and all are of course good riders. The pay is good, and, "for a spell" as one of them said, the work was "well enough." And as the evening closed in, and we began to enter a country of dark jungle-looking land, the scene seemed as appropriate as possible for a Texan adventure. But nothing more exciting than cicadas disturbed our sleep. Somebody said they were "katydids," but they were not—they were much katydider.

CHAPTER XXVIII.

Nature's holiday—Through wonderful country—Brown negroes a libel on mankind—The wild-flower state—The black problem—A pie-bald flirt—The hippopotamus and the flea—A narrow escape—The home of the swamp-gobblin—Is the moon a fraud?

IN the morning everything had changed. Vegetation was tropical. Black men had supplanted brown. Occasional tracts of rich meadow, with splendid cattle and large-framed horses wading about among the pasture, alternated with brakes of luxuriant foliage concealing the streams that flowed through them, while fields of cotton in lusty leaf, gigantic maize, and league after league of corn stubble, showed how fertile the negro found his land. And the wild flowers—but what can I say more about them? They seemed even more beautiful than before.

There is something very striking and suggestive in these impressive efforts of Nature to command, at recurring intervals, a recurring homage. Thus, for one interval of the year the rhododendron holds an undivided empire over the densely-wooded slopes of the great Himalayan mountains in India. All the other beauties of mountain and valley are forgotten for that interval of lovely despotism, and every one who can, goes up to see " the rhododendrons in bloom." Nature is very fond of such " tours de force," thinking, it may be, that men who see her every-day marvels and grow

accustomed to them require now and then some extra·
ordinary display, like the special festivals of the ancient
Church, to evoke periodically an extraordinary homage.
Lest the migration of creatures should cease to be a thing
of wonder to us, Nature organizes once in a way a monster
excursion, sometimes of rats, sometimes of deer, but most
frequently of birds, to remind man of the marvellous instinct that draws the animal world from place to place or
from zone to zone. For the same reason, perchance, she
ever and again drives butterflies in clouds from off the
land out on to the open sea, and, that the perpetual miracle
of Spring may not pall upon us, she gives the world in
succession such breadths and tones of colour that even the
callous stop to admire the sudden gold of the meadows, the
hawthorn lying like snowdrifts along the country, the bridal
attire of the chestnuts, or the blue levels of wild hyacinth.
As the priestess of a prodigious cult, Nature decrees at
regular intervals, for the delight and discipline of humanity,
a public festa, or universal holiday, to which the whole
world may go free, and wonder at the profusion of her
beauties.

The track was, in places, very poor indeed, the cars
jumping so much as to make travelling detestable and
travellers "sea-sick." And then Dallas, with an execrable
breakfast, and away again into the wonderful country, with
cattle perpetually wandering on to the track and refusing to
hear the warning shriek of the engine. The country was
richly timbered with oak and willow and walnut, with park-
like tracts intervening of undulating grassland. Here the
stock wandered about in herds as they chose, and except
for a chance tent, or a shanty knocked together with old
packing-cases and canvas, there was no sign of human
population. But in the timbered country every clearing had

the commencement of a settlement, the tumble-down
rickety habitation with which the African, if left to his
own inclinations, is content.   And wonderfully picturesque
they looked, too, these efforts at colonization in the middle
of the forests, with the creepers swinging branches of scarlet
blossoms from the trees, and the foliage of the plantains,
maize and sugar-cane brightening the sombre forest depths.
But the heat must be prodigious, and so must the mosquitoes.

It was Sunday, and after their kind the children of Ham
were taking " rest."   Parties of negresses all dressed in the
whitest of white, with bright-coloured handkerchiefs on their
heads, or hats trimmed with gaudy ribands and flowers,
and sometimes wearing, believe me, *gloves*, were pro-
menading in the jungle with their hulking, insolent-
mannered beaux.   They looked like gorillas masquerading.
In his native country I sincerely like the negro.   But
here in America I regret to find him unlovely.   I am
told that individual negroes have done wonders.   I *know*
they have.   But this does not alter my prejudice.   I think
the brownish American negro of to-day is the most deplorable libel on the human race that I have ever encountered.   And I cannot help fearing that America has a
serious problem growing into existence in the South.   The
brown-black population is there formulating for itself, apart
from white supervision, ideas of self-government, morality,
" independence," and even religion, that may make any
future intervention of a better class a difficult matter, or
may eventuate in the contemporary growth of two sharply-
defined castes of society.   I find the opinion universally
entertained in America that the brownish-black man is *not*
a sound or creditable basis for a community, and now that
I have seen in what numbers and what prosperity he has

established himself in the South, I cannot but think that he may be found in the future an awkward factor in the body politic and social.

The country in fact appears to be breeding helots as fast as it can for the perplexity of the next generation.

To the north of us as we travelled was a large Indian reservation, and at more than one station I saw them crouching about the building. But I should not have mentioned them had it not been that I saw a white man trying to buy a cradle from a squaw. He offered $20 for it, but she would not even turn her head to look at the money. It is quite possible that the mother thought he was bargaining for the papoose as well as the cradle. But I was assured that these women sometimes expend an incredible amount of labour and indeed (for Indians) of money also upon their papoose-panniers. One case was vouched for of an offer of $120 being refused, the Indians stating that there were $80 worth of beads upon the work of art, and that it had taken eleven years to complete.

How beautiful Texas is! And what a future it has! For half a day and a night we have been traversing grazing-land, and for half a day fine timber growing in a soil of intense fertility. And now for half a day we are in a pine country, sometimes with wide levels of turf spreading out among the trees, sometimes with oak and walnut so thickly inter-mingled with the pines that the whole forms a magnificent forest. Passion-flowers entangle all the lower undergrowth, and up the dead trees climbs that fine scarlet creeper which is such an ornament of well-ordered gardens of some English country houses. But here in Texas the people, as usual, have not had time yet to think of adornments, and their ugly shanties therefore remain bare and wooden. They are of course only ugly in themselves, that is to say, in material, shape, and condition, for their surroundings are delightful and location perfect. There is of course a good deal of " the poetry of malaria," as I heard a charming lady say, about some of these sites. For it is impossible to avoid the suspicion of agues and fevers in those splendid clearings, with the rich foliage mobbing each patch of cotton, grapes, or maize.

Whenever we happen to slacken pace near one of them an interesting glimpse of local life is caught. Negroidal women come to the doors or suddenly stand up in the middle of the crops in which, working, they were unperceived. From the undergrowth, the ditches, and from behind fences, appear dusky children, numbers of them, a swart infantry that seems to me to fill the future with perplexity. Are these swarms going to grow up a credit to the country ? Have they it in their breed to be fit companions in progress of the progeny of the best European stocks ?

The abundance of wild life, too, is very noticeable. Wherever we stop we become aware of countless butterflies and insects busy among the foliage, and the voices of strange birds resound from the forest depths.

But other sites appear to me perfection. Take Marshall for instance, or Jefferson. Which is the more beautiful of the two ? Some of the " commercial " settlements, just beginning life with a railway-station, six drug stores, and seven saloons, have situations that ought to have been reserved for honeymoon Edens. They are " hard " places. Law as yet there is none except revolver law, and that is pitiless and sudden and wicked. For Texas, the beautiful flower state, blessed with turf and blessed with pines, has still the stern commencements of American life before it— that rapid, fierce process of civilization which begins with cards and whisky and murder, which finds its first protection in the " Vigilantes " who hold their grim tribunals under the roadside trees, but which suddenly one day wrenches itself, as it were, from its bad, lawless past, and takes its first firm step on the high road to order and prosperity and the world's respect. For every intelligent traveller these ragged, half-savage, settlements should have a great significance and interest. Before he dies they may be Chicagos or San Franciscos. And these men, with their mouths full of oaths and revolvers on their hips, are the fathers of those future cities. They will have no immortality though in the gratitude of posterity. For they will shoot each other off in those saloons, or the Rangers will shoot them down on the flower prairies beyond the forests. But they will have done their work nevertheless. Nature in every part of her scheme proceeds on the same system of building foundations upon ruins. Whole nations have to be killed off when they have prepared and preserved the ground as it were for those that are to follow. Whether they are nations of men, or of beasts, or of plants, she uses them in exactly the same way. Everything must subserve the ultimate end.

But I did not intend to moralize. The negress waiter at Longview (where we dine very badly) reminds me how practical life should be. *She* never stops to moralize. On the contrary, she just stands by the window, swallowing all the peaches and fragments of pudding that the travellers leave on their plates. Two he negroes wait upon us. But it looks as if they were there to feed the negress rather than to feed us. For they keep rushing in with full dishes to us and rushing off with the half empty ones to her. And there she stands omnivorous, insatiable, black. Everything that is brought to her of a sweet kind she swallows. Not as if

A a

she enjoyed it, but as if she must. It was like throwing things into a sink. She never filled up.

And then, through the splendid tropical country, to Marshall. I must return to Marshall, Texas, some day and be disillusioned, or else I shall go down to my grave accusing myself of having passed Paradise in the train, and not " stopped off " there. What an exasperating reflection for a death-bed ! I should never forgive myself. But perhaps it is not so beautiful as it seems. In any case studies " from the life " would be immensely interesting. I caught a few glimpses which entertained me prodigiously. There was the negro dandy walking painfully in patent-leather boots that were made for some man with ordinary feet, with a fan in his hand and a large flower in his button-hole, an old stove-pipe hat on his head, and a very corpulent handleless umbrella under his arm. There was another, similarly caparisoned, escorting three belles for a walk in the neighbouring jungle, the ladies all wearing white cloth gloves and black cloth boots that squelched out spaciously as they put their feet down. And alas ! there was the black coquette, with her bunch of crimson flowers behind her ear, her black satin skirt and white muslin jacket, her parasol of black satin lined with crimson—and how she flirts up the green slope, with a half-acre smile on her face ! She looks back at every other step to see which, if any, of the black men, or the brown, or the yellow, on the station platform is going to follow her expansive charms, and so she disappears, this piebald siren, into the groves, her parasol flashing back Parthian gleams of crimson as she goes. But every one, man, woman, or child, black, brown, or yellow, was a study, so I must go back to Marshall some day.

At present, however, we are whirling away again through the lovely woodland, and the whole afternoon passes in **an** unbroken panorama of forest views, with great glades of meadow breaking away to right and left, and patches of maize and cotton suddenly interrupting the stately procession of timber. And then Jefferson. Is Jefferson more prettily situated than Marshall? I cannot say. But Jefferson lies back among the trees with an interval of orchard and corn-land between it and the railway line, and looks a very charming retreat indeed. A fat negro comes on board on duty of some kind connected with the brake, and a witty little half-breed boy comes on after him. The fat negro is the brown boy's butt. And he nearly bursts with wrath at the hybrid urchin's chaff, and threatens, between gasps, a retaliation that cannot find utterance in words. But the brown boy is relentless, and though the train is rapidly increasing in its speed, he clings to the step and taunts the negro who dare not leave his look-out post. But he knows very well where the fat man will get off, and suddenly, with a parting personality, the little wretch drops off the step, just as a ripe apple might drop off a branch. And then the fat man has to get off. The speed is really dangerous, but he climbs down the steps backwards, thinking apparently only of his tormentor, and still breathing forth fire and slaughter; and then lets go. Is he killed? Not a bit of it. He lands on his feet without apparently even jarring his obese person, and when we look back, we see that he is already throwing stones at the small boy, whose batteries are replying briskly. I wonder if the hippopotamus ever caught the flea? And if he did, what he did to him?

And I remember how the Somali boys in Aden used to drive the bo'sun to the verge of despair by clambering on to the ship and pretending not to see him working his way round towards them with a rope's end behind his back, and how at the very last moment, almost as the arm was raised to strike, the young monkeys used to drop off backwards into the sea, like snails off a wall.

But is this Bengal or Texas that we are travelling through? The vegetation about us is almost that of suburban Calcutta, and the heat, the damp steamy heat of low-lying land, might be the Soonderbuns. And here befell an adventure. We were nearing Atalanta. The train was on a down grade and going very fast indeed, perhaps half a mile a minute. I was sitting on my seat in the Pullman with the table up in front of me and reading. At the other end of the car was a lady with some children sitting with their backs to me. Further off, but also with his back to me, was the conductor. Each "section" of a car has two windows. The one at my left elbow had the blind drawn down. The other had not. On a sudden at my ear, as it seemed, there was a report as of a rifle; the thick double glass of the window in front of me flew into fragments all over me, and the woodwork fell in splinters upon my book. I instantly pulled up the blind of the other window and looked out to see who had "fired." But of course at the speed we were going, there was no one in sight. I called out to the conductor that some one had fired through the window. He had not heard the explosion, nor had the lady. So their surprise was considerable. And while I was looking in the woodwork for the bullet I expected to find, the conductor picked *off my table* a railway spike! Some wretch had thrown it at the passing train, and the great velocity at which we were travelling gave the missile all the deadly force of a bullet. "An inch more towards the centre of the window, sir, and you might have been killed," said the brake-man. A look at the splintered woodwork, and the bullet-like groove which the sharp-pointed abomination had cut for itself, was sufficient to assure me that he was right. But think of the atrocious character of such mischief. The man who did it probably never thought of hurting any one. And yet he narrowly missed having a horrible crime on his head. "If we could have stopped the train and caught him, we would have lynched him," said the conductor. "A year or two ago a miscreant threw a corn cob into a window, very near this spot too. It struck a lady, breaking her cheek bone, and bursting the ball of her left eye. We stopped the train, caught the man, and hanged him by the side of the track then and there."

And then Atalanta, in a country that is very beautiful, but with that poetry of malaria which suggests a peril in such beauty. And gradually the land becomes swampy, and the old trees, hung with moss, stand ankle-deep in brown stagnant water. The glades are all pools, and where-ever a vista opens, there is a long bayou stretching down between aisles of sombre trees. It is wonderful in its unnatural beauty, this forest standing in a lagoon. The world was like this when the Deluge was subsiding. There is a mysterious silence about the gloomy trees. Not a bird lives among them. But in the sullen water, there are turtles moving, and now and then a snake makes a moment's ripple on the dull pools. Sunlight never strikes in, and as I looked, I could not help remembering all the horrors of the slave-hunt, and the murder at the end of it, in the dark depths of some such horrid brake as these we pass. What a spot for legends to gather round! Has no one ever invented the *swamp-goblin ?*

For an hour and more we pass through this eerie country, and then comes a change to higher land with a splendid growth of pine and walnut and oak all healthily rooted in dry ground. But towards evening we come again into the swamps, and the sun goes down rosy-red behind the water-logged trees, till their trunks stand out black against the ruddy sky and the pools about their feet take strange tints of copper and purpled bronze. And suddenly we flash across the track of the narrow-gauge line to New Orleans—and such a sight! The line pierces an avenue, straight as an arrow, for miles and miles through the belt of forest. On either side along the track lie ditches filled with water. But to-night the ditches seem filled with logwood dye, and the wonderful vista through the deep green trees is closed as with a curtain, by the crimson west!

It was only a glimpse we got of it, but as long as I live I shall never forget it, the most marvellous sight of all my life.

No, not even sunrise upon the Himalayas, nor the moonlight on the palm-garden in Mauritius — two miracles of simple loveliness that are beyond words—could surpass that glimpse through the Texan forest. It was not in the least like this earth. Beyond that crimson curtain might have been heaven, or there might have been hell. But I am not content to believe that it was merely Louisiana.

And now comes Texakharna with its sweltering Zanzibar heat, but an admirable supper to put us into good humour, and a beautiful moonlight to sit and smoke in. If the sunset was weird, the moonlight was positively goblinish. Such gloom! Not *darkness* remember, but gloom, blacker than darkness, and yet never absolutely impenetrable. At least so it seemed, and the fire-flies, flickering in thousands above the undergrowth and up among the invisible branches, helped the fancy. And the frogs! Was there ever, even in India in " the rains," such a prodigious chorus of batra-

chians? And the katydids! Surely they were all gone
mad together. But it was a delightful ride. Sometimes
in the clearings we caught glimpses of negro parties, the
white dresses of the women glancing in and out along
the paths, and the sound of singing coming from the huts
in the corners of the maize-patches.

Here at the corner of a clearing stands a cottage, a
regular fairy-tale cottage " by the wood," and in the moonlight it looked as if, " really and truly," the walls were made
of toffy and the roof was plum-cake. At any rate there
were great pumpkins on the roof, just such pumpkins as
those in which Cinderella (after they had turned into
coaches) drove to the Prince's ball. And I would bet my
last dollar on it that the lizards that turned into horses were
there too, and the rats, and in the marsh close by you
might have a large choice of frogs to change into coachmen.

And yet, I cannot help thinking, there is a good deal of
false sentiment expended upon the moon, the result of a
demoralizing humility which science has taught the inhabitants of " the planet we call Earth." We are for ever being
warned by our teachers against the sin of pride, and being
told that the universe is full of " Earths " just as good as
ours, and perhaps better. We are not, they say, to fancy
that our own world is something very special, for it is only
a little ball, spinning round and round in the firmament,
among a number of other balls which are so superior to it
that if our own insignificant orange came in contact
with them we should get the worst of the collision. Nor
are we to fancy that the moon is our private property, and
grumble at her shabbiness, as our planetary betters have a
superior claim to their share of her, and this sphere of ours
ought to be very thankful for as much of the luminary as it
gets.

Now, to my thinking, there is something distinctly degrading in this view. Englishmen maintain patriotically that Great Britain is the Queen of the Sea; why, then, should not we Earthians, with a larger patriotism, say that our planet is the best planet of the kind in the firmament, and, putting on one side all petty territorial distinctions, boldly challenge the supremacy of the Universe itself? Depend upon it, if any presumptuous moon-men or Jupiterites were to descend to Earth and begin to boast, they would be very soon put down, and I do not see, therefore, why we should not at once call upon all the other stars and comets to salute our flag whenever we sail past them on the high seas of the Empyrean. As it is, we are taught timidity by science, and told that whenever a filibustering comet or meteor—the pirates and privateers of the skies— comes along our way we are to expect instant combustion, or something worse. Why are they not made to drop their colours by a shot across their bows? or why, when we next see a meteor bearing down upon us, should we not steer straight at it, and, using Chimborazo or Mount Everest, or the dome of St. Paul's, or the Capitol at Washington as a ram, sink the rascal? A broadside from our volcanic batteries, Etna and Hecla, Vesuvius, Erebus, and the rest would soon settle the matter, and we should probably hear no more for a long time to come of these black-flagged craft who go cruising about to the annoyance of honest planets. The same unbecoming apprehensions are entertained with regard to the moon. Yet it is absurd that we should be afraid of her. The Earth, by its velocity and weight, could butt the moon into space or smash her into all her original fragments, could bombard her with volcanoes, or put an earthquake under her and make a ruin of her, or turn the Atlantic on to her and put her out. The moon is really our own property, something between a pump and a night light, and, if the truth must be told, not very good as either. Twice a day she is supposed to raise the water of our oceans, but we have often had to complain of her irregularity; and every night she ought to be available for lighting people home to their beds, but seldom is. As a rule, our nights are very dark indeed, owing to her non-attendance; and even when she is on duty the arrangements she makes for keeping clouds off her face are most defective. If the Earth were to be half as irregular in the duties which she has to perform there would soon be a stoppage of everything, collisions at all the junctions, accidents at the level crossings, planets telescoped in every direction, and passengers and satellites much shaken, if not seriously injured. But the Earth is business-like and practical, and sets an example to those other denizens of the firmament which are perpetually breaking out in eruptions, getting off the track, and going about in disorderly gangs to the public annoyance. Why, then, we ask, ought our planet to be for ever taking off its hat to the flat-faced old moon, who is always trying to show off with borrowed light, makes such a monstrous secret of her "other side," is perpetually being snubbed by eclipses, and made fun of by stars that go and get occultated by her?

But there are objections to discarding the luminary, for it is never a graceful act to turn off an old dependant, and, besides, the moon is about as economical a contrivance as we could have for keeping up the normal average of lunatics, giving dogs something to bark at by night when they cannot see anything else, and affording us an opportunity of showing that respect for antiquities which is so becoming.

But what business the Man in the Moon has there, remains to be decided; and who gave him permission to go collecting firewood in our moon, remains to be seen. For it is well to remember that a very distinguished French savant has proved that the moon is the private property of the Earth. We used, he says, to do very well without a moon once upon a time ; but going along on our orbit one day, we picked up the present luminary—then a mere vagabond, a disreputable vagrant mass of matter, with no visible means of subsistence—" and shall, perhaps, in the future pick up other moons in the same way." As a matter of fact then, he declares the moon to be a dependant of our Earth, and says that if we were selfishly to withdraw our "attraction" from it, the poor old luminary would tumble into space, and never be able to stop herself, or, worse still, might come into collision with some wandering comet or other, and get blown up entirely. We ought, therefore, to think kindly of the faithful old creature ; but we should not, all the same, allow any length of service to blind us to the actual relations between her and ourselves—much less to make us frightened of the moon.

But the man in the moon should be seen to. He is either there or he is not. If he is, he ought to pay taxes : and if he is not, he has no right to go on pretending that he is.

CHAPTER XXIX.

ARKANSAS remains on the mind (and the traveller's note-
book) as a vast forest of fine timber standing in swamps.
There are no doubt exceptions, but they do not suffice
to affect the general impression. And if I owned Arkansas
I think I should rent it to some one else to live in ; especially to some one fond of frogs. For myself, I feel no tenderness towards the monotonous batrachian. Even in a bill
of fare the tenderness is all on the frog's side. But on
the whole, I like him best when he is cooked. In the
water with his " damnable iteration" of Yank ! yank ! yank !
I detest him—legs and all. But served "à cresson," with a
clear brown gravy, I find no aggressiveness in him. It
gets cooked out of him : he becomes the gentlest eating
possible. Butter would not melt in his mouth, though it
does on his legs. There is none of the valiant mouse-
impaling "mud-compeller" about him when you foregather
with him as a side dish. Aristophanes would not recognize
him, and the "nibbler of cheese rind" might then triumph
easily over him. Yet to think how once he shuddered the
earth, and shook Olympus ! The goddess that leans upon a
spear wept for him, and Aphrodite among her roses trembled.

But here in Arkansas, on a hot night in "the Moon of Straw-berries," what a multitudinous horror they are these "tuneful natives of the reedy lake !" Like the laughter of the sea, beyond arithmetic. Like the complainings of the plagued usurers in Hell, beyond compassion. I cannot venture my pen upon it. It is like launching out upon "the tenth wave," for an infinite natation upon cycles of floods. It is endless ; snakes with tails in their mouths ; trying to correct the grammar of a Mexican's English.

But, seriously ; was ever air so full of sound as these Arkansas swamps "upon a night in June !" It fairly *vibrates* with Yank ! yank ! yank ! And yet over, and under, and through, all this metallic din, there shrills supreme the voice of strident cicadas, without number and without shame, and countless katydids that scream out their confidences to all the stars. It is really astonishing ; a *tour de force* in Nature; a noisy miracle. I wonder Moses did not think of it, for such a plague might have done him credit, I think. At all events, the ancestors of Arabi Pasha would have been egregiously inconvenienced by such a hubbub. It is no use trying to talk ; *yank*—Katy *did*—yank—yank. That is all you hear. So you may just as well sit and smoke quietly, and watch the moon-lit swamps and wonderful dark forests go by, with their perpetual flicker of restless fire-flies, twink-ling in and out among the brushwood. If they would only combine into one central electric light ! All the world would go to see them—the new "Brush-light." But there is very little sense of utility among fire-flies. They flicker about for their own amusement, and are of a frivolous, flighty kind ; perpetually striking matches as if to look for something, and then blowing them out again. They strike only on their own box.

But here comes a station—"Hope." We are soon past

Hope; and then comes another swamp, with its pools, that have festered all day long in the sun, emitting the odours of a Zanzibar bazaar, and standing in the middle of them apparently are some clearings already filled with crops, and a hut or two cowering, as if they were wild beasts, just on the edge of the timber where the shadows fall the darkest. What kind of people are they that live in this terraqueous land? No race that is fit to rule can do it. No, nor even fit to vote. Some day, no doubt, the wise men of the world will dig up tufts of wool, and skulls with prognathous jaws, and label them " Negroids of the swamp age." Or they may fall into the error of supposing that the wool grew all over their bodies equally, and some Owen of the future discourse wisely of " the great extinct anthropoids of Arkansas." For in those wonderful days that are coming—when men will know all about the wind-currents, and steer through ocean-billows by chart, when doctors will understand the small-pox, and everybody have the same language, currency, religion, and customs duties, and when every newspaper office will be fitted with patent reflectors, showing on a table in the editor's room all that is going on all over the world, and special correspondents will be as extinct as dodos, and when many other delightful means of saving time and trouble will have come to pass—then, no doubt, as the Mormons say, all the world will have become " a white and a delightsome people," and the commentators will explain away the passages in the ancient English which seem to point to the early existence of a race that was as black as coals, and lived on pumpkins in a swamp.

And still we sit up, long past midnight, for never again in our lives probably shall we have such an experience as this, so unearthly in its surroundings—forests that crowded in upon the rails and hung threateningly over the cars, pools that lay glistening in the moonlight round the foot of the trees, the air as thick as porridge with the yanking of brazen-throated frogs, and the screaming of tin-lunged cicadas, yet all the time alive with lantern-tailed insects—just as if the clamour of frogs and cicadas struck fireflies out of each other in the same way that flint and steel strike flashes, or as if their recriminations caught fire like Acestes' arrows as they flew, and peopled the in-flammable air with phosphorescent tips of flame—a battery of din perpetually grinding out showers of electric sparks.

And to make us remember this night the cars bumped abominably over the dislocated sleepers and the sunken rails, as the Spanish father whipped his son that he might never forget the day on which he saw a live salamander; and the engine flew a streamer of sparks and ink-black smoke, till it felt as if we were riding to Hades on a three-legged dragon. But it came to sleep at last, and we went to bed, leaving the moonlit country to the vagaries of the fireflies and the infinite exultations of the frogs.

Awaking in the morning with " the grey wolf's tail " still in the sky, what a wonderful change had settled on the scene! The same swamped forests on either side of us : the same gloomy trees and the same sulky-looking pools ; but a dull leaden Silence supreme ! Where were the creatures that had crowded the moonlight? You might live a whole month of mornings without suspecting that there were any such things in Arkansas as frogs or katydids or fireflies !

I should have gone to sleep again if I had not caught sight of our new porter, or brakeman. He happened to be laughing, and the corners of his mouth, so it seemed to me, must have met behind. I need hardly say he was a negro. But at first I thought he was a practical joke. I took the earliest opportunity of looking at the back of his neck, to see what kept his head together when he laughed. But I only saw a brass button. I should not have thought that was enough to keep a man's skull together, if I had not seen it. And he was always laughing, so that there was nearly as much expression on the back of his head as on the front. He laughed all round.

I felt inclined to advise him to get his mouth mended, or to tell him about "a stitch in time." But he seemed so happy I did not think it worth while.

Is it worth while saying that the swamp forest continued? I think not. So please understand it, and think of the country as a flooded forest, with wonderful brown waterways stretching through the trees, just as glades of grass do elsewhere, with here and there, every now and again, a broad river-like bayou of coffee stretching to right and left, and winding out of sight round the trees, and every now and again a group of wooden cabins, most picturesquely squalid, and inhabited by coloured folk.

Does anybody know anything of these people? Are they cannibals, or polygamous, or polyandrous, or amphibious? Surely a decade of unrestricted freedom and abundant food in such solitudes as these, must have developed some extraordinary social features? At all events, it is very difficult to believe that they are ordinary mortals.

The hamlets are few and far between, and it is only once or twice during the day that we strike a village *nomine dignus.* Looking at a garden in one of these larger hamlets, I notice that the hollyhock and pink and petunia are favourite flowers; and it is worth remarking that it is with flowers as with everything else—the imported articles are held in highest esteem. Writing once upon tobacco cultivation in the East, I remember noting that each province between Persia and

Bengal imported its tobacco from its next neighbour on the west, and exported its own eastward. It struck me as a curious illustration of the universal fancy for "foreign" goods. So with flowers. It is very seldom that the wild plants of a locality arrive at the dignity of a garden. In England we sow larkspurs; in Utah they weed them out. In England we prize the passion-flower and the verbena; in Arkansas they carefully leave them outside their garden fences. And what splendid flowers these people scorn, simply because they grow wild! Some day, I expect, it will occur to some enterprising settler that there is a market abroad for his "weeds"; and that lily-bulbs and creeper-roots are not such rubbish as others think.

Then Poplar Bluff, a crazy-looking place, with many of its houses built on piles, and a saloon that calls itself "the XIOUS saloon." I tried to pronounce the name. Perhaps some one else can do it. Then the swamp reasserts itself, and the forest of oak and walnut, sycamore and plane. But the settlements are singularly devoid of trees, whether for fruit or shade. The people, I suppose, think there are too many about already.

And now we are in Missouri—the Mormons' 'land of promise,' and the scene of their greatest persecutions. It is a beautiful State, as Nature made it; but it almost deserves to be Jesse-Jamesed for ever for its barbarities towards the Mormons. No wonder the Saints cherish a hatred against the people, and look forward to the day when they shall come back and repossess their land. For it is an article of *absolute belief* among the Mormons, that some day or other they are going back to Jackson County, and numbers of them still preserve the title-deeds to the lands from which they were driven with such murderous cruelty.

It was here that I saw men working a deposit of that " white earth " which has done as much to bring American trade-enterprise into disrepute as glucose and oleomargerine put together. In itself a harmless, useless substance, it is used in immense quantities for " weighting " other articles and for general adulteration ; and I could not help thinking that the man who owns the deposit must feel uncomfortably mean at times. But it is a paying concern, for the world is full of rascals ready to buy the stuff.

And, after all, one half the world lives by poisoning the other.

A thunderstorm broke over the country as we were passing through it, and I could not help admiring the sincerity of the Missouri rain. There was no reservation whatever about it, for it came down with a determined ferocity that made one think the clouds had a spite against the earth. Moss Ferry, a ragged, desolate hamlet, looked as if it was being drowned for its sins : and I sympathized with pretty Piedmont in the deluge that threatened to wash it away. But we soon ran out of the storm, and rattling past Gadshill, the scene of one of Jesse James' train-robbing exploits, and sped along through lovely scenery of infinite variety, and almost unbroken cultivation, to Arcadia.

But this is "civilization." In a few hours more I find myself back again at the Mississippi, the Indus of the West, and speeding along its bank with the Columbia bottom-lands lying rich and low on the other side of the prodigious river, and reminding me exactly of the great flat islands that you see lying in the Hooghly as you steam up to Calcutta—past the new parks which St. Louis is building for itself, and so, through the hideous adjuncts of a prosperous manufacturing town, into St. Louis itself.

Out of deference to St. Louis, I hide my Texan hat, and

disguise myself as a respectable traveller. For I have done now with the wilds and the West, and am conscious in the midst of this thriving city that I have returned to a tyrannical civilization.

And I take a parting cocktail with the Western friend who has been my companion for the last three thousand miles.

" Wheat," says he, with his little finger in the air.

And I reply, " Here's How."

THE END.

73216